D0948701

CAMBRIDGE STUDIES IN EARLY MODERN HISTORY

Editors

J. H. ELLIOTT   H. G. KOENIGSBERGER

CHRONICLE INTO HISTORY

CAMBRIDGE STUDIES IN EARLY
MODERN HISTORY

*Edited by Professor J. H. Elliott, King's College, University of London, and
Professor H. G. Koenigsberger, Cornell University*

The idea of an 'Early Modern' period of European history from the fifteenth to the late
eighteenth century is now finding wide acceptance among historians. The purpose of
Cambridge Studies in Early Modern History is to publish monographs and studies which
will help to illuminate the character of the period as a whole, and in particular to focus
attention on a dominant theme within it – the interplay of continuity (the continuity of
medieval ideas, and forms of political and social organization) and change (the impact of
new ideas, new methods and new demands on the traditional structures).

CHRONICLE INTO HISTORY

AN ESSAY ON THE INTERPRETATION OF HISTORY IN FLORENTINE FOURTEENTH-CENTURY CHRONICLES

LOUIS GREEN

Senior Lecturer in History
Monash University

CAMBRIDGE
AT THE UNIVERSITY PRESS
1972

Published by the Syndics of the Cambridge University Press
Bentley House, 200 Euston Road, London NWI 2DB
American Branch: 32 East 57th Street, New York, N.Y.10022

© Cambridge University Press 1972

Library of Congress Catalogue Card Number: 71–186249

ISBN: 0   521   085179

Printed in Great Britain
at the University Printing House, Cambridge
(Brooke Crutchley, University Printer)

DG
735.8
.G74

CONTENTS

ALMA COLLEGE
MONTEITH LIBRARY.
ALMA, MICHIGAN

FOREWORD

This book is based on work originally done for a thesis submitted to the University of Adelaide. At the time when, as a postgraduate student, I embarked on this subject, I received generous help and guidance from Professors Hugh Stretton and R. M. Crawford and later profited by the comments on my work by Miss Mollie Gibbs and Professor L. C. Gabel. Subsequently, when I came to rewrite it for publication, I was greatly assisted by the expert advice of Professors Nicolai Rubinstein and Charles T. Davis, neither of whom I have met, but both of whom did much to enable me to overcome the handicaps under which I laboured in attempting to write this kind of book in Australia. I must also thank Professor Sir Keith Hancock for the very practical encouragement he gave me to pursue my study of Florentine chronicles and my colleague, Dr F. W. Kent, who discussed the subject of this work with me and whose ideas on Italian family chronicles have helped to shape what I have had to say in the earlier part of the third chapter of this book on changes in the outlook of the Florentine merchant-class in the late fourteenth century. I owe a further debt to Monash University and the University of Tasmania which have provided me with financial assistance for the purchase of books and microfilm without which I would have been unable to carry on my work in this field.

Unless otherwise indicated, the translations of the quotations cited in this book from original sources are my own. Although I initially intended to give in footnotes the Italian text of all the passages I quoted or summarised in this work, I ultimately decided against doing this because of the space it would have taken up and the limited usefulness of this to all but the specialist reader. Scholars who wish to refer back to the original wording of these quotations may in any case do so by consulting the works cited, all of which one would expect to be available in major libraries.

Monash University, 1971   L. G.

vi

INTRODUCTION

THE TRANSITION between one age and another can seldom be charted. Periods merge into each other, defying definition. Yet the presumption that the course of change may be followed and the transformation of one thing into another exactly traced lies at the root of historical inquiry. In this consists the paradox, the dilemma of the historian's task, particularly if his interests fall in fields such as intellectual history which concentrates on the critical points of juncture in what is assumed to be an ordered sequence of development.

The need to see in history an unbroken continuity will tend to make him read the significance of a bridge period either forwards or backwards, seeing in it either a persistence of the past or a foretaste of the future. This will enable him to draw out connected strings of relationship from what at first seems a haphazard tangle of loose threads, but at the price partly of defeating his own ends in smoothing out into the appearance of natural extension what he initially sought to explain as decisive change. In much of what has been written about the fourteenth century, traditionally accepted as the watershed between the Middle Ages and the Renaissance in Italy, there is this tendency, depending on the focus of the historian, either to highlight anticipations of the burgeoning culture of the Quattrocento or to emphasise the continuing medieval character of the period. Consequently, two half-views of it have tended to emerge, rather than a coherent, integrated picture, encompassing its at first sight contrary trends.

The one-sidedness of such approaches has its origin in the difficulty of elucidating the process of change. Why was it that at this time, as at other turning points in history, one state of affairs ceased to prevail and another began gradually to displace it? Is the impression that this was so due to a failure to recognise in innovation merely a later stage in the development of what had preceded it? Or was it that some factor, formerly quiescent or absent, was able at this point for the first time to give a new direction to change?

The difficulty of answering questions such as these arises not only from inadequacy of knowledge (there is a point beyond which the germination of ideas cannot, because of its very nature, be traced), but also for methodological reasons. Explanation presupposes assumptions about the nature of change. Consequently, basic questions must either challenge these assumptions, in which case they lack a framework within which they can be tested, or work back to them. Inquiry into them leads in the one case to bafflement, in the other to a return, through a circular argument, to one's starting point.

This, of course, does not necessarily imply the complete relativism of historical explanation. All it means is that models of explanation are tools, each useful and valid within certain limits, but inapplicable beyond them. A model which presupposes that in history changes occur from one state to another cannot yield meaningful explanations of such changes. The only way of approaching this particular problem is to postulate that the basic elements of all historical situations are the same and to regard changes as results of re-combinations of them. In other words, the states which alter must be considered as superstructures grounded on a base of which they reflect a particular arrangement. Any shift of the centre of gravity of their foundations will, then, occasion their collapse and their eventual replacement by a new structure consistent with the changed balance of its base.

In tracing the emergence of the Renaissance out of the Middle Ages, the general practice has been to identify the first appearance of novel characteristics in the transitional period and to link these with the peculiar conditions of the environment which produced them. Thus Burckhardt related what to him were the distinctive features of the Renaissance – individualism, naturalism, freedom from the inhibitions of the past – to the political state of Italy and the survival in the country of urban and classical traditions which elsewhere in Europe had been overshadowed by feudalism. Others have found in the early appearance of capitalism in the Italian city-states the clue to the location and character of the first evidences of the Renaissance.

The objection to this kind of explanation by association, is not that it establishes false connections (obviously a new culture is influenced by the environment from which it springs), but that it is not sufficient to account for the occurrence of the change itself unless it is assumed that the old medieval values could not be adapted to accommodate the particular conditions prevailing in Italy at the time. Only by positing the incompatibility of medieval civilisation with capitalism or social fragmentation, in other words by defining two mutually exclusive states, one medieval and pre-capitalist or pre-humanist, the other modern and capitalist or humanist, can it be argued that such environmental changes in the later Middle Ages made the Renaissance necessary.

Yet this presupposition is not only contradicted by the fact that all of the social and economic factors which are supposed to have brought on the Renaissance co-existed for a considerable time with a distinctly medieval culture. It also pre-judges the whole question of the origin of the Renaissance.

A study which involves the problem of the transition from the outlook broadly labelled medieval to that broadly labelled Renaissance cannot therefore assume the existence of two self-contained categories between which a line of demarcation can at some point be drawn. It should rather aim at reconstructing the mechanism of change by which a set of ideas, adequate for one period, came later to be discarded in favour of another set that were composed largely of the same elements and satisfying the same kinds of needs, but which nevertheless had a completely different emphasis and tendency.

The Florentine chronicles of the fourteenth century offer an excellent field for the examination of this process, at least in its initial stages. Written within the framework of a medieval conception of history in a society out of which the Renaissance culture of the following century was to grow, they bring out both the tensions and inter-relations between tradition and innovation. Their relatively naive character detracts to some extent from their usefulness as evidence of the final form the new outlook was to take but at the same time makes it easier to find in them traces of its formation which they make it possible to locate within the context of circumstance. Their authors wrote with no intention of novelty so that whatever changes of direction are perceptible in their interpretation of history issue from the need to adjust old values to new conditions. Their links with the past are much clearer than those of men like the humanists who had already taken up a consistently new posture. Merchants by trade, active participants in the political life of their city by virtue of their social position, the fourteenth-century Florentine chroniclers were concerned not to venture into originality in a field in which they knew themselves to be amateurs, but to set down the events with which they were familiar and to place these in a general historical scheme that would graft their age meaningfully within the texture of time.

The chronicler, according to one of their number, the Lucchese Giovanni Sercambi,[1] wrote as one 'instructed neither in theology, nor in laws, nor in philosophy, nor in astrology, medicine, or any of the seven liberal arts, but as a simple man of few intellectual attainments'. Unpretentiously, the chroniclers, apologetic for their lack of erudition and literary sophistication, claimed to do no more than set down the facts that had come to their notice in the strict order of their occurrence. They wrote in the vernacular for an audience of men like themselves, trained for a business career and

---

[1] Giovanni Sercambi, *Le croniche*, ed. S. Bongi (Rome, 1892), I, 118 (I, 64–5).

experienced in the ways of the world, but outside the ambit of learning. Their attitude to the cultural traditions of their civilisation was one of extreme deference. In an age when professional theologians were becoming critical of the all-embracing philosophical synthesis of the thirteenth century, they sought as far as possible to lodge their matter-of-fact recital of events within the structure of systematically worked out providential interpretations of history which assumed an order that fourteenth-century scholastics were more and more inclined to call into question. It has been pointed out that, because no university existed in Florence until 1354, a man of Dante's scholarship could take as the basis of his world picture the rapidly dating philosophy of Thomism;[1] the chroniclers who lived during and after his lifetime, being even further removed from the currents of academic speculation, accepted with the naive certainty of the reverent but uninitiated the postulates of prevailing theological doctrine as they crudely understood them, and grounded on them their reading of the significance of history.

To some extent, it was the consciousness of their distance from the sources of moral and intellectual authority that gave to their work its insistent concern with the explication of events in terms of the final meaning or pattern of the historical process. While their chronicles were not organised thematically to show up trends of development, they were interspersed with digressions intended to point out the lesson of particular incidents. Taken together, these do constitute a statement of a general view of history which ties in the interests and preoccupations of the Florentine merchant class of the fourteenth century with the overall medieval conception of a world ordered, both in space and time, according to a predetermined divine design. One senses in the chronicles of this period something more than the usual medieval predilection for the accumulation of factual information, although this of course is there, and something different from, say, Otto of Freising's Augustinian rejection of the semblances of earthly things for the eternal verities of Christianity: there is evident in them an effort to use their interpretation of the detail of historical occurrence to draw the world of their own experience within the sanctioned scheme of the medieval universe.

What had happened was not merely memorable to them because it created that sense of the antiquity of institutions on which earlier medieval chroniclers had been so prone to insist in tracing back the history of the people, city or monastery on behalf of which they wrote, often to semi-

[1] E. Garin, 'La cultura fiorentina nella seconda metà del 300 e i "barbari britanni"', *Rassegna della Letteratura Italiana*, 64 (1960), 185.

legendary origins. Nor were they on the other hand prepared to assert the irrelevance of the past to the final issues of human life. They did not, like Otto of Freising, compare history to the savage world of the sea, which the Christian had to leave on one side as he passed by it on the path to salvation:

In the deep we see the lesser swallowed up by the greater, the weaker by the stronger, and at last the strongest – when they can find no other prey – tear themselves to pieces...All these things the prudent reader will be able to find in the course of this history. It is plain therefore that the citizens of Christ ought not, as do the creeping things of the sea, to plunge themselves into the salty sea or trust themselves rashly to the treacherous gales; they ought rather to sail by faith in a ship – that is, the wood of the Cross – and in this present time to busy their hands with the works of love, that they may be able by traversing the highways of this life to reach safely the harbour of their true country.[1]

Instead of so dismissing history, a chronicler such as Giovanni Villani saw it as material through which the will of God revealed itself. It could be made to demonstrate the consistency between the working of the human world and the principle of divine justice.

This difference in approach has its counterpart in the relationship of the two kinds of writers to their society. Both Otto of Freising and Giovanni Villani were practical men, intimately concerned with politics and public affairs. But while one was the uncle of the Emperor Frederick Barbarossa, a bishop and statesman and military commander, a person of considerable learning whose culture had been formed by contact with some of the finest intellects of his day in the period of emergence of the civilisation of the High Middle Ages, the other was a mere shareholder in the Florentine banking and trading company of the Peruzzi, active in civic politics to the extent required of a member of his class but by no means prominent in them, widely travelled and well informed because of his business connections, with mental horizons broad in some senses, yet limited in others both because of the narrowness of the community which provided the scope for his activities and because of his relative isolation from the intellectual currents of his time. Otto of Freising lived at the very heart of his world, Giovanni Villani in awareness of what was taking place at most levels in it from international politics to the trivialities of everyday life in Florence, but at some distance from the true centres of power and cultural initiative. There was a disparity between what he needed to know and understand and what he himself was that drew him naturally to the role of an observer. The

[1] Otto of Freising, *The Two Cities*, ed. Evans and Knapp (New York, 1928), vi Prologue, 360.

discharge of his occupation did not exhaust his relations with his world: because of the eccentricity of his position within it he had to attempt to come further to terms with it through an effort of description and interpretation.

Paradoxically, it was Otto of Freising who could, in his world chronicle *The Two Cities*, dispose of time as a mask concealing the ultimate truth of history, while Giovanni Villani, less sure of himself, had to find that truth immanent in the web of events. In so far as the incentive to look at things historically comes from a sense of the incompleteness of the present, Otto of Friesing was moved by the urge to balance time against a complementary eternity without which it lost aim and significance, Giovanni Villani by the need to validate the immediate reality of the world by buttressing it with a meaningful past.

Discussing the Renaissance attitude to antiquity, Panofsky[1] has likened the consciousness of distance between the past and the present to the fixed distance between the eye and the object in focused perspective, seeing in the sense of separation between the observer and his field of vision, common to both, the quality most clearly setting apart the outlook of the Renaissance from that of the Middle Ages. Giovanni Villani's view of the past lacked this objectivity of perception; yet it could be said that his relationship to it marked the first step towards such a detachment: by his very eagerness to demonstrate the mechanism of history in terms of the salient issues of his own time and place he betrayed an unconscious sense of the possible contradiction between the world of his experience and the overriding order within which he sought to place it. The intentions of his interpretation were still anachronistic in that for him the meaning of the past had of necessity to conform to the religious and moral presuppositions of the present, but in the self-consciousness of his method there was already a hint of historical perspective, presuming the need to conquer and master in history an at least conceivable alien space.

This ambivalence was bound to produce difficulties both for Giovanni Villani and his successors. Each shift in the balance of political forces was bound to create dislocations in a pattern of interpretation based on the polarities of a particular historical situation. Thus the compulsion to match fact with meaning could not but distend out of its former shape the very view of history which Giovanni Villani had sought to justify. To the impulse to bridge a sensed distance was then added a movement to preserve the same relative position between the subject-matter of history and the conceptual framework which held together its significance.

[1] E. Panofsky, *Renaissance and Renascences in Western Art* (Stockholm, 1960), p. 108.

6

In the disturbed conditions of fourteenth-century Florence, when both internally and externally the clear Guelph–Ghibelline antagonism of the thirteenth century gave way before more complex power-groupings, the terms of interpretation underwent subtle yet nevertheless real changes that tended more and more to extract explanation from its theological setting and give it a secular and, at least in appearance, rational character. The concept of providence tended to be replaced by that of law, still admittedly tinged with moral overtones, but seen increasingly as operating through natural rather than supernatural processes.

This gradual and largely unconscious slide towards a more neutral and more objective approach to history was accompanied by changes in the relationship between the viewpoint of the chronicler and his historical ideals. Where even for Giovanni Villani the points of identification between the ends and mechanism of history lay within the ambit of immediate experience, in so far as all issues were ultimately referred back to the ever-present question of choice between right and wrong, the godly and the ungodly, for his brother Matteo and even more for Goro Dati the interpretation of the significance of historical development depended on an appeal to the rather vaguer and more remote authority of moral virtue and classical excellence. With the weakening of the role of providence in explanation, came a recession of standards of evaluation from the area in which the action with which the chroniclers were concerned was played out, to a region outside it that could provide independent yardsticks for it to be judged. Although the basic pattern into which events were seen as falling remained the same, there was a shift of standpoint from, as it were, immersion in history to contemplation of it. With this went an identification of the Florentine present with the Roman past and the consequent creation both of a sense of historical depth and of a view of history as, at least potentially, a comparative study.

It is true of course that the Florentine chroniclers of the fourteenth century did not attempt to develop the possibilities inherent in the change of outlook their works reflect. They continued by and large to limit themselves to commentary on any events that appeared to them worthy of note and did little to modify the form of their presentation in order to bring out new emphases in their approach to the past. Nevertheless, in a negative sense, their contribution was important, or at least revealing, in its indication that even those who clung most insistently to the more traditional and conservative mode of historical writing were edging their way towards the modern historical consciousness that was to be more clearly expressed later in the works of the humanists.

The line of development discernible in the Florentine chronicles of this period is interesting not because it reaches the point of fruition but because it illustrates the part which even resistance can play in bringing about and shaping change. The transition from chronicle to history in this case was not a natural evolution, the succession to a more advanced stage of historical writing from a more primitive one, but a halting metamorphosis in which the shell of the old both constricted and helped to provoke the growth of the new. The mechanism of change was not just a means by which something that had not existed before could come into being but a determining condition of the form and balance of what did emerge. In this sense its very erratic, one might almost say haphazard nature, becomes significant not so much in explaining what happened as in relating the resultant historical consciousness to its antecedents and so offering a clearer perception of the assumptions and formal presuppositions underlying it. The circumstances in which it became fixed are important not only as the precipitants of its formation but as the mould of its distinctive characteristics.

I

GIOVANNI VILLANI

WRITING IN the thirty-sixth chapter of the eighth book of his chronicle, Giovanni Villani claimed that he had been inspired to write his work while on a visit to Rome on the occasion of the jubilee proclaimed by Pope Boniface VIII in 1300. According to his own testimony it was then that he was struck by the need to do for his own city what the great historians of antiquity whom he had read, 'Virgil, Lucan, Valerius and Paulus Orosius', had done for Rome. Faithful to the traditional belief that Florence was the 'daughter and creature of Rome', and considering that it 'was rising and about to perform great things like Rome in her decline', he found it a worthy task to collect what information he could on its origins and early history and continue his account of its progress, so long as it might please God to grant him life, into his own times.[1]

Modern scholars[2] have thrown doubt on Villani's assertion that he was moved to write his work as early as 1300, since it can be established from internal evidence that its text, at least in the form in which we know it, cannot have been composed before the 1320s or 1330s. Whether his statement ought therefore, as Professor Aquilecchia has recently suggested,[3] be taken as a rhetorical device to link the composition of the chronicle with the ideal date of Dante's *Divine Comedy*, or whether it should be read to mean that it was on this occasion that Villani first conceived the design of his work and began collecting material for a history, the earliest parts of which were only to be set down in their final form more than two decades later, the use of the terms employed in this deservedly famous passage is nevertheless significant. For, while there had been Florentine chronicles before Villani's, it was only with his that a Florentine view of history emerged that wove together the early legends concerning the city's foundation, and the information about its early history recorded in the annals which Villani

---

[1] Giovanni Villani, *Cronica*, ed. F. G. Dragomanni (4 vols., Florence, 1844–5), VIII, 36.
[2] C. Cipolla and V. Rossi, 'Intorno a due capi della cronica malispiniana', *Giornale Storico della Letteratura Italiana*, VIII (1886), 231–41; F. Neri, 'Dante e il primo Villani', *Giornale Dantesco*, XX (1912), 1–31. On the question of the dating of Villani's *Chronicle* see Appendix II.
[3] G. Aquilecchia, 'Dante and the Florentine Chroniclers'; *Bulletin of the John Rylands Library*, 48 (1965–6), 48–51.

used as his sources with a coherent interpretation of the role of Florence in the political struggles of his own time and of the century or so preceding it. We do not know whether it was the sense of his city's historical destiny, perceived on that day in 1300 in Rome, that made him want to show how and why Florence had grown and prospered, and what conclusions were to be drawn from its rise about the nature and meaning of history. But we can say that at some point, probably later than the experience to which he alluded, or which he might even have invented, he was prompted to construct a work that would not merely absorb into a continuous narrative such facts as he could glean from the available sources but also act as a demonstration, covering both the past and his own life-time, of what to him was the singular destiny of Florence as an heir to Rome and as an ally of the Papacy and champion of the Guelph cause.

The legends which the Florentine chronicles[1] prior to Villani's had recounted, provided a general conception of the relation of Florence to the Roman heritage which Giovanni Villani accepted and upon which he built, but these earlier works did not really anticipate his particular interpretation of the significance of the history of Florence and the political events of his time. This he owed in part to another of his sources, the chronicle of Martin of Troppau[2] which provided him with the material for his propapal account of the Guelph–Ghibelline conflict of the early thirteenth century, but more to the immediate circumstances of his own age.

Giovanni Villani belonged to a generation which had witnessed the rapid rise of Florence to prominence as an Italian state, following the resolution in favour of the Guelph cause which it had supported, of the struggle between the Papacy and the Empire in the previous century. Its triumphant and seemingly irresistible progress as both a commercial and political power had been accompanied by the consolidation, through the introduction of a guild-based form of government, of the dominant position within the city of the merchant-class to which he belonged. It was the conjunction of these developments that undoubtedly impressed Giovanni Villani with the significance of the historical moment at which he was, or pretended to be, inspired to compose his chronicle.

Of the conditions that induce men to write history not the least important is the awareness of having reached a stage from which it can be seen to have

---

[1] The best collection of these is O. Hartwig *Quellen und Forschungen zur ältesten Geschichte der Stadt Florenz* (2 vols., Marburg, 1875; Halle, 1880); P. Santini, *Quesiti e ricerche di storiografia fiorentina* (Florence, 1903), pp. 89–144 contains a further chronicle of this group not published by Hartwig, which however Giovanni Villani does not appear to have directly used as a source.

[2] *Monumenta Germaniae Historica Scriptorum*, XXII, 397–482.

shape, becoming not merely a series of isolated events but a landscape in time, revealed from this vantage point in all its unifying contours. In the case of Giovanni Villani, such a historical consciousness was the outcome of several promptings: his sense of the new found dignity of his city, his conviction that, both as the successor to Rome and the ally of the Church, it enjoyed a singularly favoured position as its recent history illustrated, and most of all perhaps by the urge to give expression, in the vernacular tongue which the men of his class could readily understand, to a view of the world in which practical good sense derived from success the confirmation of divine approval. It was the coincidence of the arrival at self-confidence of an active, literate, but as yet inarticulate calling, with a set of historical conditions appearing to endorse its claim for a place within the medieval world order, that fixed in clarifying focus Giovanni Villani's subject: the history of his city interwoven with the great events of his time.

Giovanni Villani was, however, not only a man of his age and a writer who was influenced by the example of his distinguished contemporary, Dante, in trying to make of his historical narrative and the record of the occurrences of his own time a means to edify and instruct his fellow-citizens. He was also a merchant, against the background of whose career his great work took shape, reflecting the prejudices and practical values of his profession and to some extent even moulded, in its later books, by the vicissitudes of his life.

From what we can discover of him, it is clear that Giovanni Villani was very much a typical well-to-do Florentine burgher, living over a time span, the first half or so of which favoured men of his kind, but the latter portion of which, by bringing problems which affected both the state and the economy with which he had identified his interests, tended to reverse the optimism of his earlier years. Born no later than 1276,[1] he early formed an association with the Peruzzi Company, then one of the leading trading and money-lending firms in Florence. In 1300 he became one of its shareholders, being at the same time a member of the Arte del Cambio or Bankers' Guild. In the same year, he went to Rome, his presence there being occasioned not only by Boniface VIII's famous jubilee of that year but by the discharge of his duties as an agent of his company at the papal Court.[2] Between 1300 and 1307 he travelled widely as its representative. From Rome he returned to Florence being present in 1301 to witness the decisive

[1] The fact that he became a shareholder in the Peruzzi Company on 1 May 1300 means that he must have been at least 24 at this date. See A. della Torre, 'L'amicizia di Dante e Giovanni Villani', *Giornale Dantesco*, XII (1904), 41; F. P. Luiso, 'Indagini biografiche su G. Villani', *Bullettino de'Istituto Storico Italiano per il Medio Evo*, 51 (1936), 3.

[2] Luiso, 'Indagini biografiche su G. Villani', pp. 6–7.

events of the struggle between the Whites and the Blacks.[1] The following year he left for Flanders where he looked after the interests of his firm intermittently until 1307,[2] journeying between Bruges and Florence at least once, as is evident from a reference in his chronicle[3] to his passage through Sion in the Alps late in 1303. Around 1307, he came back to settle in Florence where he probably married his first wife shortly afterwards.[4] His formal association with the Peruzzi Company seems to have ceased in 1308 when his brother Filippo replaced him as a shareholder; however, he continued to act on its behalf in property transactions in Siena in 1309 and 1310.[5] By 1322 he had investments in the rival firm of the Buonaccorsi[6] which suggests that, after an initial period of exclusive association with one company both as shareholder and agent, he was now in a more independent financial position.

Following a pattern usual among the Italian merchants of his day, Giovanni Villani served an itinerant apprenticeship in international commerce and banking until, in his early thirties, he had acquired the means to establish himself in his native city. Henceforth he was able to enjoy the fruits of an industrious youth and devote himself to civic affairs. He first held office in 1316 as one of the Commissioners for the Mint;[7] was Prior at the end of the same year and the beginning of the next, and again in 1321-2 and 1328;[8] in 1322 he was among those citizens charged with devising economic sanctions against Pisa[9] and was also entrusted with the task of superintending the construction of the new city wall, a full description of which was to appear in his chronicle.[10] These were the highlights of a public career that included the occupancy of lesser offices in the period between 1316 and 1341. In these years, Giovanni Villani, though not belonging to one of the major families of Florence, would have enjoyed considerable prestige as a successful merchant and respected man of affairs.

---

[1] VIII, 49.

[2] Luiso, 'Indagini biografiche su G. Villani', pp. 10–25.

[3] VIII, 64. Giovanni Villani's presence in Florence, presumably as a result of his return from Flanders at the end of the previous year, is attested in VIII, 72.

[4] Luiso, 'Indagini biografiche su G. Villani', p. 34.

[5] G. Milanesi, 'Documenti riguardanti Giovanni Villani', *Archivio Storico Italiano* (N.S.), IV, pt 1 (1856), 3–12.

[6] P. Fanfani, 'Instrumento dell'accordo e compagnia fatto tra Giovanni Villani e Filippo e Francesco e Matteo', *Il Borghini*, III (1865), 520 ff.

[7] G. Arias, 'Nuovi documenti su Giovanni Villani', *Giornale Storico della Letteratura Italiana*, XXIV, An. 17 (1899), 383.

[8] E. Mehl, *Die Weltanschauung des Giovanni Villani* (Leipzig–Berlin, 1927), pp. 5–6. For useful summaries of Giovanni Villani's career as a civic official, see also R. Palmarocchi, *Cronisti del Trecento* (Milan–Rome, 1935), pp. 836–7 and the same author's, *I Villani* (Turin, 1937), pp. 12–28.

[9] Arias, 'Nuovi Documenti su G. Villani', p. 387.

[10] IX, 256–7.

His improved social status was reflected in his second marriage to Monna dei Pazzi who, though somewhat *déclassé* through being a widow, nevertheless came of old patrician stock considerably more distinguished than his. She was, it seems, to prove something of a trial to him, getting him into trouble by breaking the sumptuary laws the puriticanical Florentine merchants had imposed to prevent their womenfolk from sporting too much finery, and consequently causing him to complain, in a rather disgruntled passage, of the 'disordinate appetite of women which overcame the reason and good sense of men'.[1]

The last decade of Giovanni Villani's life was to see a sudden collapse of his fortunes and social position. In 1338, the bankruptcy of the Buonaccorsi ruined him and brought him the humiliating experience of imprisonment for debt in the notorious Stinche prison in Florence.[2] The subsequent failure of the Bardi and Peruzzi Companies which struck a crippling blow at the commercial life of the city further embarrassed his financial position. The political eclipse of the solid burgher element in the community, as a result first of the tyranny of the Duke of Athens and then of the prevalence of the relatively more democratic regime that followed it, at the same time removed him from the active participation in civic politics, which had figured prominently in his life for a full quarter of a century. It was with understandable bitterness that he was to deplore the admission to positions of power of 'artificers, manual workers and idiots...newcomers from the country or outsiders who cared little for the Republic and knew even less how to direct it...'[3] His was the complaint of a man whose old age had been crowned with poverty and disappointment and who, having nearly fifty years before conceived his great work out of pride and confidence in his city and its merchant elite, had lived to see the position of both decline dramatically, entailing his own financial and social failure. His closing days were clouded with a gloom that tinged his writing with apocalyptic foreboding which the Black Death, claiming him as one of its victims in 1348, seemed signally to confirm.

Not only did Giovanni Villani's lifetime span the most dynamic period in Florentine history, but his experience brought him into contact with most of the areas of activity which decisively influenced its course. He had been at the Papal Court and, as a member of the Peruzzi Company, bankers

---

[1] X, 11. Giovanni Villani's second marriage took place between 1323 and 1327. See Luiso, pp. 35–6. The pardoning of Giovanni Villani's wife by Charles of Calabria for her violation of the Florentine sumptuary laws (which provoked the passage cited) is documented by N. F. Faraglia, 'Alcune notizie intorno a Giovanni e Filippo Villani il Vecchio', *Archivio Storico per le province napoletane*, XI (1886), 554–61.

[2] Arias, 'Nuovi Documenti su Giovanni Villani', p. 388.

[3] XII, 43.

to the King of France, would have been familiar with, if he did not know at first hand, the intrigues surrounding the clash between Philip the Fair and Boniface VIII. As a civic official, he had immediate access to all information available to the Florentine Republic and would furthermore have derived from his various terms of service invaluable experience of practical affairs.

The close association between his own interests, those of the business enterprises on which Florentine prosperity depended and of the state he played an active part in administering would have given him that sense of the grounding of principles of policy in everyday decision that underlay, in his case as in that of classical historians such as Thucydides and Polybius, an insistence on the importance and relevance of history to the immediate issues of politics. Like the Greek men of action who turned to the recording of events because they believed these had a lesson to teach which would be valid in other times and places, Giovanni Villani was concerned predominantly with his own age. Unlike them, however, he had, as a Christian and a writer conscious of belonging to an extended tradition, to graft his record of the present on to the stem of a past that could give it roots both in an antiquity, reassuring in its aura of pristine virtue and sanctity, and in the Christian time scale within which it alone could acquire a more than ephemeral meaning. As he himself expressed it in the opening chapter of his chronicle, 'because our beginnings go back a very long way, the recounting in brief of other ancient histories seems to me necessary to our undertaking; and it may be diverting, useful and of comfort to our citizens that are and will be to consider that, in being virtuous and of great achievement, they are the descendants of a noble progeny and virtuous people, such as were the ancient, good Trojans and brave and noble Romans. And so that our work may be more praiseworthy and good, I invoke the aid of our Lord Jesus Christ, in whose name every work has a good beginning, middle and end.'[1]

Poised between his veneration for a semi-legendary antiquity and the omnipresent demands of his religion, Giovanni Villani grounded his account of his city's history in the elaboration of a tradition by which the diversification of humanity stemmed from the Tower of Babel, and the Trojans and Romans were the links between the world of biblical times and the original Florentines. In tracing through this line of development, or rather affiliation he was doing little more than re-stating what he had discovered in his sources. In recording the early growth of his city, he also drew directly or indirectly upon previous historical writings, such as the

---

[1] I, I.

Chronica de origine civitatis,[1] Sanzanome's *Gesta Florentinorum*,[2] the so-called chronicle of Brunetto Latini[3] and the work described by Hartwig as the *Gesta Florentinorum*, which is not to be confused with Sanzanome's chronicle of the same name.[4] These were for the most part perfunctory recitals of events, yet already adumbrating some of the cherished beliefs of the Florentines about their origins to which Giovanni Villani was to give renewed expression. It was from them that he derived the idea of the opposition of the Florentines and Fiesolans[5] that figured so largely in the mythology of the Florentines about their past, not only as a peculiarity of their history, but also as an explanation of their dissensions,[6] due allegedly to the merging in them of two incompatible peoples, and to their aspiration to realise in themselves the virtue and nobility of the Romans and quell the rudeness stemming from their Fiesolan ancestry. It was these, too, that suggested the landmarks dominating the early centuries of the city's history: its original foundation by the Romans, its destruction by Totila, its re-erection by Charlemagne with the aid of the Romans and against the resistance of the Fiesolans who were to pay for their opposition by the later destruction of their town and the absorption of its surviving population in that of its former enemy. On this framework of fact Giovanni Villani was to hang his conception of his city's chequered destiny, growing out of a fusion that was to perpetuate its inner divisions. Symbolically the statue of Mars, erected at the head of the Ponte Vecchio to impart its regenerative virtue to a rebuilt Florence,[7] was, according to him, to attract to itself in 1215 the murder of Buondelmonte Buondelmonti that was to set in train, with the Guelph–Ghibelline conflict, the civic strife that would henceforth disturb the city. The germs of growth and disintegration were thus seen as inherent in the circumstances of its origin.

Much of this legendary background to Florentine history was the common inheritance of Giovanni Villani's generation and was to colour not only the early books of his chronicle but also Dante's references to his city's past in the *Divine Comedy*. The similarities between the views of the two writers on this subject have in fact prompted the claim, made specifically by

---

[1] Hartwig, *Quellen und Forschungen zur ältesten Geschichte der Stadt Florenz*, I, 35–65.

[2] *Ibid.* I, 1–34. Also published in *Cronache dei Secoli XIII & XIV* (Florence, 1876), 125–54.

[3] Hartwig, *Quellen und Forschungen zur ältesten Geschichte der Stadt Florenz*, II, 221–37. Also published by P. Villari.

[4] *Ibid.* II, 271–96.

[5] N. Rubinstein, 'The beginnings of political thought in Florence: a study in medieval historiography', *Journal of Warburg and Courtauld Institutes*, V (1942), 198 f.

[6] I, 28.

[7] III, I.

Ferdinando Neri,[1] that Villani's interpretation of history derived from the work of his more illustrious contemporary. While it seems likely that the two men knew each other[2] and certain that Villani, as the younger and less distinguished of the two, was influenced by the personality and writings of his great compatriot, to see in the outlook of the one mere reflection of that of the other, would seem to overstate the case. Such a view overlooks the extent to which the supposed debt of Villani to Dante was constituted of elements that were part of the common heritage of both and the degree to which there were divergences between, or differences of emphasis in, their treatment of the events of their time. Giovanni Villani was after all a supporter of the Black Guelphs while Dante had been a leading White. Consequently, even though he was objective enough in his statement of facts to condemn the duplicity of Charles of Valois and the excesses of the Blacks in 1301,[3] Villani's interpretation lacked the clear imperialist bias of Dante's presentation of the political issues of his age. For Giovanni Villani, the Church remained the embodiment of the forces of righteousness in history, in spite of the aberrations of its Pastors, and the Emperors of the Hohenstaufen line, particularly Frederick II, the incarnation of evil in so far as they opposed its interests or defied its pronouncements. Dante worked from quite other premises which implied that the political claims of the Papacy represented an arrogation of powers which properly fell within the imperial or secular sphere of divinely constituted authority.[4] Both poet and chronicler were hostile to the Capetian monarchy and Boniface VIII, but they differed in the intensity of their condemnation, as they did in the tone of their references to the conflict between Papacy and Empire. The extent of this disparity is obscured by the fact that Dante did not explicitly elaborate an interpretation of history. This has to be deduced from his digressions and his placing of key historical figures in the *Inferno* or *Purgatorio*. If comparison is made on this basis between his judgments and Giovanni Villani's, it immediately becomes clear that Villani's archvillains, Frederick II and his illegitimate son, Manfred, the one depicted in his chronicle as the archetype of worldly evil,[5] the other as parricide, poisoner and usurper,[6] receive far gentler treatment from Dante who

---

[1] F. Neri, 'Dante e il primo Villani', p. 26. For a discussion of this question, see also E. Mehl, 'G. Villani und die Divina Commedia', *Deutsche Dante Jahrbuch*, x (1928), 173–84.

[2] A claim to this effect was made by Giovanni Villani's nephew, Filippo, in his commentary on the Divine Comedy. For a discussion of this and other evidence for the friendship between Dante and the chronicler see A. Della Torre, 'L'amicizia di Dante e Giovanni Villani', pp. 33–44.

[3] VIII, 49.

[4] *Inferno*, I, 127 ff; *Paradiso*, XXVII, 55 ff.

[5] VI, I.

[6] VI, 41; VI, 45.

relegates the former to the Inferno and the latter to Purgatory merely because of the heresy of the one and the excommunication of the other.[1] On the other hand, Charles of Anjou, whom Villani regarded favourably as a champion of the church and whom he censured only for his execution of the youthful Conradin, was to be found in Dante's purgatory among the negligent rulers and castigated for his treatment of Provence and the South of Italy.[2] The death of St Thomas Aquinas, attributed by Villani to Charles's physician,[3] was laid by Dante directly at the door of his master. While both writers often drew their facts from the same source, they gave them clearly contrasting emphases.

What the two men shared, apart from a common store of information about the Florentine past, was a more general affinity of view as to the responsiveness of history to the will of God and, subject to divine intervention and the preservation of free will, to astrological influences. Dante and Villani both limited the power of the stars in the same terms, while allowing the general efficacy of their sway over human affairs.[4] While Dante did not place the events of his time within a divinely ordained scheme as Villani attempted to do, his presumption in *Monarchia*[5] that the creation of a world empire by the Romans immediately prior to the incarnation of Christ proved that it was sanctioned by God, coupled with his belief that miracles confirmed this, indicates a remarkable closeness in the presuppositions of the two men as to the dependence of the course of history on supernatural forces. Even here, however, the consistency of the views of both with the general outlook of their time makes it difficult to attribute Villani's opinions on these points with any certainty to the influence of Dante. All that can be said is that, as Professor Aquilecchia has shown,[6] verbal parallels between the text of his chronicle and passages in the *Divine Comedy* indicate that Villani was, at the period when he actually composed his work as it now stands, familiar with the great poem of his contemporary. The question of how far he was indebted to Dante for the factual information contained in its earlier books is hard to resolve, in the absence of a proper critical edition of Villani's *Chronicle*, because of the uncertainty which still prevails as to the exact identity of its sources.[7] In the existing state of knowledge, the most likely possibility appears to be that both Dante and Villani drew their pre-conceptions concerning early Flor-

---

[1] *Inferno*, x, 119; *Purgatorio*, III, 112 ff.
[2] *Purgatorio*, VII, 113, xx, 67–9.   [3] IX, 218.
[4] For Dante's views, see *Purgatorio*, XVI, 65 ff.
[5] *Monarchia*, Bk II.
[6] G. Aquilecchia, 'Dante and the Florentine Chroniclers', p. 49.
[7] For a discussion of the current state of scholarly opinion on this question, see Appendix I.

entine history from the same body of written records and oral traditions, that Villani in addition took over from Dante's work certain turns of phrase and metaphorical expressions, together with some judgments on particular situations (his comment on the humiliation of Pope Boniface VIII at Anagni[1] is a case in point). At the same time, Villani's approach to history was essentially different from Dante's, partly because he started from a contrary ideological position, and partly because his aim was not to show, as Dante attempted to do, that men's fate in the next world corresponded to their merits in this one, but rather that, even in this life, divine justice manifested itself in the actual resolution of earthly conflicts and the actual consequences of human actions.

When one compares Villani's *Chronicle,* on the one hand with earlier Florentine historical writings, on the other with passages of historical relevance in the *Divine Comedy,* what is surprising is the degree of originality it displays not, in the material it contains, but in its treatment – in the weaving of the web of historical incident into patterns of significance, in the use of anecdote and digression to underline the lessons of events and, above all, in the fullness and circumstantiality of its narrative detail. These qualities are shared by only one other Florentine historical work of the period, Dino Compagni's chronicle, but this could hardly have had an influence upon him since, being a denunciation of the Black faction victorious in the civic conflict of the opening of the fourteenth century, it was carefully concealed in his lifetime and came to light only two hundred years later.

Dino Compagni's work[2] in some ways challenges comparison with Villani's. Both exemplify the growing concern of the generation living in Florence around 1300 with the elucidation of historical processes, both reflect the increased self-awareness and sophistication of the social group from which their authors were drawn. Yet in intention, range and character they differ markedly. Dino Compagni's chronicle is of narrow compass: a tight, coherent rendering of a single dramatic episode, it has the unity, pace and quality of a literary work. The evil of civic discord arises, triumphs and then consumes itself in the sudden, ominous deaths of its progenitors. By nature, it is less history than *exposé*; not calm, measured, untidy with the haphazard interlacing of events, but passionate and as economically drawn together into lines of significance as a play. All proceeds as repercussion from the vibration of a single centre. It is not

---

[1] VIII, 63.

[2] Dino Compagni, *Cronica,* ed. I. del Lungo, *Rerum Italicarum Scriptores,* n. ed., IX pt 2. For a full discussion of this work, see I. del Lungo, *Dino Compagni e la sua cronica* (3 vols., Florence, 1879–80).

a chronicle in the same sense as are those of Giovanni Villani and his successors and, though it illustrates more perfectly in many ways than they do an awakening historical consciousness, it is not the kind of work on which a tradition could have established itself.

Complete in itself, exhausted in the unique situation it sets itself to describe, it does not, like the extended historical accounts of the chroniclers proper, lend itself to continuation or development. As a self-sufficient entity, it is more interesting than its larger, more diffuse counterparts written later in the century; but it is correspondingly less valuable as an example of an evolving form and lacks, through its very concentration, those loose ends of incidental comment or indiscriminate assembly of material which in the longer chronicles offer inadvertent indications of changes in mood and outlook.

Giovanni Villani's work has none of the dramatic intensity of Compagni's but within its ostensibly universal framework it allows a broader confrontation with the historical process. Its scope forbids the tight organisation of material that characterises Compagni's short history, as it does its simplicity of conclusion. Where patterns show in the form of interpretation they do so unintentionally – unthinkingly accepted assumptions materialised in the shaped outlines of events. It neither captures a single historical moment nor expresses one crystallised state of its author's consciousness but, like one of Uccello's panoramic perspectives, follows the confusion of action from successive, unco-ordinated points of vision. Its clarity derives not from any kind of ordering through structure, but from honesty and perceptiveness of observation and from an inherited sense of form that invests human behaviour with a simple, self-rectifying rhythm. The idea of justice, not in the modern sense as an end to be achieved, but in its primitive connotation of a property of life, a law compelling the restoration of moral equilibrium, pervades the historical narrative and gives each of its segments, that is amenable to being moulded by it, unity and meaning.

Two anecdotal episodes in Giovanni Villani's *Chronicle* illustrate the operation of this principle. The first concerns Count Ugolino della Gherardesca, otherwise notorious for his place in Dante's *Inferno*[1] where he eternally appeased the hunger from which he and his children had perished by gnawing the skull of Archbishop Ruggieri who had decreed the terrible manner of their death. In Villani's work he appears, not wreaking vengeance for his end, but at the peak of his delusive fortunes. At a feast prepared for his birthday he drew aside a wise and valorous courtier called

---

[1] *Inferno*, XXII, 124 ff., XXIII, 1–90.

Marco Lombardo,[1] to impress him with the magnificence of the festivities and the grandeur and power which it implied, asking him what he thought of it. 'The wise man', according to Villani, 'replied immediately saying, "You are more prone to mischance than any nobleman in Italy." Perturbed by Marco's words, the Count said "Why?" And Marco replied, "Because you lack nothing but the wrath of God".'[2]

Beneath its moral overtones, the story bears a resemblance to that of Polycrates of Samos[3] in Herodotus. In each case, excess is seen by the perceptive to violate the law of measure and so entail catastrophe. Inordinate good fortune must attract its compensation of disaster. For Giovanni Villani, however, the classical notion of an irresistible yet also inexplicable fate has become transmuted into the Christian conception of retribution for sin. 'Hubris' generates 'nemesis', but only because guilt has been incurred through moral transgression, so that finally it is evil rather than departure from the mean of human action that invites calamity. This is clear from another episode which also illustrates the pattern such incidents assumed in Giovanni Villani's *Chronicle*. Guidotto della Torre, having driven from Milan the head of the rival Ghibelline faction, Matteo Visconti, cannot resist the temptation of gloating over his enemy's misfortune and sends a courtier to ask him how he fares in his exile and when he expects to return to Milan. The envoy, promised a palfrey and a miniver robe for his pains, seeks out Matteo whom he finds in much reduced circumstances. He asks the former tyrant whether he will help him earn a palfrey and a miniver robe by answering two questions. 'Willingly' replies the cunning Matteo, realising immediately from whom they come. To the first question, he answers, 'It seems to me that I fare well for I know how to live in accordance with the times.' To the second he says, 'Tell your Lord, Master Guidotto, that when his sins exceed mine I shall return to Milan.' Guidotto, informed of these replies, acknowledges their wisdom: 'Well have you earned the palfrey and the robe,' he tells his courtier, 'for these are indeed the words of the wise Master Matteo.'[4] Later, of course, with the descent of Emperor Henry VII into Italy, Matteo's prediction is fulfilled: the Della Torre lose control of Milan and the Visconti re-assert their dominance over the city.[5]

Underlying this anecdote there is both the idea that success must of necessity expend itself and the belief that evil is unerringly punished. Guilt accumulates as, in the Greek view of fate, does the debt incurred by

---

[1] Marco Lombardo also appears in *The Divine Comedy* (*Purgatorio*, XVI, 40 ff.) but his role in it is merely to enlighten Dante on the uses and limitations of astrology.

[2] VII, 121.   [3] Herodotus, *Histories*, III, 40–3, 120–5.

[4] VIII, 61.   [5] IX, 9 and 11.

excessive good fortune. The outcome of an event reflects the moral quality of the occasion that has brought it forth, but the time it takes to reveal itself is proportionate to the gravity of its cause. Human action – in its broadest sense history – thus falls into a wave-like rhythm, the period of which is governed by the strength of its initial impulse. If this is trivial and simple, its consequences follow presently: for instance, prosperity which engenders pride, envy and arrogance promptly leads to civil strife;[1] undue rejoicing soon brings in its train causes of woe, as in 1333 when the Florentine carnival was followed by disastrous floods, worst in their incidence where the festivities had been most intense.[2] Those who take life lightly have it suddenly and dramatically shown to them that it is in earnest, as Giovanni Villani took pains to point out in describing how, when the populace of Florence had gathered to witness a realistic depiction of hell contrived for them on barges on the Arno, the collapse of the overloaded Ponte alla Carraia sent many of them, as the advertisement for the spectacle had with unintended irony promised, 'to learn tidings of the other world'.[3]

An offence which is immediately manifest, which requires no interval of time for its full iniquity to be revealed, can be promptly punished. But the greater the evil, the longer is its lease of life and, correspondingly, the graver is its penalty. The cycle of sin and retribution is drawn out in proportion to the severity of its cause, the most serious violations of the natural order being those with the most far-reaching historical repercussions. Of these, defiance of the Church was, in Giovanni Villani's scheme of things, the most significant in that it brought into direct confrontation the forces endowed with divine approval and those representing the most flagrant expression of human self-will. Besides, the conflict between the Papacy and the emperors of the Hohenstaufen dynasty which had contributed to the making of the situation which Villani sought to justify not only illustrated the sequence of zenith and decline, but also had the historical importance to constitute an appropriate centre-piece for a providential interpretation of history. In describing it, Villani was careful to highlight its significance as a contest as much between moral principles as between political forces.

This portrait of the Emperor Frederick II with which his dramatic account of these events opens, shows this ruler as the very embodiment of worldly excellence and spiritual depravity:

This Frederick...was a man of great deeds and great worth, learned in letters and of natural talents, universal in all things, and he knew the Latin language and our vernacular, German, French, Greek and Arabic, was copious in all virtues,

---

[1] VIII, 1 and 39. [2] X, 216. [3] VIII, 70.

bountiful and courteous in giving, valiant and skilful in arms, and was much feared.

Yet also he was dissolute in many forms of lust, and kept many concubines and catamites after the manner of the Saracens; he wanted to abandon himself to all the bodily pleasures and led an almost epicurean existence, heedless that there would ever be another life, this being one of the principal reasons why he became an enemy of churchmen and of the Church.[1]

That Frederick II and his sons 'lived and ruled with much worldly glory' was for Giovanni Villani an essential pre-condition of the overthow of their dynasty and their extinction as a family. But what distinguished their fate from that of more venial offenders were the tendency and scale of their actions. The worldliness of the Hohenstaufen was seen by Giovanni Villani not merely as a private fault, but as the root of a corruption threatening the whole body of Christian society. Their opposition to the Papacy, while being inspired by personal motives, reflected the desire to replace the Church's ascetic, spiritual ideal with that of human self-gratification. Thus, in describing Frederick II's first excommunication, pronounced on him by Pope Honorius III, Giovanni Villani emphasised the connection between the Emperor's repudiation of papal claims and his whole proud and self-indulgently sensual manner of living: 'he was not willing to bow in obedience to the Church; on the contrary, he was obstinate, living in a wordly way in all bodily pleasures'.[2]

The Church had been Frederick's guardian and supporter in his early struggles to preserve his inheritance; he owed to it his success; this, however, brought out in him not gratitude but an arrogance that disdained the humility of homage to his former protector and refused to brook any impediment to the satisfaction of his desires. Such, according to Giovanni Villani, was the background of a conflict which the Emperor was allowed initially to prevail that his designs might fully reveal themselves until, after his final excommunication and deposition by Innocent IV at the Council of Lyons, 'God in a short time took from him all honour, estate, power and greatness and showed him His wrath...'[3] Where previously nothing had seemed to stand in his way, his armies being everywhere victorious, rebellions against him in Milan and Faenza crushed, the Popes driven from the country and his Ghibelline supporters triumphant in the cities of Italy, now all turned just as decisively against him. The rout of the forces he had sent to besiege Parma was followed by the defeat and capture of his son Enzo before Bologna. Finally, in 1250, he himself died in Apulia, murdered, so Villani claimed, by his own illegitimate son Manfred – a sinner falling

[1] VI, 1. [2] VI, 14. [3] VI, 24.

in turn a victim of sin, deceived into believing he could put off his end (which the necromancer Michael Scot had foretold would occur in a place named after a flower) by avoiding Florence only to find the prediction ambiguously fulfilled in the tiny, obscure village of Firenzuola.[1]

Fitting though its circumstances (embroidered as they were by Guelph legend) must have seemed to Giovanni Villani, Frederick II's death did not suffice to expiate the guilt he had incurred. His sons, succeeding to his inheritance, had also to bear the penalty which it entailed. Conrad, his immediate heir, died soon after ascending his throne, he too poisoned, in Giovanni Villani's version of events, by his half-brother Manfred, once again the unintending instrument of divine judgment.[2] Manfred himself who now usurped power, rightfully the due of Conrad's infant son Conradin, was next to feel the wrath of God which manifested itself, however, only when Manfred had, as a result of the Ghibelline victory of Montaperti, reached the highest point of his deceptive fortunes.[3] Opposed by Charles of Anjou, whom the Pope had called in as a last, desperate measure to check the Hohenstaufen ascendancy, he confidently confronted his adversary from an unassailable position on the heights of Benevento. According to Giovanni Villani, had he waited two or three days, he would have had the army encamped on the plain below him at his mercy without striking a blow, since it had neither food for its troops nor fodder for its horses. Moreover, delay would have enabled reinforcements to reach him. Against all considerations of prudence however, he chose to attack immediately, rashly and unnecessarily hazarding his cause to the test of battle. To Villani his decision, being naturally inexplicable, could only signify a divinely inspired suspension of his normal caution: 'God deprives of sense him to whom he wishes ill.'[4] His action, at this critical point in the struggle between the forces supporting and opposing the Church, was governed not by reason but by a divinely ordained fatality: meeting Charles of Anjou on the battlefield to which he had been irresistibly drawn, he was defeated and killed.

After his death, of the ill-fated progeny of the Emperor Frederick II, only the youthful Conradin remained. He too was destined to perish. Seeking to retrieve the former possessions of his family by an expedition to Italy in 1268, he lost the battle of Tagliacozzo, fled, was captured and executed by Charles of Anjou.

Villani's comments on the final extinction of the Hohenstaufen dynasty throw a revealing light on his understanding of the historical mechanism that bore earthly powers up to success, and then down to failure. They

---

[1] VI, 41. [2] VI, 44. [3] VI, 84. [4] VII, 7.

begin by drawing the expected moral conclusions: 'And so in Conradin ended the lineage of the House of Swabia, which enjoyed such great power in its emperors and kings, as has been previously stated. But surely it is evident from reason and experience that whosoever raises himself against the Church and is excommunicated must come to a bad end in soul and body; and therefore the Church's sentence of excommunication, just or unjust, is always to be feared, for very clear miracles have occurred, and this anyone who reads ancient chronicles may see from the emperors and lords of the past who were rebels and persecutors of the Church.'

Then, however, they go on to add to this condemnation of the Hohenstaufen that of the agent of their final overthrow who is castigated for his execution of the luckless Conradin. 'For this sentence King Charles was much reproved, by the Pope, his cardinals and whoever was wise, since he had captured Conradin and his retainers in battle and not by treachery, and it would have been better to have kept him in prison than have him killed. Some said that the Pope assented, but we give no credence to this for he was considered a saintly man. And it seemed that, on account of the innocence of Conradin who was of such a tender age to be condemned to death, God revealed a miracle against King Charles, for not many years later, God sent him great adversities when he believed himself to be at the height of his power, as in the course of this history we shall presently mention.'[1]

Depending on whether Giovanni Villani is looking forward or back in history, the death of Conradin assumes a different character. In one sense, it is the culminating act of divine retribution and as such historically and morally necessary. Yet on the other hand, it is a reprehensible deed which must be duly atoned for since it infringes justice. Charles of Anjou has fulfilled the will of God, but in so doing has committed an offence for which he must pay by the defeat of his hopes when his power has equalled that of the rulers he has overthrown.

This moral contradiction exposes the imperfect merging, in Giovanni Villani's interpretation, of two potentially irreconcilable elements. The pattern of rise and fall which he has imposed on his account of power-politics is a carry-over from the classical idea of fortune. The insistence that goodwill prevail and evil be discomfited stems from a providential view of history inconsistent with the action of a neutral and implacable fate. The only way that the two conceptions can be reconciled is by ascribing to the surfeit of success which, according to one, brings on decline, the connotation of sin that, according to the other, is the cause of human woe. The tendency of power to corrupt can thus be exploited to fuse together two

---

[1] VII, 29.

independent explanations of worldly misfortune. What this implies, however, is that temporal authority can not only not endure; it can also not escape the moral transgressions which must precede and justify its degradation.

Even those whose historical role has initially been that of supporters of the Church must therefore suffer the consequences of their God-given good fortune, not because this is bad in itself, but because of the pride and greed it engenders in them. The French monarchy which through its traditional alliance with the Papacy had become the leading power in Europe was, like Charles of Anjou, not immune from this fate. Giovanni Villani's prognostications of its coming decline began characteristically when Philip the Fair seized and expropriated the Italian merchants in his kingdom.[1] The subsequent defeat of the French at Coltrai by an army of mere Flemish burghers lent colour to these predictions and he drew from it the vague but pointed conclusion that it had occurred 'not without good reason and divine judgment for it was an almost impossible event'.[2] The outrage committed on Pope Boniface VIII at Anagni and the dissolution and dispossession of the Templers presently provided the pretext for more explicit condemnation and for the anticipation of the future 'shaming and adversities' of the French crown.[3] Philip the Fair, succumbing to the lure of power, was now caught in its trammels. His dramatic death in a hunting accident in 1314, preceded by the adultery of his three daughters-in-law and followed by the decease, in sudden succession, of his sons, brought down the vengeance of God. This was prompted, according to Giovanni Villani, not only by the seizure of Pope Boniface but also by the disregard by the Capetians of prohibited degrees of consanguinity in marriage.[4] Divine disfavour, revealed in the extinction of the dynasty, further manifested itself in the reverses of its successors. The defeat of the French at Crecy by the numerically much inferior English army of Edward III was due – so Giovanni insisted – to the sins of the French kings, culpable on this occasion on account of the injustice of their demands and their tardiness in undertaking a promised crusade.[5]

The decline of France, if less drastic in its outcome than the downfall of the Hohenstaufen, illustrated the operation of the same law. Earthly glory drew all to the edge of the same precipice. The only difference was that some had further to fall than others. A remark which Giovanni Villani attributed to Charles of Anjou, at the time when he first heard of the rebellion of the Sicilian Vespers that was to rob him of his recent conquest of Sicily, aptly illustrates how the blending of providence and fate qualified

[1] VII, 147.   [2] VIII, 46.   [3] VIII, 92.   [4] IX, 66.   [5] XII, 67.

the action of both in the ensuing conception of a deserved yet also destined decline. 'Since it has pleased you, Lord God, to make my fortunes adverse, may it please you that my descent should be by little steps.' (*Che il mio calare sia a petitti passi.*)[1]

Once the fatal tide had turned, the downward trend was accepted as inescapable, only the degree of its incidence could then be modified by human repentance or divine intercession. Like a physical law, it was of the nature of things and so open to mitigation but not elimination.

Underlying Giovanni Villani's moral reading of history, an older element, partly assimilated, partly obtrusive, thus discloses itself. While his interpretation is at first sight purely of his age, reflecting its prejudices and subjecting all to its religious preconceptions, on a closer view it reveals the sediment of earlier layers of influence. Like the culture of which it was an expression, it was a composite of successively absorbed ways of thought, itself structured by history. Its roots reached down to the magical belief in the limited term of the spiritual vitality of a man or people which the concept of fate had rationalised and to which the overlay of Christianity now gave moral justification. It transformed primitive conceptions, clothing them however in a shell of significance which anchored them in a particular set of historical contexts.

In a similar way, Giovanni Villani's conception of the role of the supernatural in history echoed age-old superstitions which had in medieval times acquired the Christian garb of faith in miracles and other divinely ordained signs. Here too the merging of otherwise disparate elements implied no inconsistency. The world picture which his interpretation reflected wove together the belief, of animistic origin, in the sympathy between physical reality and spiritual forces, with the Christian sense of direction and moral purpose in history. Nature responded to violations of human justice. The stars in the courses influenced men's actions, if only in their tendency. And miraculous predictions momentarily lifted the veil of an otherwise inscrutable future. But all of this preserved its conformity with the will of God, which manifested itself as much in these exceptional suspensions of the normal laws of the world or instances of celestial influence, as in the eventual vindication of a divinely ordained justice in the ordinary course of human affairs.

The omen played an essential part in Giovanni Villani's representation of history as a confirmation of its wider spiritual significance. If the fate of the wicked provided the ethical lesson to be learned from the past, miracles, prodigies and portents were palpable demonstrations of God's power over

---

[1] VII, 62.

this world. Even more, they constituted a necessary complement to the working out, through natural means, of the historical pattern: while divine retribution righted the balance upset by a violation of the moral order, an omen reflected the disturbance produced by such a violation in a corresponding suspension of the laws of nature. An abnormality at one level translated itself into one at another appropriate to the occasion which had brought it forth.

The link which Giovanni Villani traced between an unusual incident in Florence and the humiliation and death of Pope Boniface VIII illustrated his conception of the character of omens. It appears that the Pope had presented the city of Florence with 'a young and handsome lion'. An ass, laden with wood, which happened to be brought into the courtyard of the Palace of the Priors where the cub was tethered unexpectedly attacked it, 'either because of its fear of it or through a miracle,' and kicked it to death in spite of the efforts of the bystanders to save it. This, according to Giovanni Villani, 'was considered a sign of great changes and things to come, of which many occurred in these times to our city. But certain educated men claimed, that the prophecy of the Sybil was fulfilled, where it had said: "When the domesticated animal will kill the King of the Beasts, then the dissolution of the Church will begin", and soon this manifested itself in Pope Boniface himself as will be seen from the next chapter'[1] (which dealt with the assault on him at Anagni).

The essential elements of the portent are all present in this little story. First there is the inversion of the natural order of things, the killing of the fiercest, most majestic beast by the most timid and contemptible, an event which, to a superstitious mind, would have seemed so exceptional and incredible as to be accountable only through a supernatural cause. Then, there is the connection between the lion and the Pope which localised the significance of the omen: as Boniface VIII's gift, the lion became his symbol, its ignominy and death the anticipation of his former master's. Lastly, there is the association between the freakish happening and a previous prediction connecting the world of everyday things to the Sybilline prophecies foretelling the ultimate dissolution of this world and revealing the secret of the signs that were to herald this apocalyptic event. Read with the correct key, the killing of the King of Beasts by an ass yielded its esoteric sense as a prefiguration of the coming dissolution of the Church.

The omen was at once a clue to the underlying significance of history and a relic of a submerged and imperfectly assimilated layer of Giovanni Villani's cultural inheritance. At one level, it reinforced his insistence on

---

[1] VIII, 62.

the divinely ordained justice of history, indicating when superficial appearances were against it that the deeper currents of change, evident only to those who could perceive the signs, would ultimately rectify any seeming prevalance of evil. At another level, it pointed to the cataclysmic area beyond the frontiers of order out of which came the forces of destruction, unleashed by a vengeful God, that, towards the end of time, would help to consume the fabric of this world.

Most closely related to the actual unfolding of the historical pattern were the cases of foreknowledge that, even as the forces of evil prospered, disclosed their eventual discomfiture. Among them was the trance-induced vision of Pope Clement IV foretelling the defeat of Conradin at Tagliacozzo, vouchsafed him by divine inspiration since 'he was a man of holy life'.[1] Or again there was, at the very time when the news of the assault on Pope Boniface VIII at Anagni was being borne to France, the revelation to the Bishop of Sion in the Swiss Alps, through which the couriers passed, of the misfortunes of Philip the Fair would incur as a result of it:

The Bishop of Sion who was a man of upright and holy life, on hearing the news was all but stupefied, standing for a space in silence, thunderstruck with astonishment at the seizure of the Pope. And recovering himself, he said openly in the presence of many good people: 'The King of France will be overjoyed at this news, but I have it by divine inspiration that for this sin he is condemned by God, and great and various perils and adversities, bringing shame upon him and his descendants, will afflict him very soon and he and his sons will remain disinherited from the kingdom.'[2]

The seers through whom these insights into the future were communicated were both, it will be noted, 'men of holy life', converted at the critical moment into vehicles of divine revelation. Giovanni Villani saw in Petrarch's mentor, Dionigi di Borgo San Sepolcro, another such prophet who foresaw the death of Castruccio Castracane, the tyrant of Lucca, at a time when this ambitious ruler seemed on the point of prevailing over Florence. The learned and pious Augustinian, then at the University of Paris had heard from Villani of the danger in which his city lay and had replied reassuringly: 'I see Castruccio dead; and at the end of the war you will have the lordship of Lucca by the hand of one whose arms will be black and red, with much trouble, expense and shame to your Commune and short will be the time you enjoy it.'

'We had this letter from Paris' Villani explained, 'at the time when Castruccio had the above mentioned victory at Pistoia and, we having written back to the master that Castruccio enjoyed greater pomp and power

---

[1] VII, 28.   [2] VIII, 64.

than ever before, he presently replied to me: "I reaffirm what I wrote to you in the other letter; and if God has not altered his judgement and the course of the stars, I see Castruccio dead and buried." And when I received this letter, I showed it to my fellow priors, I being then of their number, for a few days before Castruccio had died, and the judgement of Master Dionigi was prophetic in all its particulars.'[1]

From what Villani says, it is not clear whether the worthy Master Dionigi owed his intimation of Castruccio's imminent end to direct divine revelation or to a discernment of the future in the stars; but whatever its source, it was of a pattern with those which had thrown a gleam of light forward in time on to the fate of the last, surviving Hohenstaufen and of Philip the Fair. In either eventuality, the hidden springs of history had momentarily been exposed to reveal the significance in the larger design of the particular incidents which appeared transiently to distort its outline.

For if the natural course of events could in a sense be considered to devolve independently of God's immediate intervention, it was nevertheless geared to coincide with the movement of higher streams of reality, such as the celestial or the spiritual, through an awareness of which its inner structure and prevailing direction could be derived. Thus, both clairvoyance and astrology were means to augury; yet the character of the indications they provided differed. If a vision of the future could be set down to a divinely conceded miracle, prediction from the stars was governed by humanly definable rules. Hence it was difficult to square with the providential nature of Giovanni Villani's interpretation of the past. Either history obeyed the will of God, or it was governed by the configuration of the heavens – unless the latter were seen itself as part of a divinely constructed mechanism which, like the clockwork universe of the seventeenth and eighteenth century theists, stood as an intermediary between the conception and the realisation of the dictates of providence.

Astrology was consequently awkward; yet it could not be dispensed with. Not only was its validity an accepted scientific assumption of the age, but it also wove into Giovanni Villani's world-view as another manifestation of the sympathy between physical phenomena and human life. Between the stars and men there were links which confirmed the interaction and interdependence of fatality and the course of nature. Thus the deaths of the great, such as Pope Gregory IX,[2] Philip V of France[3] and Pope John XXII[4] had, according to Giovanni Villani, their astral counterparts in preceding eclipses. Comets could also signify impending deaths, though they more usually presaged the passing of something larger than the life

[1] x, 86.   [2] VI, 27.   [3] IX, 131.   [4] XI, 20.

of man. That of 1264, for instance, announced the end of the Hohenstaufen dominance in Southern Italy, presently to be terminated by Charles of Anjou's victory over Manfred. In support of his interpretation of this, Giovanni Villani invoked the authority of Statius and Lucan who had both held that a comet indicated an imminent change of government. He added, however, from his own experience that the appearance of this particular comet had coincided with the onset of Pope Urban IV's final illness and its diminution with that pontiff's death.[1] In general, he viewed comets with misgiving, especially if they fell within Virgo, a sign of human connotation. That of 1314, late in Virgo, he regarded as responsible for the pestilence which broke out two years later, as well as for the death of Philip the Fair and his sons.[2] That of 1340 'at the end of the sign of Virgo and the beginning of that of Libra' portended, according to him, the serious plague epidemic of the same year which killed off (if his own testimony is to be credited) more than one sixth of the population of Florence.[3]

Similar prognostications could be inspired by eclipses, if these were in signs such as Cancer, normally indicative of the world's ascendance. When the sun was partly obscured in Cancer in 1339, Villani foresaw famine and plague. In fact, a tempestuous season followed which ruined crops and produced a dearth of grain and wine.[4] The plague did not eventuate until the following year by which time it could be more plausibly accounted for by reference to the comet of that year mentioned above. There was some juggling here of the effects supposedly due to astrological influences, for not only did an eclipse and a comet predict the same result, but another partial solar eclipse nine years earlier, but in the same sign as that of 1339, was linked to a different consequence, namely the decline of the city of Lucca which evidently shared with the world its ascendance in Cancer.[5]

Prediction by the stars could clearly be a tricky business and, in Giovanni Villani's case, seems to have resolved itself into a search in his historical narrative for the likely repercussions of vaguely defined astrological tendencies. Comets meant changes or pestilences, or even the advent of some important political figure such as Charles of Valois whose arrival in Italy in 1301 followed the appearance of one and from whose coming (as Villani put it) 'Italy and our city of Florence had many revolutions.'[6] Eclipses signified death and decline. Conjunctions of planets had varying effects depending on their combination and position in the zodiac. For instance,

---

[1] VI, 92.   [2] IX, 65 and 80.   [3] XI, 114.   [4] XI, 100.   [5] X, 157.

[6] VIII, 48. When no such historical figure appeared on the scene after a comet had been seen, it was considered more generally to have ushered in political change – for instance the two comets of 1337 were considered to have presaged the expulsion of the Papal Legate from Bologna (XI, 68 and 70).

the prevalence of war in 1325 was laid at the door of the conjunction of Mars and Saturn in that year.[1] In 1328, a crop failure was put down to the presence of Saturn at the end of the sign of Cancer and on the point of entry into Leo. Interestingly, Giovanni Villani described this situation as a recurrent phenomenon:

Saturn, according to the pronouncement of poets and astrologers, is the God of the workers, but its influence extends rather to a great degree over the tilling and sowing of the soil; and when it is found in adverse and contrary houses and signs, such as are Cancer and even more Leo, it endows the soil poorly with its virtues, for it is by nature sterile, as is the sign of Leo; so that it produces dearth and sterility and not fertility and abundance. And this we have seen from experience at times in the past, and those who understand these matters are satisfied that this was so at these times which occur every thirty years and sometimes every quarter of that period, depending on the conjunctions of good and bad planets.[2]

The cyclical nature of planetary movements carried with it the implication of regularity in the changes they influenced. Since particular conjunctions were repeated, so must the effects they produced return. Thus, astrology could be an aid to the study of history, revealing in it critical turning points which corresponded with configurations of the stars conducive to radical change.

Giovanni Villani himself elaborated this conclusion in discussing the triple conjunction of Saturn, Jupiter and Mars in 1345. The recurrence of a conjunction of the two former planets at twenty-year intervals produced, in his opinion, or in that of the astrologers who advised him, a natural periodicity in history.

Now he who will read this chapter may say, 'What is the use to the present treatise of knowing this astronomy?' We reply to whoever is discreet and prudent and wishes to investigate the changes that have occurred in former times in our country and elsewhere that, reading chronicles, he will very well be able, by understanding events that are past, to predict future ones, acknowledging that this conjunction in this triplicity of aerial signs[3] occurred initially in these present times in the year 1305 in the sign of Libra, and then in 1325 in the sign of Gemini. [That of 1345 was in Aquarius.] Very manifest to everyone were and are the innovations in our city and elsewhere which made themselves freshly felt from one conjunction to the next, roughly every twenty years or slightly less, these being lighter, and approximately every sixty years, which are more pronounced and change triplicity. And again it is easily possible to distinguish the

---

[1] IX, 327. [2] X, 118.

[3] The term *triplicity* refers to the division of the signs of the Zodiac into four groups of three, each associated with one of the four elements: earth, air, fire and water. Every sixty years this conjunction would move from a sign dominated by one element (namely air) to that under the influence of another (in this case water). See L. Thorndike, *History of Magic and Experimental Science* (8 vols., London, 1923–58), III, 340–1.

innovations and discords, of the Church against Empire, and the other innovations of the ancient Florentine people, and of the transmission of sovereignty from King Manfred to King Charles which in two hundred and forty or rather two hundred and thirty eight years will have occurred on twelve occasions in twelve signs, innovations which, in those earlier times, consisted of the passage beyond the seas [the Crusades] and among other great things, the transfer of the Kingdom of Naples to King Robert Guiscard. And he who searches back nine hundred and sixty, or rather nine hundred and fifty three years, returning to the first [conjunction], the most powerful of all, the forty eight conjunctions having elapsed, will find the beginning of the fall of the power of the Roman Empire at the coming of the Goths and the Vandals into Italy and many disturbances of the Church etc.[1]

This passage constitutes, on Giovanni Villani's part, an interesting though to a certain extent uncharacteristic excursion into an astrological interpretation of history. His periodisation of the past in terms of conjunctions of Saturn and Jupiter has no organic relation to his broader historical outlook but is introduced arbitrarily to justify a digression which might otherwise seem irrelevant to his readers. It derives, as the opening of the chapter which contains his remarks makes clear, not from his own investigations but from the need to set information obtained from professional astrologers in the context of events. Advised by 'Master Pagolo' (presumably Paolo Dagomari)[2] of the conjunction of Saturn and Jupiter on 28 March 1345, and of its attendant phenomena, of which the most important were the proximity of Mars and a simultaneous eclipse of the moon, and convinced of the exceptional gravity of these indications for future developments, he felt constrained to extend the inferences drawn from them to cover the broad compass of past history. He thus superimposed retrospectively an interpretation which he had disregarded in his own previous account of events.

Despite the relatively extraneous nature of his astrological speculations, these are not however altogether without significance as an element in the composite structure of his view of change. In his examination of the idea of civic decline in the work of Giovanni Villani's slightly older contemporary, the Paduan humanist Albertino Mussato, Rubinstein[3] has underlined

---

[1] XII, 41.

[2] G. Villani's nephew Filippo in his short biography of Paolo Dagomari ascribes to this astrologer the corrections of the Toledan Tables which in XII, 41, his uncle attributes to Master Pagolo. It is clear from the contexts that they refer to the same man. See *Le vite d'uomini illustri fiorentini* (Florence, 1847), ed. F. G. Dragomanni, p. 45. For a modern account of Dagomari's life and work see Thorndike, *Magic and Experimental Science*, III, 205–12.

[3] N. Rubinstein, 'Some Ideas on Municipal Progress and Decline in the Italy of the Communes', in D. J. Gordon (ed.), *Fritz Saxl: A Volume of Memorial Essays* (London, 1957), p. 182.

the astrological origin of the concept of recurrent historical cycles, demonstrating the indirect influence on the thought not only of Mussato but of others such as Armannino Giudice and Villani, of the prevailing scientific preconceptions of the age. The prestige of astrology at the time was such that not only did its validity go unquestioned but the pattern of occurrence it implied provided the frame for more general notions of change. Together with the idea of fortune (also in all likelihood ultimately of astrological derivation) it created a predisposition to represent history as a sequence of rises and falls, punctuated at regular intervals by moments of crisis in human affairs.

To this extent, the influence of ways of thinking traceable to astrology was compatible with Giovanni Villani's sense of the self-exhausting tendency of worldly power; yet astrology itself, at least in its fully determinist form, could, as he himself saw, conflict with the basic postulates of his religious and moral world view.

Consequently, he was at pains to re-echo, whenever he had cause to explain anything by reference to the stars, the reservations of theologians as to the conditional or tendential nature of their effects on the sub-lunar world. He was quick to condemn anyone like Cecco d'Ascoli who was burnt at the stake in 1327, ostensibly for having held that even the Incarnation and Crucifixion of Christ had been dictated by stellar necessity.

For all that he was a great astrologer, he was a man of vain and worldly life, and he had presumed through the audacity of that science of his upon forbidden and untrue matters, for the influence of the stars does not entail necessity nor can it be against man's free will, nor more particularly the prescience of God which guides, governs and disposes all according to His will.[1]

Even when he acknowledged the power of the stars, Giovanni Villani hastened to add that they were mere instruments for the fulfilment of God's will. Thus, in discussing the cause of a great flood which submerged parts of Florence in 1333, he followed a detailed explanation of it in terms of astrological influences with a disclaimer of their final responsibility for the disaster, in so doing recapitulating the arguments of certain unnamed theologians who had engaged in a dispute on this point with some 'natural philosophers and astrologers':

On the above questions, the wise clerics and masters in theology replied devoutly and reasonably, saying that the reasons alleged by the astrologers could be true in part, but not of necessity, except to the extent that it pleased God; for God is superior to the whole course of the heavens and he causes to move and rules and governs; and the course of nature is to God as the hammer to the blacksmith, for

---

[1] x, 40.

with it he can fashion many kinds of things as he has imagined them in his mind. Likewise and more particularly, the course of nature and the elements and even the diabolical, are by God's command the people's whips and hammers to punish sins; and it is not possible for our perishable nature to foresee the abyss and eternal decree of predestination and prescience of the Most High, poorly as we know even his created works visible to us. And so that readers may draw some profit from this question, we say that God has authority as omnipotent Lord of the universe to send and permit his judgments on the world, according to the course of nature, and when it pleases Him supernaturally and again against nature; and he does it for two ends, either through gracious mercy, or in the execution of justice.[1]

To clinch his point, Giovanni Villani proceeded to instance the miraculous acts of God in the Bible and the various calamities which had occurred since to purge the sinfulness of man, capping all this with a demonstration that the flooding of Florence, like earlier natural disasters, had stemmed not from physical causes but divine retribution. His proof consisted not only of a catalogue of Florentine vices – pride, covetousness, fraudulence in trade and usury, envy, the vanity of women (he could not let himself forget their 'disordinate spending and ornaments'), gluttony and lust but also of a reported vision which he had at first hand from the Abbot of Vallombrosa who had it from the mouth of the very holy hermit who had experienced it. This good man had evidently been interrupted at his prayers by a cavalcade of demons, one of whom on being interrogated as to their mission, had answered, 'We are on our way to submerge the city of Florence for its sins, if God permits it.'

God's will, it seems could be manifested indiscriminately by demons or the stars, in this case acting together to fulfil His judgment. Clearly, for Giovanni Villani, the problem of reconciling the predictable movements of heavenly bodies with the miraculous nature of divine intervention did not arise since ultimately the planets and celestial spheres, like good and evil spirits, were so much machinery to be manipulated at will in order to preserve the consistency between physical phenomena and human deserts. To the astrologers as men of learning he was prepared to defer: did not their science in any case afford a useful means for discovering God-given signs in the skies? But to their pretensions to do more than read omens he stolidly opposed the obtuseness of his faith in an order of things in which every level of reality was and, despite the laws of nature, must remain responsive through divine intervention to the great moral drama of existence, according to which everything in man's experience finally found its place in a scale of religiously sanctioned rewards and punishments.

[1] XI, 2.

Astrology was thus yet another mirror of the ways of providence; but one that caught above all hints of foreboding. For, underlying the very conception of this science which Giovanni Villani had appropriated to the use of his interpretation of history was the expectation of catastrophe at points in time when the abnormal complexion of the heavens found its counterpart in earthly prodigy or disaster. The cyclic movement of the stars seems, from the earliest Babylonian speculations about them, to have suggested the possibility of the end of the world when all the revolutions of the heavenly bodies had been completed, so imparting apocalyptic overtones to the whole area of thought which drew its inspiration from astrology. In Giovanni Villani's work, the connection between stellar influences and presentiments of calamities on a cosmic scale is not explicit; astrological predictions constitute a late addition to his view of history and are only superficially integrated into it. It is possible, however, to discern in his chronicle traces of a deeper level of apocalyptic beliefs which, simply because it is more fully absorbed into his preconceptions, colour his attitude to the strange and ominous without immediately betraying its origins.

The explanation he gives for the sudden eruption of the Tartar invasions is a case in point. The story he tells is quaint and, on the face of it, seems no more than another of those picturesque flights of the imagination with which medieval minds loved to embroider their accounts of the unusual. According to it, the Tartars were descended from those tribes of Israel which Alexander the Great had, because of their brutalized way of life, enclosed in the mountains of Gog and Magog in order to prevent them from mixing with and so contaminating the other nations of the world. Their continued confinement had been effected by means of an ingenious device: huge trumpets designed to emit a loud noise whenever the wind blew through them had deluded the cowardly and dim-witted Tartars into believing that Alexander's army was still there, ready to pounce on them should they emerge. In time, however, owls had made their nests in these trumpets, so silencing them, and encouraging the Tartars (who in the meantime 'living like beasts, had multiplied into an innumerable number') to break out of their mountain fastness and over-run the surrounding regions.[1]

Ludicrously improbable though it is, this tale was the outcome not of a passing fantasy but of a long and distinguished evolution. Giovanni Villani's immediate source for it was the *Liber Peregrinationis* of Ricold of Monte Croce, a Florentine friar who had spent some time in Syria,[2] but the

---

[1] v, 29.

[2] J. C. M. Laurent, *Peregrinatores Medii Aevi Quattuor* (Leipzig, 1864), XI, 2–14.

legend which this writer had elaborated by introducing the flamboyant details of the trumpets and owls went back much further, first to the Alexander romances which had proliferated in both Moslem and Christian lands in the Middle Ages, beyond them to the eschatological predictions of the Koran[1] (themselves influenced by the Alexander legends), and the Old Testament,[2] earlier still to the apocalyptic strain in traditions of Mesopotamian origin which seeped into the religious speculations of the Jews after their return from Babylon. A. R. Anderson, in an able and illuminating study,[3] has traced the diversification of the whole family of myths which stemmed initially from the belief that the end of the world would be preceded by a term in which the powers of evil, personified in the giants Gog and Magog, would have freedom to wreak havoc on humanity before they were consumed, in a final cataclysmic clash with the forces of good. Through one line of descent this original conception issued in a conviction in the impending reign of an Anti-Christ,[4] through another which Anderson has examined it produced, as a result of the confusion of Gog and Magog with the lost tribes of Israel and these in turn with the Parthians who had allegedly been driven by Alexander the Great beyond the Caspian Gates, in the superstitious dread of a demonic, bestial people, shut up in mountains from which they would ultimately break out to spread death and devastation among men. Some of its attributes and putative origin had been ascribed by Josephus to the Scythians,[5] Jordanes to the Huns,[6] Otto of Freising to the Avars,[7] so that even before the appearance of the Tartars it had come to be identified with one or other of the wild Steppe peoples who periodically swept down upon the settled regions of Asia and Europe and by their depredations and primitive way of life evoked the spectre of an elemental diabolical force.

In the traditions on which Giovanni Villani drew, the prodigious carried the connotation of the sinister and threatening, of the reversal of the natural order of things. Within the ambit of the normal functioning of the world, imperfect though it was, justice prevailed. Violence, defiance of the will of

[1] Koran, XVIII–XXI. [2] Ezekiel, XXXVII–XXXIX.
[3] A. R. Anderson, *Alexander's Gate, Gog, Magog and the Enclosed Nations* (Cambridge Mass., 1932). With reference to Villani, see particularly pp. 84–5.
[4] In *Pseudo-Methodius*, the principal medieval source for apocalyptic predictions outside the Scriptures, the two strains are in fact re-associated with the inclusion of Gog and Magog in the eschatological scheme that embraces the belief in Anti-Christ. See E. Sackur, *Sibyllinische Texte und Forschungen* (Halle, 1898), p. 74.
[5] Josephus, *Wars of the Jews* (3 vols., London, 1889–90), VII, 7, 4. Josephus has the Scythians enclosed by Alexander not in a mountain but at Lake Maeotis where Jordanes also places the original Huns.
[6] Jordanes, *Gothic History* (Princeton, 1915), XXIV, 38–40.
[7] Otto of Freising, *The Two Cities*, V, 9, p. 338.

God were ultimately cancelled out, neutralised by the operation of divine providence made manifest in history. But beyond lay an area of chaos out of which the world had once come and to which it would one day return. And of this the monstrous and preternatural were signs.

Towards the end of Giovanni Villani's chronicle, the tendency to revert to an apocalyptic reading of omens grew more pronounced. In the middle books of his work, the course of events had easily accommodated itself to an interpretation according to which the balance always tipped finally in favour of the forces of righteousness. But when the fortunes of Florence suffered such reverses, involving Giovanni Villani himself, as the bankruptcies of the Bardi and Peruzzi companies which brought ruin to the city, the tyranny of the Duke of Athens which temporarily suspended its liberties, the plague of 1340 which decimated its population, his mood became more pessimistic and he was ready to see in any natural disaster or adverse portent evidence of an impending and general catastrophe. As the twelfth and last book of his history progressed, like its author's life, towards its truncated end, it was shot through with increasingly ominous references to unfavourable astral configurations, plagues, tempests, fires, earthquakes and strange lights in the sky.

One can trace the intensification of his sense of impending calamity through the last chapters of his work. In reporting the onset of the pestilence of 1347, the renewal of which was to carry him off in the next year, Giovanni Villani's attitude was still one of concern rather than alarm. He was prepared to treat with reserve the foreboding of the astrologers who had claimed to predict it.

And this plague was previously foretold by the masters in astrology who said that at the vernal equinox, that is, when the sun entered the beginning of Aries last March, the ascendant of this solstice was the sign of Virgo, and its master, that is the planet Mercury, was in the sign of Aries in the eighth house, which signifies death; and had it not been that the planet Jupiter which is fortunate and connotes life, was present with Mercury in this house and sign, the plague would have been unending, if it had pleased God. But we must believe and hold it as a certainty that God permits these pestilences and other afflictions to people, cities and countries as a punishment for sins and not only through the course of the planets and stars but whenever it pleases him and when he wishes, as Lord of the universe and the course of the heavens, to make the course of the stars accord with his will...[1]

Villani's emphasis at this stage was still on the punitive nature of such tribulations, but already, even in rejecting the possibility that the stars might decree the extinction of humanity there was a hint that God, acting

[1] XII, 74.

through them, might be preparing for mankind an act of retribution of more than usual severity. Further untoward occurrences, such as storms and other violent atmospheric disturbances that brought the fearful Florentine populace out on a three-day pilgrimage, as well as disastrous fires which burnt out more than twenty houses and caused several deaths, deepened this into an apprehension lest divine justice might have something yet worse in store for his sinful and unrepentant fellow-citizens:

And take note, reader, how many tempests, famines, plagues, devastations, storms, thunder-bolts, fires and discords among the citizens have occurred this year in our city of Florence. Please God that these signs correct our shortcomings and sins so that God may not condemn us to a greater judgment, which must be feared, so far are faith and charity lacking among citizens.[1]

By the beginning of 1348, Giovanni Villani's misgivings had found confirmation in severe and widespread earthquakes, extending over Northern Italy and parts of Germany, and preceded at the close of the previous year by a singular and menacing omen:

This year on the 20th December, in the morning after sunrise there appeared in Avignon in Provence where the Papal Court is, above the palaces of the pope, as it were a column of fire which remained there for the space of an hour and was seen by all the courtiers who marvelled greatly; and notwithstanding that this could have been produced naturally by the rays of the sun in the manner of the rainbow, it was nevertheless a sign of future and great events...[2]

The earthquakes themselves had for Giovanni Villani even more terrible connotations. Writing what chance or destiny were to make the last lines of his chronicle he asked the reader once again to note that 'these devastations and perils of earthquakes are great signs and judgments of God, and not without good reason and divine permission; and are among those miracles and signs that Jesus Christ, preaching to his disciples, predicted should appear at the end of the world'.[3]

Thus broken off, its expectations half-fulfilled by the seemingly illimitable toll of the ensuing Black Death, the conclusion of Giovanni Villani's chronicle strains beyond the margins of history to encroach on the realm of last things, his belief in which had in any case informed so much of the interpretation he had given to the natural course of change. For, if Giovanni Villani's world view was medieval and Christian, it was also framed for this very reason by an encompassing spirituality that at once contained time and governed its inner meaning and form. Underlying his presuppositions as to the tendency of history to revert ultimately to a moral equilibrium, as

[1] XII, 91.   [2] XII, 121.   [3] XII, 124.

to the role of the minatory omen and the inter-dependence of the natural and supernatural, was the original presumption of a finite time, ordered by the pattern of rise and fall, perforated to reveal passing glimpses of eternity, destined eventually to annul itself in its culminating apocalypse. The different strata of Giovanni Villani's interpretation show the infusion of magical, fatalistic and astrological elements into the sub-soil of his thought; yet finally all these influences are really no more than successive assimilations of variants of the same basic conception: the imposition on human action of the corrective rhythm of cosmic forces, restoring its balance and betraying its aberrations by corresponding disturbances in the physical and psychic worlds.

The sources of this lie far deeper than the Christian tradition in the early history of primitive magical practices and Eastern religions. What is surprising about its presence at the root of Giovanni Villani's assumptions about history is not that it is there – this after all is what one would expect in view of the outlook and cultural inheritance of the age – but that its implications evoke the kind of critical justification he attempts to give them. He does not take for granted; he seeks to prove and, in doing so, links an accepted set of presuppositions as to the immanence of supernatural influence in the natural world with a particular interpretation of the events leading up to his own time. To draw a specific lesson from the immediate past, he introduces the Trojan horse of demonstration from evidence into an area of preconceptions which had previously always been secured from critical questioning because it had remained undefined.

Giovanni Villani, the Guelph, the orthodox medieval Christian, was also the shrewd Florentine merchant, the perceptive observer of the political and economic life of his day. Such sense as he had of historical structure he derived from tradition; but despite this the whole tone of his writing, the way he spelt out what he believed in terms of what he knew and saw, was governed by habits of mind that were inquisitive, pragmatic, inimical to the acceptance of conclusions without argument or proof. History he saw as a form of experience which, like the accumulated wisdom of business practice, could teach the prudent to avoid the mistakes of the past. This was quite literally true of the hints on political behaviour he scattered at appropriate points in his chronicle to bring out errors in the ways of the foolish: thus, he cautioned his readers against personal ambition and the fickleness of the populace which he found evidenced in the fall of Giano della Bella,[1] against self-interest and factional spirit which led to the failure of the efforts of the Florentines to acquire Lucca in 1341,[2] against the power of

---

[1] VIII, 8.   [2] XI, 130.

39

envy and the jealousy of riches which had been responsible for the confiscation of the property of wealthier citizens by the relatively democratic regime established in 1345 after the expulsion of the Duke of Athens.[1] But it also applied to the other, broader inferences Giovanni Villani drew from history, the source of which lay really in his religious and moral beliefs, but which he still insisted on deriving from the factual evidence of his narrative of events. Unable to break himself of the inclination to read the past as a set of examples illustrating rules of conduct, yet predisposed by his whole outlook to allow only one kind of conclusion to emerge from them, he could not but enter the dangerous terrain of circular argument in which the very possibility of a discrepancy between what he wanted to prove and the material he might use to do it – a possibility admitted in the demonstrative character of his approach but nevertheless destructive of the basic postulates of his position – would lead him on to define what had previously seemed self-evident in an effort to cover all possible loopholes, to clothe the nakedness of assumptions in the deceptively protective armour of fact.

Of necessity the promptings of experience and the rules of morality had to point in the same direction, and history became the link for reconciling apparent contradictions between them. This was the principle on which Giovanni Villani worked and the one which he bequeathed to his successors. It meant that, as circumstances changed, so too did the character of history which, as the factor balancing the equation, had to adapt itself to the variations in the two terms which it joined. The way that it did this was largely influenced by the values and attitudes of the urban, merchant community to which the Villanis and their fellow chroniclers belonged. As a novice in the chronicler's craft, Giovanni Villani had, despite the practical tone and descriptive fullness of his narrative, deferred to the view of history he had inherited. His brother Matteo who continued his work after his death and the other Florentine chroniclers of the late fourteenth and early fifteenth century increasingly broke away from it to continue, in altered political and social circumstances, to meet the demands it had satisfied. Elements which had been present in Giovanni Villani's account of his times but which had been peripheral for him to the mainstream of history acquired a central importance, so modifying the whole character of his interpretation while maintaining many features of its form.

That aspect of his work, out of which these later developments were to spring, is beyond the scope of this chapter which has been primarily concerned with the elucidation of the formal texture of his view of history. It

---

[1] XII, 44.

will be discussed later in relation to the emergence of more realistic pre-occupations in the works of his successors. However, in order not to give an unbalanced picture of Giovanni Villani's chronicle, some reference needs to be made to its other characteristics. Though its diffuse subject matter is drawn together by inherited notions of measure, justice and divine providence, it is not these that give it its historical value, nor its undoubted, if quaint and stilted charm. It is rather the fullness, intricacy and the variety of the information it provides and the little idiosyncratic asides which reveal a personality, insatiably and unselectively curious, often prejudiced and self-opinionated, yet at the same time perceptive of every striking detail of his surroundings. As Burckhardt[1] was the first to state, and as has been frequently remarked since, Giovanni Villani was among the earliest to display an interest in statistics of population, revenue, expenditure and food supply.[2] His figures, though probably slightly exaggerated, have been found by modern students of the subject[3] to be surprisingly reliable, suggesting that he had access to sources then available to the communal authorities but now lost. The chapters which contain these estimates, are also a rich mine of information on aspects of Florentine life and economic activity at this period of which we would otherwise know little. We learn from them of a remarkably extensive system of popular education catering for 8,000–10,000 children at its lowest, primary level, for 1,000–1,200 in more advanced commercial schools and for 550–600 in grammar schools. We are told how many officials the Commune employed and what they were paid, how many lawyers and doctors practiced in the town, how many bankers there were, how many apothecary's shops, how many bakers' ovens, how much grain was needed to supply flour for the bread baked in them, how much wine had to be brought in to quench the thirst of the Florentine populace and how many animals were required to provide it with meat. We discover also the number of workshops engaged in the textile industry, the basis of the Florentine economy, and how many people it supported. The growth in population and changes in character

---

[1] J. Burckhardt, *The Civilisation of the Renaissance in Italy* (London, 1944), pp. 50–1.

[2] XI, 92–4.

[3] On this question, see the following articles, all in the *Archivio Storico Italiano*: N. Rodolico, 'Note statistiche su la populazione fiorentina nel XIV secolo' Ser. V, 30 (1902), 241–74; G. Pardi, 'Disegno della storia demografica di Firenze' Ser. VI, 1, An 74 (1916), pp. 49–51; A. Sapori 'L'attendibilità di alcune testimonianze cronistiche dell' economia medioevale' Ser. VII, 12, An 87 (1929), pp. 19–30; E. Fiumi, 'La demografia fiorentina nelle pagine di Giovanni Villani' An 108 (1950), pp. 78–158; E. Fiumi, 'Economia e vita privata dei fiorentini nelle rivelazioni statistiche di Giovanni Villani' An 111 (1953), pp. 207–41. Rodolico, the earliest to write on this subject, expressed some reservations about Giovanni Villani's statistics, but the other authors listed have, on the whole, dismissed his criticisms and by and large accepted the chronicler's estimates.

of manufacture over the previous thirty years are recorded; production, it appears, had actually fallen, as had the number of workshops, but with the improvement in the quality of the cloth made, the value of the output had increased.

Such a social and economic profile of the city in exact, statistical terms is unique for the period and reflects Giovanni Villani's direct involvement, not only in civic affairs, but in the application to the problems of urban administration of the rationalised methods of business-practice evolved by the great Florentine trading companies. Accurate estimates of revenue, food requirements and population had by this time become as necessary to the government of Florence, dependent as it was on finance for defence and imports to feed the inhabitants of the city, as precise indications of market conditions, the availability of raw materials, the state of demand and the extent of assets and liabilities were to companies such as the Bardi and Peruzzi, then engaged in far-flung and complex commercial operations. There was a natural carry-over from the approach adopted in one field to that taken in the other as there was from the recourse to precise quantitative measurement for practical ends to the more disinterested concern displayed by Giovanni Villani with facts and figures for their own sake. Habits of mind that had arisen from necessity in one context became generalised in the other into an undifferentiating curiosity that took in not only particulars of the economic life of Florence, but also outbreaks of epidemics,[1] the erection of churches,[2] bridges,[3] and town walls,[4] the last of which Giovanni Villani was singularly qualified to describe as one of the commissioners charged in 1324 with supervising the construction of the third circuit of walls to gird the city. Miracles and exceptional manifestations of religious piety such as the outburst of flagellant zeal in 1310[5] also of course caught his attention: nothing that either practical training or superstitious belief drew to his notice escaped being recorded. The essential point, however, is not the variety of his observations, but the faith in the intrinsic value of information which they reveal. All that had happened seemed to him worthy of remembrance for the lessons it would teach the future, as to the greatness of Florence in his day, the unprofitability of wickedness, or the unfailing concern of God for human affairs. In so far as the writing of history stems from a sense of the usefulness of knowledge of the past and of the deducibility of certain simple principles from it, Giovanni Villani was a historian. His tragedy was that he did not see the incompatibility between the neutral event and the positive conclusion towards which,

---

[1] x, 61; xi, 114; xii, 84.
[2] viii, 7; viii, 9; xi, 12.
[3] v, 41; vi, 50; xii, 46; xii, 72.
[4] viii, 31; ix, 256–7.
[5] viii, 121.

whether he admits it or not, the historian seeks to advance. In trying to prove from experience that human action was governed by divine providence, Giovanni Villani set expectations for the correspondence between the actual course of events and the working out of historical tendencies that, as circumstances altered, could only be realised by forcing standards of interpretation to vary with changing realities. In the effort to endow historical fact with an enduring meaning, he instead made meaning depend upon fact, the transformations of which could not but be transferred to the interpretations of history that rested upon them.

2

MATTEO VILLANI

It is set down in Holy Writ that, sin having corrupted all the ways of man's flesh, God sent the flood over the earth; and, through his mercy, preserving humankind in the eight souls of Noah, his three sons and their wives in the ark, all the rest of the race he submerged in the flood. Since then, as in time people have multiplied, there have been several individual floods, plagues, infections and pestilences, famines and many other ills that God has permitted to afflict men for their sins. But from what one can gather from written records, there has been from the general flood till now no universal judgment of plague so all-embracing as that which came in our day.[1]

Thus, after the brief prologue to his first book, Matteo Villani opened his chronicle. The tone set is unmistakable and characteristic. This was to be the record of tribulations and human perversity. He went on to explain how he came to undertake his work.

The author of the chronicle called the chronicle of Giovanni Villani, citizen of Florence, to whom I was closely linked by ties of blood and affection, having yielded up his soul to God in this plague, I resolved in my mind, knowing more, after many grave misfortunes, of the world's calamities than it had revealed of its prosperity, to take up at this point, as at a renewal of time and of the world, our varied and calamitous material, bringing together annually, within the capacity of one weak understanding, events that appear worthy of remembrance so that in times to come a surer testimony to them may be had.

In long, tortuous sentences, he was to continue his brother's chronicle until he too, fifteen years later in 1363, succumbed to the plague. The terrible pestilence overshadowed the work which owed both its beginning and end to its ravages. As Matteo Villani's own words made clear, it also served to distinguish in his mind the period which he was to describe from that in which Giovanni Villani had so dutifully recorded events.

The Black Death, like the Flood, became for him one of those epochal turning-points in history which did not perhaps so much change its course as alter the character of the resultant age. Matteo Villani was not inspired to write differently or see anything significantly new in the years that followed the great plague of 1348. His narrative, like his brother's, is arranged in the customary, chronological chapters or entries: only the prologues prefaced to his books give a hint of an interest in more general historical questions. His approach is equally conventional; the tone is moral, the choice of material undiscriminating, the treatment descriptive rather than thematic. Yet, despite this, the promise of his initial chapter is not altogether belied by what follows. If there is not much sign of a renewal of time and of the world in his gloomy account of events, at least there is a sense of severance from the past, a tendency to re-examine the realities of the situation in the wake of the all-transforming shock of the plague.

Matteo Villani's conclusions as to its effects are not encouraging: he found that, far from repenting of their sins, those who had lived through the Black Death gave themselves up to earthly pleasures, so inviting even further the wrath of God.

One would have believed that the men whose lives God had mercifully preserved, having seen the extermination of their neighbours and heard the like of all the nations of the world would have become of better disposition, humble, virtuous and Catholic, avoiding iniquity and sins, full of love and charity towards each other. But no sooner had the plague died down than the contrary was seen; for men finding themselves few in number and abundant in inheritance and legacies of landed wealth, forgetting the past as though it had never occurred, gave themselves to the most shameful and dishonest life, such as they had not previously led...And the lower classes [*minuto popolo*], men and women, because of the excessive abundance in which things were available, were not prepared to work at their usual crafts, wanted the dearest and most delicate foods for their sustenance and married at will, dressing children and low-born women in all the beautiful and expensive clothes of honourable dead ladies. And without any restraint almost the whole of our city rushed into dishonest living; and so too, and worse, did other cities and provinces of the world. And according to the reports which we have been able to hear, unscathed by divine wrath, considering the hand of God to be tired, people nowhere held themselves back, living in continence. But according to the prophet Isaiah, the wrath of God is not lessened, nor his hand tired but he has much compassion in his mercy, and therefore holds his hand, to bring sinners to conversion and penitence, and punishes leniently.[1]

The Black Death did not make Matteo Villani's categories of judgment different from his brother's, but it did set human experience, as he saw it, in a new light. Man was incorrigibly evil; God, though merciful, could only react to his transgressions by inflicting yet more natural calamities upon the world. History could therefore only be a series of disasters interspersed with periods when heedless human folly had free play. Writing of a recurrence of the plague in 1358, Matteo Villani likened men's disregard of such divine warnings to the indifference of animals in a slaughter-yard to their

---

[1] I, 4.

impending death: 'seeing others in the butcher's hands slaughtered with a knife, they leap joyfully in the meadow as though it would never happen to them'.[1]

Whereas for his brother the sequence of events built up in time into a structure embodying a divine ordained plan, for Matteo it could only illustrate the interaction of two permanent and unalterable conditions – men's fecklessness and its counterpart in the physical and political disturbances which it evoked. What history could teach was consequently not that, underlying the seeming confusion of life, there was a morally just order, but rather that the adversity of the times had its origin in the weakness of man's nature:

considering that through the stain of sin the human race is altogether subjected to temporal calamities, to much misery, to innumerable ills, which make their way into the world in various manners and diverse and strange movements and times, such as are the disturbances of wars, the agitation of battles, the fury of peoples, the changes of kingdoms, the depredations of tyrants, pestilences, plagues and famines, floods, fires, shipwrecks and other dire things, the men whose times we are entering, astonished as though through ignorance, may wonder at them the more strongly, understand divine justice less and perceive little the lesson and remedy of the adversity if the memory of similar cases in times past does not give them some instruction and if they do not know how to qualify duly those cases that disclose the clear face of prosperity, covering up beneath the thick veil of ignorance the ruinous issue and dubious end of mortal things.[2]

Giovanni Villani had written to glorify his native Florence and, indirectly, to elaborate and defend the Guelph view of thirteenth century Italian history. Other motifs had only incidentally entered his work. Matteo's purpose was by contrast from the very beginning to expose human shortcomings as the cause of the natural and other disasters that overwhelmed his age. Giovanni Villani had of course also aimed to reveal the deceptiveness of worldly good fortune; but this was in the context of situations in which the temporary triumph of the forces of evil had to be explained away as a necessary prelude to their discomfiture. In Matteo's case there was no such discrimination: the sins of men were as universal in incidence as the natural scourges which punished them. This made for a profound difference in his approach to history despite his continued acceptance of the medieval view that misfortunes were the penalties of human failings.

The pessimism engendered by the Black Death was in itself sufficient to push the equation between men's lot and his deserts back into these terms. Everywhere things seemed to be going wrong, and this was only explain-

---

[1] x, 46.　　　　[2] I, Prologo.

able, on the basis of the presuppositions of the age, by an equal deteriora-
tion in the morality of social and political action, signs of which were in any
case not far to seek in the demoralised atmosphere which, as Matteo Villani's account indicates, the plague had stimulated.

For if some, like the devout chronicler himself, saw in the pestilence
a manifestation of divine wrath, prompted by men's sinfulness, others like
Boccaccio reacted to the sense of the precariousness of human life which
it inspired by an intensified urge to enjoy its pleasures while the opportuni-
ties lasted. As the description of its effects both in Matteo Villani's history
and in the *Decameron* made clear,[1] fear had acted during the epidemic as
a solvent of all social ties and conventions: wives had left husbands, parents
children in order to escape an infection that meant almost certain death.
Those who did not seek immunity in isolation had thrown themselves
into wild and dissolute living to banish the terror of the plague and to
snatch what joy they could from a life that might at any moment be taken
from them. Doctors, helpless against the disease, either quickly succumbed
to it or sought survival by avoiding patients; priests died, the last rites
were no longer administered, church services seldom held. All that had, up
till the outbreak of the pestilence, served to sanction, and so to set the
limits of, allowable behaviour fell temporarily into abeyance. Men now did
as they pleased; land was no longer cultivated, the crafts were neglected,
private property ceased to be respected as the survivors occupied the
houses, helped themselves to the clothes of the dead. The sick were left to
die on their beds and then buried in mass-graves. Normal emotions of pity,
affection, devotion and shame gave way before the all-powerful urge for
self-preservation.

Once the epidemic ended, of course, life began to resume its accustomed
course, but things were never quite the same again. The rules of morality
had been shaken by the licence of the plague year. Marchionne de Coppo
Stefani (or Bonaiuti) records,[2] in the immediately ensuing period, a series of
spectacular thefts, notable for the participation in them of men of good
family and elevated social rank who would normally have had no motive to
steal and who seem at this time to have been drawn to it by bravado or the
general slackening of the previous respect for property. Men of the lower
orders were also affected by the collapse of formerly sacrosanct values. The
most important influence responsible for their freer conduct in the years

---

[1] 1, 2. G. Boccaccio, *Decameron* Giornata Prima, Prologo. Marchionne di Coppo Stefani,
Cronaca fiorentina, ed. N. Rodolico in *Rerum Italicarum Scriptores*, n. ed. (Città di Castello,
1927), gives an even fuller account (R. 634, pp. 230–2) of the plague's effect, on which the
above summary is largely based.

[2] Stefani, *Cronaca fiorentina*, R. 659, pp. 243–4.

following the Black Death was, of course, their enhanced bargaining power as a result of the sudden contraction of the work-force, but the erosion of class barriers and of social discipline in the exceptional conditions created by the plague helped equally to encourage a mood of self-indulgence among those whom necessity had previously constrained to self-denial. If the pestilence had shaken society free of many traditional restraints, other influences were soon to intensify its disruptive effects. In Florentine politics, the period following the expulsion of the Duke of Athens in 1343 had, even before the Black Death, seen a shift in the centre of gravity of power. The lesser guilds had, in the revolution following the ousting of the tyrant, obtained a share in the government greater than any which they had previously enjoyed. This, of course, had met with the disapproval of Giovanni Villani[1] as it did with that of his brother,[2] and furthermore created strains within the structure of a political system heretofore designed to express the will of the rich, burgher class. The great families of the city had been temporarily weakened by the bankruptcies of the trading companies in which their money had been invested, but as prosperity revived so also did their pretensions and they bore with ill-will a regime that did not reflect their uncontested predominance. The situation was complicated by disputes which arose over clerical immunities: at first it was a question only of a clash between the Communal government and the Avignon papacy over the subordination of the Florentine clergy to the jurisdiction of the city, necessary to safeguard its tottering banking houses from pressure exerted by ecclesiastics to secure repayment of their debts.[3] Eventually, however, the issue broadened out into a more general opposition between the claims of the city and the liberties of the church, as a result in part of the unpopularity of the Inquisitor, Piero d'Aquila, and in part of the anti-clerical temper of many of the supporters of the new regime who may perhaps have been influenced by the Fraticelli and other heretical sects.[4] In 1355 there was further friction because of the execution of a priest by the civic authorities and the imposition of taxes on the clergy.[5] By this time, the consistently anti-clerical posture of the representatives of the lesser guilds in the government was making into natural allies of the Church the

[1] Giovanni Villani, *Cronica* XII, 43; XII, 72.

[2] II, 2; III, 56.

[3] A. Panella 'Politica ecclesiastica del Comune fiorentino dopo la cacciata del Duca d'Atene', *Archivio Storico Italiano* An. 71, II (1913), 271–370. With reference to the controversies between the Church and the Commune of Florence at this period, see also G. A. Brucker, *Florentine Politics and Society* (Princeton, 1962), pp. 132–9, 157–9.

[4] Panella, 'Politica ecclesiastica', pp. 313–14.

[5] F. Baldasseroni, 'Una controversia tra stato e chiesa nel 1355', *Archivio Storico Italiano*, Ser. v, 37 (1906), 39–49.

great families entrenched in the exclusive Parte Guelfa, the self-appointed guardian of the integrity of Florentine traditions.

The alignment so formed was to last until 1378 and constitute one of the basic conditions colouring Florentine attitudes to the Papacy in the three decades following the Black Death.

Another factor which was to have even greater effect in modifying the previously pro-papal orientation of Florentine foreign policy was the changing character of the political situation in the Italian peninsula in the mid-fourteenth century. The establishment of the papacy at Avignon in 1305, followed as it was by the seizure by various petty tyrants of large sections of the former states of the Church, weakened the basis of the traditional papal–Florentine alliance. While the pope and the leading Tuscan Commune still had a common interest in resisting imperial claims and in restraining Veronese and Milanese expansionary designs, the real aims of their policy began to diverge about the middle of the century. After the death of the Emperor Henry VII in 1313, the Ghibelline menace ceased to weld into a single party all those who had for various reasons wanted to exclude imperial influence from the peninsula. The papacy became far more concerned with regaining possession of its lost territories, while Florence was absorbed in conflicts with neighbouring states in an effort to extend its boundaries or to prevent powerful rivals from expanding theirs to the detriment of its interests. The polarising effect of the Guelph–Ghibelline antagonism gave way before the flexible demands of changing political circumstances which might make Florence and the Papacy allies at one moment and enemies the next.

Traditional sentiment, of course, continued to influence Florentine opinion in favour of the papal connection until about 1350 when the emergence of Giovanni Visconti, Archbishop of Milan, as the dominant ruler in Lombardy brought out, despite the threat which this posed to both Florence and the papal territories, discrepancies in the interests which each sought to protect. In the course of the devious intrigues as a result of which the Milanese in 1350 induced the tyrant Giovanni Pepoli to yield Bologna to them, Clement VI came to suspect that the Florentines were less concerned to restore the city to the Church to whom it rightfully belonged than to acquire for themselves an influence over its government.[1] He was therefore not very sympathetic to their pleas for assistance when, in the following year, Giovanni Visconti invaded Tuscany. With Bologna by this time irretrievably lost to the Milanese tyrant, the pope preferred negotia-

---

[1] F. Baldasseroni, 'La guerra tra Firenze e Giovanni Visconti', *Studi Storici*, XI (1902), 365–407; XII (1903), 4–94.

tion with him to the prolongation of a costly war which could now only serve Florentine interests. Effectively abandoned by the Papacy, Florence had in turn to break with precedent by invoking the aid of the Emperor Charles IV. The shock of the disillusionment caused by the Pope's failure to come to the aid of Florence was softened in 1352 by the inclusion of the city in the truce between Clement VI and Giovanni Visconti.[1] Even so, it had left its mark and events in the next three or four years were to deepen the impression it made.

The next pope, Innocent VI, by embarking on a rigorous policy of reconquest in Romagna through the agency of the shrewd and energetic Cardinal Albornoz, made it virtually certain that further strains would develop in the long-lived but by now rather threadbare friendship between the Papacy and the Tuscan Commune. For if Florence claimed to be a loyal daughter of the Church and an enemy of tyranny, it was none the less clearly more expedient for her to have the neighbouring province of Romagna divided into a number of petty principalities than united under the control of a strong, revitalised pontifical state. Families such as the Malatesta whom Albornoz sought to crush the Florentines had every reason to try to keep in power. Aware of this, Innocent VI increasingly played an independent game in Italian affairs, isolating Florence by winning Charles IV over to his side with the promise of imperial coronation in Rome. Florence, faced for once with a reconciled Empire and Papacy, was helpless and, in 1355, found itself compelled to buy off Charles IV with a grant of 100,000 florins.[2] This humiliating experience brought home once and for all the bankruptcy of the old Guelph policy of the republic. Its future diplomacy would clearly have to take account of the emergence of the Church as a rival political power in Italy and substitute a flexible attitude to the making and unmaking of alliances for its previous constancy to the papal cause.

Two influences had, thus, in the years just before and after the Black Death, tended to undermine the time-honoured attachment of the Florentines to the Papacy; on the one hand, there was a rise of anti-clericalism deriving from the special position of the clergy within the city and the need which the new regime felt, for financial and other reasons, to abrogate it; on the other there was resentment at the unwillingness or inability of the Church to give Florence adequate military or diplomatic support, first against Giovanni Visconti in 1351 and then against Charles IV in 1355.

---

[1] *Ibid.* See also G. Mollat, *The Popes at Avignon* (London, 1963), pp. 122-5.

[2] F. Baldasseroni, 'Relazioni tra Firenze, la chiesa e Carlo IV', *Archivio Storico Italiano*, Ser. v, 37 (1906), 53-4.

The effect of these was not only to modify the outlook of Matteo Villani's Florentine contemporaries towards the Church; it also shook their confidence in what had, until then, been one of the pillars of their world. Together with the financial disasters of the 1340s, the plague, the ravages of the mercenary companies, one of which under Fra Moriale was to devastate Florentine territory and hold the city to ransom in 1353,[1] it bore witness to the undependability of all human resources, even those which had previously appeared divinely sanctioned. Self-interest was the motive governing the actions of the princes of the church no less than that of other mortals.

Matteo Villani's pessimism sprang from two sources. On the one hand it grew out of an awareness of the natural calamities and political and other reverses that distinguished his age. On the other it reflected a loss of confidence in his city's destiny as a result of the collapse of the supports that had previously sustained it. The pre-dominance of the Black Guelphs during the first four decades of the fourteenth century had given rise to an identification of the fortunes of Florence with the ascendancy of its rich burgher class and the success of its pro-papal foreign policy. From the 1340s on both of these became the victims of changed circumstances. And, for the time being at least, nothing took their place as guide-lines for a sense of civic political identity.

To make matters worse, the middling sorts of men from whom chroniclers such as Matteo Villani and Marchionne di Coppo Stefani were drawn, found themselves caught in the cross-currents of factional rivalry. Out of sympathy with the popular or lesser guild element in the new civic administration, they were equally at odds with the exclusive group controlling the Parte Guelfa. Later, when this upholder of privilege resorted to the stratagem of 'admonishing' as Ghibellines and so depriving of political rights those who threatened its interests, Matteo Villani was to be among its victims.[2] Rejected by the intransigent conservatives, yet attached to the traditional conception of a Florence ruled by men of substance and established family, he was isolated by a polarisation of forces that excluded from the centre of the political stage solid middle-of-the-road burghers like himself. Not committed to the policies of the civic government as his brother had been up to the final decade of his life, he was inclined to regard politics as a spectator rather than as a participant and concern himself less with lauding the triumphs of Florence than with deploring its factional

---

[1] III, 89. See also G. Gerola, 'Fra Moriale in Toscana', *Archivio Storico Italiano*, Ser. v, 37 (1906), 261–300.

[2] G. A. Brucker, 'The Ghibelline Trial of Matteo Villani (1362)', *Mediaevalia et Humanistica*, 13 (1960), 48.

struggles, such as that between the Ricci and Albizzi families that rent the city apart in the 1350s.

Yet, he inherited from Giovanni Villani, if not the aim of celebrating the greatness of Florence and giving its rise significance within the context of universal history, at least the tendency to go to extremes in drawing from a transitory impression of prosperity or adversity an absolute categorisation of an age. Thus the Black Death assumed historically the proportions of the Flood, and the vices of the men of his day, together with misfortunes of his time, became sure signs that the lowest depths of human depravity had been reached: '...according to the judgment of many men of discretion the world has never been worse nor more contaminated by every vice, and particularly those which are most odious and displeasing to God.' Even the savagery of animals could not equal its barbarities, for the fierceness of man, evidenced in a particularly vicious execution of prisoners in Sicily, according to Matteo Villani, 'surpassed the cruelty of tigers and the ferocity of the most savage beasts that the earth produces.'[1]

Whereas for Giovanni Villani history had been the vindication of justice, for his brother it was the chronicle of the evil and the woes of man. For the one, it had shown how imperfect realities could serve a perfect ideal; for the other, it revealed the unbridgeable distance between the dictates of conscience and the testimony of experience. Yet if Matteo Villani's world was the expression of a moral chaos, his purpose in describing it was to make a thing of order out of the very fabric of confusion, to oppose to what existed the principle of what properly ought to be. Hence, on the one hand, his tentative approach towards what one might describe as a rhetorical conception of the historian's task and, on the other, his concern to define standards of behaviour which not so much issued from the actual evidence of human action as compensated for it. There is a tendency in Matteo Villani's work towards seeing history as something which, even if he himself was not equal to presenting it as such, ought ideally to hold up to reality a model superior to itself. It is in this sense that one ought perhaps to read such deferential references as the following to the proficiency of the rhetoricians, unattainable by a chronicler:

As the wise have it, speaking and writing should be apposite to the subject dealt with and from this principle proceeds the art of eloquence that is called rhetoric which, joined to a noble intelligence, better disposes and makes more aggreeable that which is being discussed; of this science, we know nothing, as our writing shows, and hence from our rough but true writing the eloquent may derive not diversion but profit. This it has pleased me to say in as much as the bestial

---

[1] IX, I.

cruelties alien to all humanity of which we have presently to speak would, to be better described merit the eloquence of Cicero; but we shall put them on record in our accustomed vernacular, avoiding words which through their association with grammar would be little understood by the vulgar for whom we write.[1]

Although the formula that Matteo Villani uses here is conventional, the self-deprecating tone of his remarks is none the less revealing. To give adequate force to what is being said rhetoric would be essential; in view of the audience for whom the chronicle is intended it cannot, however, be employed. There is a suggestion of inferiority, an acceptance of limitation. Giovanni Villani had likened his task to that of the great historians of antiquity. Though he would not have claimed to equal their skill, his subject – the rise of a great city – was fit to be compared to theirs – the decline of Rome. Matteo on the other hand is conscious that the essence of history as a literary form resides in execution rather than in substance. Although in general his position is much closer to his elder brother's than to that of his son, Filippo, on this point he had passed the critical dividing-line between the outlook of the chronicler and of the humanist.

Yet he does so only in the sense that he is aware of a possibility which he feels himself incapable of exploiting. Realisation in this as in so much else lay beyond his grasp; and it is in this precisely that the significance of his nostalgic reference to Cicero lies. It is another of the co-ordinates by which he plots his exclusion from the area of notable achievement. History has ceased to be a chart revealing the rocks and shallows of the past, the shapes of change, from a continuation of the lines of which present action could take its direction; it has become instead exposure of the inadequacy of things in which external standards exist to measure and show up the shortcomings of the prevailing reality. These standards define themselves not by reflection of the material that is judged but in contrast to it: they are an indication of what is missing in the imperfect state of the world.

Order, liberty, peace are all prized for their absence. Whereas for Giovanni Villani the natural had necessarily to be complemented by the supernatural which alone provided the meaningful key to its underlying structure, for his brother the natural was in itself something to be striven after to correct its deformations revealed in the actual experience of life. Humanity, in the ideal sense at least, thus became a value in its own right. It was no longer appropriate to ask, in judging an action, what cause it served. Rather it was its effect that mattered, whether it added to or lessened

---

[1] VIII, 81. See also VIII, 1 in which Matteo Villani discusses the respective merits of eloquence and force of arms as means of achieving power over men, and comes down in favour of the former.

the sum of human misery. This comes out very clearly in Matteo Villani's reaction to an incident in which some Genoese adventurers, having taken the Moslem city of Tripoli in North Africa by guile, returned with the gains to fill Genoa with Saracen slaves. Instead of seeing this as a victory for Christendom and an act of divine retribution against the infidel as perhaps one might have expected, he considered it a 'just judgment of God' that in a brief space of time nearly all those who had thus profited by their treachery should have fallen upon evil days and been reduced once again to their former poverty.[1]

God did not take sides in his punishment of those who resorted to trickery or caused human suffering. The same standard was applied irrespective of the identity of those who had been injured. Yet despite this more humanised and generalised conception of evil, the formula used in condemning the offence was a traditional one: men sinned, by their subsequent adversities paid for their transgressions and thus learnt the meaning of divine justice.

When it came to the grounds that called forth his disapproval, Matteo Villani's emphasis was different from his brother's but he moralised in largely the same terms and shared the same assumptions as to the corrupting nature of power and the self-destructive tendency of evil. The opening chapters of the seventh book of his chronicle which deal with the French monarchy have much in common with comparable passages in Giovanni Villani's work attributing the misfortunes of the Capetian dynasty to the misdeeds of Philip the Fair and his family. Both writers discover in English victories over surprising odds at different stages of the Hundred Years' War instances of divine castigation of the French kings for their sins.[2] But whereas in Giovanni Villani's chronicle such incidents are framed within a broad historical structure opposing to defiant secular power the limiting constraint of the Church and the moral law, his brother deals with them essentially as isolated warnings intended immediately to correct natural human failings. Philip of Valois whose crimes the French defeats punish has undertaken to go on a crusade and in return has been given the right to levy church tithes in his kingdom for a number of years. But, as his later depreciation of the coinage and confiscation of the property of moneylenders indicates, he is greedy and does not keep his promise, preferring to retain the money so raised for his own use. When he loses 28,000 men in a naval battle and is beaten by the English in a skirmish, he fails to heed these signs of divine displeasure but goes on to further iniquitous financial exactions:

[1] v, 60. [2] Giovanni Villani, *Cronica* XII, 67; Matteo Villani, VII, 4.

having seen himself the judgment of God, he did not return to the virtue of humility, but crowning evil with evil, to have exceeding wealth in which he placed his trust, he licensed and gave surety to all the usurers in his kingdo m granting them permission to lend publicly, if they paid the court five per cent of what each of them was taxed by the royal officials each year.

Later, this assurance, like that to the church is repudiated; the king gains further wealth at the expense of the usurers as well as of those they have exploited; but his meanness brings his family no lasting advantage, for the disastrous French rout at Poitiers reduces the French crown to poverty and exposes the country to foreign invasion.

Subsequently, after his death hastened by disordinate lust, he being on in years and taking his pleasure with his young and beautiful wife, there followed graver afflictions of war in his kingdom: finally, King John his son and one of his [other] sons were captured in the great battle we will presently describe, from which it may be concluded that, as fraudulently the cross was taken and the holy journey promised by the King of France, so by divine judgement did his kingdom pass to his enemies; and as he wished to enrich his kingdom unduly from the property of the Church and of the other foreign merchants and usurers of his kingdom, so through a just retribution was the king impoverished and the kingdom exhausted of money and plunder; and wishing from ambition to exalt themselves above the other rulers of Christendom, they were seen to enter the servitude of prison, conquered miraculously by those weaker than themselves in power and in the number of their men.[1]

There are strong formal similarities between this and similar passages in Giovanni Villani's work: in both the punishment is shown to be a kind of inverse counterpart to the crime. But the scale of judgment has shrunk. Philip of Valois is a man of very human weaknesses. He does not defy the Church or God's law; he merely seeks his own sensual pleasure and financial advantage with complete indifference to his previous promises or the welfare of others – of the Christians in the Holy land he has undertaken to defend from the infidel, of the money-lenders he has used for his own ends, of his own subjects who suffer from his extravagance. At any point, he is free to mend his ways and thus presumably to avert the final act of divine retribution. He is not impelled forward by the logic of power, but by the failings of his own character. The example he provides illustrates, not the necessity of reining in the driving energy of man to prevent it from disturbing the balance of a divinely sanctioned order, but the vulnerability of the world to the shifting sands of human feeling, the undependability of which makes impermanence a constant condition of life. The purpose of history in this

[1] VIII, 4.

reading of it is not so much to explain the ways of providence to man but to hold up the mirror of his natural vices and so induce him to reform. Ultimately what it teaches is ethics, though still often expressed, as in the prologue of his seventh book in theological terms:

> Even the wise marvel when they see the overthrow of the most potent kings and other great rulers of whom having recollection of committed misdeeds not reformed in the time conceded by divine grace, but rather aggravated by these same rulers and their successors through disordinate presumption, they would ascribe what occurs not to a marvel but to the merciful chastisement of divine mildness and justice which, so as not to lose souls eternally, temporarily strikes and scourges, so that by their ruin, by their disastrous accidents they may recognise correct and reform themselves.[1]

The agency of divine providence is here no more than a means to moral correction; but what has been carried over from the previous conception of it is the assumed correspondence between sin and retribution, a correspondence that, as in Giovanni Villani's work, implies a condemnation of worldly excess in so far as any divergence from the approved mean in one direction entails an equal distortion of the normal pattern of events in the opposite sense. What would seem astonishing in the light of the conditions customarily governing human action becomes explicable as a counterpoise to the moral deviation which the French king's misdeeds imply. By seeking more wealth than was his due he has only brought poverty on to himself and to his country; by aiming at unwarranted power, he has incurred defeat and humiliation. As in the traditional notion of fortune which Giovanni Villani took over, the higher one tried to climb, the lower one ultimately fell. This idea Matteo Villani expressed, like his brother before him, in quite explicit terms:

> ...when you find yourself in the highest rank of temporal dignities turn your eyes to the ground and see that, the higher and more elevated the place, the greater is the ruin and fall; and perhaps you will reconcile your spirits to the fate that divine providence has conceded it, without striving beyond your calling.[2]

While Matteo Villani judged good and evil very much in relation to this world, there persisted in his thought at least this vestige of the traditional rejection of earthly values in favour of spiritual ones – the belief that undue success or prosperity must attract its complementary portion of failure and misfortune. But unlike his brother, he did not see in this swing of the pendulum from worldly triumph to disaster, grounds for disregarding the here and now in preference for the beyond. He rather drew from it the

[1] VII, I.   [1] IX, 85.

practical conclusion that one should not aim too high; if one was satisfied with one's station in life everything would presumably be all right.

Finally, what remained in his formulation of this idea which originally carried such strong religious and fatalistic overtones was a hard-headed puritanism that found a ready niche in his outlook precisely because it tallied so well with the diffidence and pessimism of his own temper. In an adverse age it was wiser not to take risks nor to rejoice prematurely at momentary good fortune. It was prudent to be aware that, sooner or later, reckoning must come. The proverb 'the extremes of joy are filled with lamentation' (the same idea also found expression in the Latin tag quoted from Saint Gregory 'Praenuntia tribulationis est laetitia satietatis')[1] was invoked to point the moral of situations in which extravagant festivities were followed by tragedy, once in connection with the Gambacorta of Pisa who entertained the Emperor Charles IV regally only to have him subsequently connive in their overthrow,[2] on another occasion with reference to Edward III of England whose sons died in the plague shortly after the Order of the Garter had been instituted with magnificent but, in Matteo Villani's eyes, frivolous pomp.[3]

The burgher's disapproval of ostentatious display, so inimical to his cardinal virtue of thrift, no doubt contributed to these strictures, but they also reveal a deep-rooted distrust of life's more promising indications. Pietro Gambacorta had apparently won the favour of the Emperor; Edward III had just concluded a favourable peace with France. Both rejoiced, and, rejoicing, were deluded since it was in the nature of things that happiness must be atoned for by sorrow.

The mutability of fortune ought, Matteo Villani felt, make men suspicious of prosperity. Whatever was could not endure. 'We have said many times that the world because of its sin does not know how to, nor can, stay at rest, as its travails of which we write bear testimony, so that our work may truly be called the book of tribulations, and of new ones.'[4] Equally, it ought to make them wary of relying on their own devices since no human effort could assure the certainty of achieving their desires. King Robert of Naples, noble, skilful and powerful, whose abilities would have led one to expect that he would prosper in all his enterprises, in fact failed in his cherished aim of conquering Sicily, thus providing an example for men to desist from ambition and from believing that 'anything could have firmness through force or could escape in time the calamities innate in the mortal and fallible things of the world.'[5] Paradoxically, his son Louis 'poor in possessions and in counsel, disobeyed by his subjects, weak in armed forces,

---

[1] II, 71.   [2] IV, 44.   [3] VIII, 47.   [4] XI, 38.   [5] VII, 39.

ill-fitted to be able to rule and keep his kingdom,'[1] succeeded through a fortuitous twist in circumstances where his father, so much better provided,
had failed. From this, Matteo Villani drew the conclusion that 'to presume
certain confidence in oneself, by reason of sense, prowess (*virtù*) or power
is on some occasions to find oneself deceived with grave perturbation of
mind.' What defeated all the resources of human skill could come about
regardless of them 'through other unanticipated ways of varying fortune.'[2]

Life was above all unpredictable. Fortune which to Giovanni Villani had
been the force that brought down the mighty from their seats when they
had exceeded the due term of their power tended to become in his brother's
work merely a capricious chance obeying no discernible principle or law.
The term was still used to suggest that worldly success must necessarily be
shortlived, but ceased to imply any definite or systematic tendencies governing the shape of action. It became synonymous with the erosion of
accident upon the bases of humanly created authority and in some cases, as
in this, with the windfall gains of totally unexpected circumstances. It was
something that one needed to be careful of, since what it brought was liable
to melt away as swiftly as it had come, while as a destructive agent it
constantly threatened anyone, the instability of whose position exposed
him to the play of chance. 'Thus unforeseen occurrence to so powerful
usurper of the state', Matteo Villani wrote of the sudden murder of a Sicilian magnate and his family by rivals resentful of the ascendancy he had
obtained over their duke, 'is to be noted as an example to those who with
the favour of deceptive fortune in future rise to similar ranks not to be
ignorant of the hidden ambushes which lie concealed in envy and in the
turbulence of unstable conditions.'[3]

Again, it was a note of practical warning that blunted the point of the old
moralistic formula. One must not aim too high, but if one does so, one
must be prudent. Otherwise the natural drift of fortune would bear one
down.

It follows that, while human ingenuity is powerless before the trend of
fortune, foresight can do something to avert its effects. The position which
Matteo Villani adopts on this point is contradictory but in line with his
essentially defensive psychology. It is unwise to expect anything from
fortune; but on the other hand it is equally inadvisable to give in to it. For
fortune is like the sea which will carry one to destruction unless one can at
times resist its flow. It is with this view of it in mind that Matteo Villani
reproaches the Florentine government, the inexperience and ineptitude of
which he is at pains to emphasise, with abandoning 'diligence and solici-

---

[1] IV, 2.   [2] IV, I.   [3] III, 77.

tude...to the course of fortune,' adding a moment later that, as a result, the Commune is led 'more by fortune than by foresight.'[1] It is also in this connotation that he speaks of fortune in the aphorism 'People rush to where fortune counts more than sense'[2] to underline the conclusion that in human affairs, impulse has more influence than reason. Fortune, in these contexts, becomes in effect synonymous with the kind of instinctive action that leaves man at the mercy of circumstances.

It is a characteristic of Matteo Villani's conception of fortune that it embodies, in the shell of a traditional idea, the gleanings of a practical, worldly wisdom. Superficially resembling his brother's, it nevertheless implies a different value, no longer pointing away from but towards a concern for practical realities. The final, though unintended effect is the recharging of a traditional concept with quite new overtones of meaning. At the same time, the discrepancy between the pragmatic character it assumes in its new form and its articulation in old, moralistic terms creates the need to endow it artificially with the sanctioning authority of time-honoured prejudices. The result is a hybrid of practical rules of action and inherited distrust of immoderation, given formal religious justification by references to the role of divine providence in endorsing it.

As a result of this transformation of the effective meaning of concepts such as fortune, the mastery of an external reality, no longer consistent with the inner promptings of conscience, displaces the subordination of that reality to a wider, ordered spiritual scheme. Two consequences follow from this: first, the correspondence between the natural and the supernatural, axiomatic to the old view of things, is no longer necessary – since divine providence now merely masks an ethical morality and worldly wisdom there is no need to invest the whole of creation with transcendental significance in order to anchor its action in a process of cosmic dimensions; secondly, the structural characteristics of the traditional interpretation of history cease to give unity to it as a whole but are applied instead to individual instances or types of human behaviour: the tendency to attribute a particular kind of result to a given cause persists but within much narrower limits, the pattern of sin and retribution being assimilated within streams of events governed by natural forces. A third incidental implication of this shift in focus is a growing concern with practical questions for their own sake. In the same sense, there is a tentative evolution of alternative, more pragmatic norms as substitutes for the dictates of a particular religious or political viewpoint.

The weakening of faith in the supernatural is evident in Matteo Villani's

---

[1] IV, 55.   [2] I, 47.

chronicle not because of any sharp departure from the practice of recording ominous happenings, astrological phenomena and other similarly unusual events, but because of their loss of significance in relation to his general interpretation of history, and sometimes of their changed character or implications. In his references to eclipses, conjunctions of planets and other celestial signs it is remarkable how often he searches for natural and particularly climatic consequences in order to illustrate their effects. Of an eclipse of the sun in 1354 he says 'of its influence we could see and understand little, except that a singular dry and cold followed the whole winter'.[1] Of the comet the astrologers called Ascone which appeared in the sign of Pisces in 1361, he stated that 'what was seen of its influence was that the winter was very fine and dry, and not too cold, very well suited to the sowing and cultivation of the soil; the spring was fresh and moist, and the summer tempered by rains, whence great abundance ensued.'[2] Most interesting of all is his commentary on the effects of the comet Negra, seen in 1351. This was traditionally associated with death, being considered of a Saturnine nature. Its appearance in 1347 (or the appearance of another comet designated Negra) had been linked by Giovanni Villani with the Black Death.[3] Matteo Villani was aware of its supposed sinister effects and did his best to make his observations live up to them; despite this, however, he could not help allowing his enumeration of its consequences stray into his favourite field of meteorology and, obviously ill at ease with the whole subject, reached only the most half-hearted and indecisive conclusions:

We made a point that year of looking out for the most singular and important events that transpired of which we could have news, and in Italy and in the Patriarchate of Aquilea there were many decapitations of great landholders and citizens which would take long to particularise. And the common plague did not break out this year; but as a result of the war of the Genoese, Venetians and Catalans, great shipwrecks took place and a great slaughter among their men and their allies, and through losses sustained at sea no fewer died on the return journey than in battle. There occured in Italy a singular mishap to the grain, vines, olives and fruits of the trees, in that, everything promising a good harvest, suddenly in the month of July there blew up a great wind-storm which stripped all the trees of their fruit and beat and flattened to the ground the ripened grain and crops with inestimable damage. A few days later the heat was so excessive that all the green crops withered and dried up. As a result of this mischance it happened that, where a rich and plentiful harvest had been expected, it was generally throughout Italy barren and poor. And there occurred in this year singular floods, which caused much damage in many places and spread through-

[1] IV, 24.   [2] X, 93.   [3] Giovanni Villani, *Cronica* XII, 98.

out Italy a general shortage of bread and an exceptional one of wine. In this same year at the beginning of December, there appeared on the seventeenth, in the morning before the break of day, a great band of fire that ran from north to south. And in this same year at the opening of December, Pope Clement VI died, together with some of his cardinals. To our slight understanding, this suffices about these signs in the sky and, having recounted part of what happened, we leave to the astrologers the influence of that which pertains to their science and we shall return to our cruder material.[1]

Though long-winded, this passage deserves to be quoted in full, for it exactly reflects the balance between deference to authority and sturdy common sense in Matteo Villani's handling of a question which he very much wanted to deal with in an orthodox manner without feeling equal to it. He lacked the automatic faith in the connection between the comet and the human world which would have enabled him unhesitatingly to define the effect of the one upon the other. Instead, he cast round haphazardly for plausible consequences in the hope that one or other of them might fit the requirements of the astrologers to whom in the end he despairingly relinquished the field.

The one distinctive feature of his extended rigmarole of possibilities is his concern for the physical as well as the fatal impact of the comet's appearance. The lights in the sky he mentioned, as well as the peculiarities of the weather he described, are recurrent characteristics of his reporting of celestial phenomena and suggest a more naturalistic interest in them and a tendency to try to establish causal connections within the realm of purely atmospheric disturbances rather than between stellar forces and man.

In his discussion of an eclipse of the moon in 1355, the direction of his line of inquiry is quite explicitly brought out:

And not knowing its influence from astrology, we will consider the effects in this following year and we see, continuously until the middle of April, very clear skies and afterwards continuous rains beyond due measure for the remainder of April and the whole of the month of May and afterwards continuous drought and intemperate heat up to the middle of October. And in these summer and autumn times there were general infections and in many parts illnesses of fever and other distempers of the human body and particularly diseases of long duration of the stomach and of the flux.[2]

Matteo Villani goes on to mention an epidemic of rabies in Calabria, animal diseases, battles in France, Flanders and Italy, an unexpectedly good wheat harvest and grape crop despite adverse weather conditions, floods and the spoiling of orchard fruit; but it is unnecessary to follow

[1] II, 44.   [2] VI, 12.

him into this excursion into the climatic and other peculiarities of the year in question which, in any case, merely repeats in different terms the substance of the last quotation. What is significant is his initial point of attack, the way that he is immediately drawn to search for variation in climate and the effect that these have had on crops. Other consequences of a political nature that are mentioned at all are vague in contrast to these precise observations which, however, have themselves no relation in astrological terms to their supposed cause, except that of coincidence of time. Hence, the impossibility of arriving at more than an exasperated disclaimer by way of an evaluation of the evidence presented. Or, as in this case, the terse, apologetic statement that these particulars would not have been set down, had it not been for the eclipse, which presumably justified the mention of anything that might conceivably be connected with it, just in case such a connection existed.

The other notable characteristic of Matteo Villani's treatment of celestial omens is his predeliction for what, in the opinion of his contemporaries, were phenomena of the atmosphere rather than of the planetary spheres. Relatively few eclipses are recorded in his chronicle by comparison with the number set down in his brother's, and the one allusion he makes to conjunctions of planets is a retrospective reference to the famous triple conjunction of 1345 which Giovanni Villani had discussed at length and which Matteo Villani brought into his account of the Black Death only to dismiss it as a possible cause of that pestilence.[1] By contrast there are repeated descriptions of lights or fires in the sky that (according to the scientific notions of the time) fell into the class of exhalations from the earth in which the astrologers of the age, following Aristotle, included comets.[2] This switch in interest goes a long way to explain the increasing tendency evident in his work to associate meteorological effects with astrological causes. Henry of Hesse, in a treatise on the comet of 1368 (composed some years after Matteo Villani's death) which Thorndike summarises was to distinguish between the influence of stars and the direct action of vapours in the atmosphere of which comets were considered to be luminous condensations. According to Thorndike's paraphrase, Henry of Hesse argued that the co-incidence of comets with plagues was due to their both arising from 'the same cause, namely pestilential vapours in the viscera of the earth, such as poison men who dig wells and whose exhalation from the earth gives rise to both comets and plagues. By such reasoning Henry tries to explain the natural ills which were supposed to follow the appearance of comets. He

---

[1] I, 2.
[2] Thorndike, *Magic and Experimental Science*, III, 115–16, 595–6.

further contends that the comet is not caused by, or associated with any particular constellation, and that it is unnecessary to invoke such astrological influence to account for the aforesaid natural accompaniments of comets. It is idle in his opinion for astrologers to base special judgments concerning rulers and regions upon comets, or indeed to make any predictions which they would not have made had the comet not appeared. Moreover, it would be impossible to make such astrological prognostication from comets, because one cannot tell exactly where the comet first appeared or connect it with certainty with any one planet or house.'[1]

Matteo Villani does not go nearly as far as this and reject the astrological influence of comets, but the emphasis he gives in his survey of their effects clearly represents a step in this direction. Whereas for Giovanni Villani a comet was above all a *sign* indicating some great future change – the death of a prominent man, the overthrow of a government, an unprecedented plague – for Matteo as for Henry of Hesse it is essentially a natural phenomenon which one would expect to act, at least in the first instance, upon the physical world. Matteo Villani does not, like Henry of Hesse, deny the power of comets over kings and countries, but he relegates suggestions as to their potential influence in bringing about political events to a subsidiary place in his tentative lists of their consequences. Their inclusion is, one feels, either an afterthought or a perfunctory concession to a previously accepted practice. His immediate reaction to celestial phenomena, search for their possible climatic implications, reveals that he regards the sky not as a reflection, enigmatic and emblematic, of human history, but as an extension of the perceptible world, constituted of the same sort of matter, subject to the same forces.

His obvious fascination with lights in the sky, that is, with a class of phenomena intermediate between the astral and the earthly, points to a growing sense of the blurring, if not the merging, of what had previously been virtually two distinct levels of reality. His interest in these presumably auroral illuminations is not original: Giovanni Villani had in 1309 noted the appearance in the air of 'a very great fire, as large as a big galley, running from north to south with great clarity so that it was visible throughout Italy.'[2]

Even so it is significant for the detailed descriptions it inspires and for the way that it brings together indications conventionally considered to be astrological in character with a probing for their atmospheric effects. Giovanni Villani had linked the nocturnal lights of 1309 with the coming of the Emperor Henry VII. For him, they were primarily an omen and

---

[1] *Ibid.* pp. 493-4.   [2] Giovanni Villani, *Cronica* VIII, 109.

required to be recorded not on their own account but because of the event they foretold. His brother, however, was clearly intrigued by these phenomena in their own right. His reports of them have the sense of actuality of lived experiences. The first he sets down, in October 1352, describes how 'on Friday evening after sunset...a huge mass of incandescent vapours' appeared above Florence, burning with such intensity that the whole sky was 'marvellously illuminated.' It must have been at a great height, for it was visible from every city in Italy. Yet despite this it seemed everywhere on the point of touching 'the summits of the towers and the tops of the trees.' Frequently it threw out great sparks of fire that looked as though they would hit the ground. So rapidly did it move that, from Italy to Hungary, it produced the same illusory effect of nearness. As soon as it faded out of sight, there followed a loud rumbling thunder like the sound of an earthquake. Its appearance caused amazement among the people and speculation among the learned who held it to be a combustion of vapours, or comet, or Asub' at the same great height as Mars and so large that, had it come down to the ground, 'it would have covered the whole of Italy, and more land'.[1]

Something of the dramatic intensity of the emotions and impressions aroused by these strange lights in the sky remains in this account, as it does in the reports Matteo Villani furnishes of other occurrences of them. He describes how on one occasion people rushed out into the streets of Florence and bells were rung because many took the reddish glow in the sky for a sign of fire.[2] The disquiet and curiosity inspired by these spectacular but mysterious phenomena can be sensed in the elaboration of detail which surrounds his record of them: again, as so often in Matteo Villani's chronicle, one feels the effort to trap the truth in a net of particulars. Everything that can be noticed is set down in case it may prove to be significant. A light in the sky is not just a light, it is a shape, a moving object, mass of flame, the visual accompaniment of a distant, thundering roar. In one instance, Matteo Villani compares the streak of fire passing overhead to a snake: a large firm head of blazing light trailing behind it an ashen serpentine coil, narrowing at the neck, broadening again at the belly and then thinning gradually towards the tail – to fade slowly from one extremity to the other.[3] On another occasion, to give an idea of the vast expanse of the reddening mass of vapour, he says in a rather beautifully descriptive phrase that 'the stars showed themselves in it like sparks in fire.'[4] Such similes capture the sensory reality of perception far better than Giovanni Villani's terse and on the whole unilluminating comparison between the size of

[1] III, 37.   [2] X, 31.   [3] III, 74.   [4] X, 31.

lights in the sky and of a galley that, in any case, completely ignores the problem of distance of which, [as we have seen, his brother was made aware by the deceptive proximity of the same lights in widely separated places.

By contrast to his suggestive descriptions of these phenomena, Matteo Villani's comments as to their possible effects monotonously re-echo the same conclusion: the lack of rain in the ensuing months.[1] To this other incidental consequences are sometimes added, for instance, a hot summer and much tertian fever,[2] poor harvests and in one case earthquakes; and in a unique reversion to Giovanni Villani's response to such phenomena, the arrival in Italy and the coronation of the Emperor Charles IV. But this last result is, considered in context, only one of those retrospective concessions to a traditional formula of interpretation that Matteo Villani felt impelled from time to time to make. After dwelling upon the usual drought, and remarking that it was only broken because the Madonna of Santa Maria Impruneta yielded to the entreaties addressed to her by a procession to her shrine, he inserts a final superfluous sentence: 'There also followed the coming of the Emperor in this year and his coronation, and the coming of great earthquakes, as we shall presently relate.'[3]

Despite such occasional references to the possible meaning of celestial signs as portents of great events, for Matteo Villani astrology has largely ceased to have the force of a fatal influence upon human affairs. Omens, those other points of connection between the physical and the psychic worlds in the animistic view of reality which Giovanni Villani had to some extent absorbed, are however recorded in his chronicle, though their relevance to history seems purely accidental. They are not worked into the texture of events as symbolic pointers to the final outcome of a patterned chain of development, but seem rather to illustrate or characterise the quality of a single incident. For example, the death of Pope Clement VI is anticipated by a thunderbolt which strikes the campanile of St Peter's and destroys its bells.[4] The appropriateness of this is underlined by Matteo Villani who, after detailing the late pontiff's vices, concludes: 'The comet Negra[5] foretold his death, the striking of St Peter's in Rome by lightning consumed his fame in vile metal'[6] (a reference to the melting-down of parts of the bells in the heat generated by the lightning).

Similarly the destruction of the statue of a winged lamb surmounting the campanile of Santa Maria Novella in Florence, also by lightning, is held to be a 'demonstration of occult judgment, considering that the friars of this

---

[1] III, 37; III, 74; X, 31.   [2] VIII, 47.   [3] III, 104.
[4] III, 42.   [5] See page 60 above.   [6] IV, 43.

place disordinately transgress the humility of the rule given them by St Dominic...'[1]

The omen in both these cases has an examplary or cautionary character, in one instance implying divine condemnation of an unworthy pope, in the other urging the friars to reform their lax and luxurious ways (with the effect that one of their number, 'the venerable master Pietro degli Strozzi', decided that the graven image of the lamb was not to be replaced upon the pinnacle of the campanile, and that in future the convent would rely for protection against lightning upon holy relics). It unmasks sin but provides no insight into the meaning of history.

An earthquake could, according to Matteo Villani, have a similar significance, as for instance when the town of Borgo San Sepolcro, alone of the cities of Tuscany, was devastated by an earthquake, this being a 'singular sentence of God' upon it for having been first place in that part of Italy to open its gates to the troops of 'the great tyrant, the Archbishop of Milan'.[2] But equally, an earthquake could portend future changes, like that of 1349, which foreshadowed political revolutions and disturbances in the countries where it occurred.[3] The idea that aberrations from the course of nature must be accompanied by corresponding deviations in the human world died hard, and Matteo Villani did not reject it. But his assumption of it was somewhat hesitant, leading more to tentative guesses than confident assertions because it lacked the backing of a coherent view of reality in which such interlocking phenomena had a logical and essential place.

His treatment of a subject in which he clearly had a morbid, fascinated interest – the birth of monstrous children – bears this out. Concern with the auspiciousness or otherwise of such prodigies of nature seems to have arisen from the tradition of the medieval bestiaries: both Giovanni and Matteo Villani allude to the birth of lion cubs, the former as an exceptionally favourable omen,[4] the latter only to correct the misconceptions of ancient authors who believed that lions could not breed in cold climates and that they died stillborn, being revived by their mothers' breath.[5] But it was reserved for Matteo, with his natural pessimism, to fasten on the most grotesque manifestation of this kind of phenomenon and, strangely, to consider it as a concomitant to the birth of lion cubs which, to his brother, had been so fortunate a sign. After describing in the most horrible particulars some deformed children who had been born, he remarked that according to the learned, this affliction had resulted from the failure of the heavens to emit their customary emanations, adding however, that this

---

[1] VIII, 46.   [2] III, 48.   [3] I, 45.
[4] Giovanni Villani, *Cronica* X, 183; XI, 67.   [5] III, 90.

deficiency seemed to have been compensated for among lions for of these three male cubs had been born on St Zenobius' Eve.[1]

The idea that aberrations from the proper course of things were related still lingers here, but effectively as something stemming from natural causes. It is exceptional physical conditions which have produced both results; neither is a symptom of a deep-set spiritual disturbance vibrating through other levels of reality. Elsewhere, however, Matteo Villani concedes that the birth of deformed children may well be a punishment for sin, though the whole tone of his explanation in this case is indecisive:

But of this and other monstrous human bodies born in our city we cannot determine whether it was the after-effect or portent of some affliction, as the ancients believed; but shameful and dishonest sins often are the reason for monstrous births, and sometimes the power of the constellations.[2]

In this as in other, similar passages, Matteo Villani is torn in two directions by his attachment on the one hand to the traditional association between misfortune and guilt, on the other by his attribution of the abnormal to malfunctions of the cosmic order. The one drew him to crude moral explanations, the other to physical ones. Giovanni Villani had been able to combine the two by fusing together the conception of a divinely ordained, morally just universe with the primitive belief in the interaction of the spiritual and material worlds. But to do this he needed the connecting link of history which demonstrated the triumph of good by invoking the correspondence of actual reality with the over-riding spiritual order. History in the sense of an explicit materialisation of a transcendental scheme joined what, in Matteo Villani's loose, morally aimless universe fell apart. Unable to impose a clear sense of direction upon change, Matteo Villani lacked the means to pull together ethical judgment and causal explanation. The fragments of what they had combined remained, but tended increasingly to attach themselves to particular situations, here pointing up an adventitious moral, there edging towards the semblance of a naturally conceived causation. Vestiges of the supernatural persisted, reinforcing moral condemnation, or patterning an apparently physical process upon traditional conceptions of astrological influence. Yet they had become effectively redundant, appealing to conventional habits of mind rather than serving the purpose of knitting life together into a significant whole. As they ceased to fulfil a meaningful function, so other motifs began to emerge, not as substitutes for them but as an alternative source of values. Giovanni Villani's outlook had proceeded from the assumption of a responsive

[1] IX, 25. [2] IV, 70.

world, Matteo's from that of a restrictive one. Consequently, he was drawn both to prize freedom and humanity and to regard them as essentially and inevitably precarious. They came to constitute ideals, manifestations of that proper natural condition of men's existence that was better than the reality of nature or man himself. Liberty, for instance, which 'in this world is certainly reputed the dearest thing that there is'[1] was a disposition towards which created beings normally tended:

As we see from experience, both men and animals are, without cause, by nature desirous of liberty and crave for it as for their own good; little birds, fondly nourished in cages, rejoice on seeing the forest, and if they can flee from the places in which they are confined, return to the woods; men who have been long in servitude, accustomed to the yoke of tyranny, if they are persistent, and see the chance to recover their liberty, strive to attain it with all their bodily feelings.[2]

The natural, in this interpretation of it, was the inner prompting of a man's or an animal's being. As in Boccaccio's more light-hearted, contemporary conception of it,[3] it opposed itself to all outward constriction. Yet, just because it was expressed so much in the form of instinct and impulse, it was subject to their limitations. It was natural for men to seek freedom, but also for them to be incapable of achieving or preserving it. Animals wanted to be at liberty; but they could be tamed, broken into a submission that would deprive them completely of their native will to be free. So also men, who besides had other vices, other weaknesses that made them frequently assist in, or encompass, their own subjection. They were ungrateful, ever ready to overthrow those whose eminence they resented,[4] and by nature changeable and eager for novelty.[5] Their passions could make them incapable of ruling themselves, like the people of Prato, who 'by not knowing how to use liberty became subjects'.[6] Or they could, out of mere spite, sacrifice their own freedom in order to destroy that of those they hated, the reason given by Matteo Villani for the submission of the Sienese to the Visconti who were thereby placed in a position to threaten the independence of Florence.[7]

Above all, men could lose the taste for liberty so that, when the opportunity came, after a long period of subjection, to regain it, they would be incapable of doing so. Thus, the people of Verona, given an unexpected chance of shaking off the oppressive rule of the Scaligeri, at a time when dissensions in that family had resulted in the flight of their ruler and his

---

[1] x, 23. [2] ix, 70.
[3] See A. D. Scaglione, *Nature and Love in the Late Middle Ages* (Berkeley, 1963), for a discussion of Boccaccio's conception of nature and the natural.
[4] v, 38. [5] x, 25. [6] i, 73. [7] i, 62.

abandonment of the city, failed to make use of it and indeed soon welcomed their tyrant back into their midst without any effort to set up a popular government. 'The people, cowardly and accustomed to servitude,' Matteo Villani commented, 'finding itself at liberty... did not know how to use the liberty and freedom which fortune had unwittingly restored to them.'[1] Similarly, when Jacopo Pepoli, isolated by his enemies, threw himself at the mercy of his Bolognese subjects, they had not the resolution to expel him, but, keeping him in power, allowed him to sell their city to the Milanese: 'already tamed by the servile yoke of tyranny, when the time for freedom came, because of poverty of spirit or their sins, they were not worthy of such a benefit, it being at that point in their power to return to liberty without opposition.'[2] Guided more by 'the course of fortune than free will' (the expression is revealing), they slipped back into the well-worn groove of submissiveness.

While, in the unstable political conditions of mid-fourteenth century Italy, freedom represented a value to be sought after, one necessary for man to realise his true nature, it was also something elusive and corruptible. Set against it as the very embodiment of the pathology of free institutions was the phenomenon of tyranny, the self-destructive cancer which grew out of the weaknesses and tensions of popular regimes. Tyranny to Matteo Villani was of the essence of the violent and unnatural. Like Bartolus of Sassoferrato,[3] he contrasted its arbitrary nature with the legitimate, authorised power of hereditary rulers. The cruelty of tyrants was not to be wondered at for they delighted in the shedding of innocent blood to maintain by terror their violently established states. Mercy and humanity which were the natural attributes of a hereditary prince were not to be expected of them.[4] Blandishments, deceptions, betrayals, the disregard of all charity, blood-relationship, honour – these were the normal resources of tyrannous ambition.[5] Treachery to them was preferable even to war in that the cost of fighting exceeded that of bribery.[6] Yet despite the sheer immorality of their methods, in the disturbed conditions of the Italian States of the period, they prevailed. But their power was, by its very nature, shortlived. Their lack of scruple which they used as a weapon against others, could equally well be used against themselves. They could trust no-one, enjoying none of the traditional loyalty accorded to hereditary sovereigns and being surrounded by men eager to pull them down so that they could take their place. It followed, according to Matteo Villani, that 'as tyrannies are

---

[1] IX, 60. [2] I, 63.
[3] See E. Emerton, *Humanism and Tyranny* (Cambridge, Mass., 1925), p. 127 for translated text of Bartolus of Sassoferrato, 'De Tyrannia' Ch. II, 3.
[4] VIII, 109. [5] III, 99. [6] IX, 71.

created as, in their rise, they strengthen and grow, so is nourished and concealed in them the cause of their confusion and ruin.'[1] And if tyranny thus bore in itself the seeds of its own destruction, those who practiced it involuntarily but irresistibly hastened their own downfall by their insatiable appetite for power: 'As the thirst of the miser for acquiring gold cannot be satisfied, so the tyrant's passion cannot be extinguished by the attainment of lordship; to devour he holds his gullet open, and the more he can destroy or consume, the more he desires.'[2]

This conception of tyranny has in it something of Giovanni Villani's belief in the self-destructive character of worldly evil. Those doomed by God encompass their own downfall through the tendency of their passions to bring about their merited ends. At this point, the providential interpretation adjoins and blends with a naturalistic one: where Manfred miraculously chose to forfeit the battle of Benevento to Charles of Anjou – because rashness was all of a piece with the defiance of the will of God for which he stood condemned – the tyrants destroy themselves because their power rests on principles that necessarily undermine it. Their overthrow, though morally justified, is brought on not because they are evil, but because of the natural tendency of the methods they use. Yet the process by which it comes about has the same pattern, is impelled by the same logic as that which, in Giovanni Villani's formulation of it, underlay the action of divine retribution. The idea of nature here grows out of that of providence, with the loss of a clear sense of a morally directed history but with the retention of the same mechanism and the same overtones of belief in the necessity of the ultimate punishment of the wicked.

The Platonic–Aristotelian conception of the natural or real as the perfected essence of the actual, which the medieval Christian world-view absorbed and to which it gave a theological colouring at this point separates itself out from the religious associations that had given it a narrow, specialised meaning. It becomes once again a vague sentimental attachment to a pure instinctive good which the imperfections of experienced reality obscure and distort. But at the same time it continues to bear the marks of its previous connection with a particular doctrine of rewards and punishments in so far as it takes for granted that the unnatural – and therefore evil – will perish of its own corruption even though there is no assertion of the converse, that the natural will, of its own impulsion, prevail.

It is this last detail which sharply distinguishes the old, theologically orientated view of history from the basically ethical naturalism of Matteo Villani's interpretation of human behaviour. In the former, providence

---

[1] VI, I.   [2] IX, 56.

ensures that right triumphs, in the latter this depends on man's capacity to learn from the past the lessons that God has written into it. Consequently, the area left to human choice is larger, and crucial in a sense that it was not before. Even the assumption that men would meet their just deserts through the operation of natural tendencies leaves open the loophole that they might be able to circumvent the effects of such tendencies by anticipating them. In this way the moral force of the process could be completely nullified. God, conceived as a power directly intervening in human affairs, could defeat all the ingenuity of a tyrant's cunning; but with that tyrant considered merely as a person obsessively driven to his doom by his lust for power or as one who would ultimately fall a victim to others' use against him of his own methods, the possibility arises that, by resorting to exceptional restraint or skill, he might be able to avoid the normally expected consequences of his actions. This, indeed, is precisely what did happen, according to Matteo Villani, in the case of Giovanni Visconti da Oleggio who was wily enough to surrender Bologna to the Church in return for the right to hold the smaller city of Fermo before his misdeeds caught up with him and who therefore was able to retire and enjoy in peace the fruits of his ill-gotten gains.

...and having committed so many cruelties, so many extorsions and robberies, like an old wolf he knew how to manage things so that he got away freely with huge quantities of money and jewels and betook himself to Fermo; he had both pulled out of the game and withdrawn to a place of peace and tranquility, leaving the Bolognese and the Legate at war; and certainly, if he was considered wise, on this occasion he showed it.[1]

Matteo Villani's barely concealed admiration reflects the ambiguity of his position. He does not disguise Giovanni da Oleggio's roguery; but on the other hand makes no effort to conceal that at times guile may be effective. However stringently tyranny, treachery and greed might be condemned, they still fall within an area of behaviour in which, so far as practical results are concerned, skill counts for more than the rightness or the wrongness of the action involved. The bias of his interpretation has subtly but decisively shifted in response to the change in his approach to the problem of controlling circumstances: morality has become merely a matter of judgment and no longer necessarily affects the resolution of a situation. The whole sphere of the practical, though certainly not exempt from assessment by its standards, can also be considered to some extent separately in the light of the actual pressures that determine success or failure in this world.

[1] ix, 76.

71

Resourcefulness becomes thus a criterion in its own right, irrespective of the justification or otherwise of the purpose it is employed for – because it is a tool in the reduction of the haphazard, accidental play of events to the service of human ends. A Machiavellian ruse by which King Peter of Aragon tricked the garrison of Lojera in Sardinia into surrender, for instance, elicits Matteo Villani's commendation as an example of how ingenuity may defeat adversity. Evidently, while investing the city, this astute ruler had heard that his Venetian allies had suffered a disastrous naval defeat in the Eastern Mediterranean at the hands of his Genoese enemies. Instead, however, of raising the siege, he spread the rumour that it was the Genoese and not the Venetians who had been decisively routed, with the result that the defenders of the place became so disheartened that they readily yielded it to him. This, according to Matteo Villani, 'confirmed the ancient proverb against sloth which says that good management overcomes bad fortune'.[1] Can Grande della Scala of Verona drew similar praise from the Florentine chronicler by the swift resolution with which he retrieved his position when it seemed effectively lost. Hearing while out of the city that one of his illegitimate relatives had seized power, he immediately returned though he had with him only a small band of men and succeeded in ousting the usurper before the latter had had time to consolidate his authority. Had he delayed, Matteo Villani considered, he would not have regained Verona for a long time, or perhaps, if his upstart successor had been able to provide adequately for its defence, he would never have done so.[2] But, acting as he did, he provided what to Matteo Villani was clearly a model of political behaviour in that it showed, as Peter of Aragon's stratagem had done, that even with luck against him, a determined and skilful ruler could achieve his ends. The realism inherent in the favourable portrayal of such conduct is of a different order from that which occasionally inspired Giovanni Villani and of which his brother's views on statecraft are to some degree a development.

Giovanni Villani was a shrewd if somewhat dour observer of the political life of his day who not infrequently felt impelled to generalise from experience in maxims intended to warn or enlighten his readers. Virtuous citizens were, for instance, urged not to become involved in politics, it being a disgrace before God and man that in this imperfect world vices always overcame virtues and jealousy and proud ingratitude prevailed over magnanimity and liberality.[3] One should also not aim at the heights of power since envy would ensure that those who hoisted a leader up would later try to pull him down, 'the ungrateful people' knowing no other reward for

---

[1] IV, 34.   [2] III, 101.   [3] Giovanni Villani, *Cronica* VIII, 8.

anyone so foolish as to attempt to serve its interests.[1] Besides, it was in the nature of things that a rapidly gained political ascendancy would be short-lived, as Cola di Rienzo's meteoric career showed.[2] Self-interest at the expense of the common good was the bane of states and the cause of the decline both of Rome and the disaster-plagued Florence of the mid-fourteenth century.[3]

Such comments anticipate Matteo Villani's moralising on practical questions but they do not reveal an interest in these for their own sake. Basically, they are reflections of prejudice projected upon actual situations to which they are appropriate. This is true even of the occasional, rare passage which expresses sentiments that would not have looked out of place in a work by Machiavelli; for instance, this one which deplores the failure of the heads of the Florentine government to lead their own troops:

the rulers of Florence did not recall what Lucan had written of Caesar: when he drew up his army, he did not say to his troops 'Go,' but 'Come,' and so acting the Romans always had victories. And so the opposite happens with lords and rulers of Communes when they do not personally lead their armies, leaving care and provision to foreign soldiers.[4]

This represents a valid generalisation from the experience of warfare in fourteenth century Italy; but it still has the quality of a judgment made from the distance of absolute standards that do not so much arise from the reality of circumstances as condemn it out of hand when it does not conform with a preconceived ideal. Giovanni Villani cannot seriously have thought good burghers like himself, elected for a temporary term to conduct the affairs of the republic, would have been effective as military commanders; what he was really concerned to do was to ascribe to the incompetence of the Florentine administration the failure to take Lucca in 1342. All he really wanted to say was that if the men responsible for directing the campaign had been there on the spot (which they could have been without leading the troops), its outcome would have been different. But seeing politics as he did in terms of edifying morals, he had to go further than this to what in fact becomes a nostalgic lament that things are not as they were in the days when rulers heroically led their armies to victory. What at first sight seems acute, realistic deduction turns out in context to be a value judgment without direct applicability to the situation to which it refers – the statement of an abstract principle rather than the prescription of a practicable method.

The immediate, pressing necessity is here still subordinate to the moral

[1] *Ibid.* XII, 43.   [2] *Ibid.* XII, 105.   [3] *Ibid.* XI, 139.   [4] *Ibid.* XI 109.

quality of the action concerned in a way that it is not, say, in Matteo Villani's treatment of a problem bearing similarly on the military ineptitude of republican governments – an urgent issue confronting Florence in the 1350s following the formation of Fra Moriale's free company in 1353. Putting pressure upon one Commune after the other, this group of professional soldiers was, as Matteo Villani described in some detail,[1] able to extort money or the right of passage in turn from each of the city-states of Tuscany when united they could successfully have resisted it. Analysing the reasons for this, he put it down to the psychological tendency of each Commune to ignore the plight of others, imagining that a danger at a distance could never become a close one: '...each Commune being far from the storm, it cared little about it'.[2] The conclusion he drew from this was not only the need for co-operation, but above all that of resistance. The companies thrived on the willingness of their victims to buy them off. The terror they inspired was not due to the force they represented but to the irresolution of those who stood in their path. Challenged, their seeming might would crumble, for like all thieves, they were essentially cowardly. An incident in which another company, led by Count Conrad of Landau, of which all Italy stood in fear, was nevertheless ignominiously routed in the best comic opera style by a mere rabble of villagers in the Apennines, armed with nothing but rocks and pitchforks,[3] showed up the emptiness of the threat they represented – as did the withdrawal from Florentine territory of the same mercenary band (when it had been re-formed) in the face of resolute opposition by the city's government. The latter episode, according to Matteo Villani proved that,

however numerous the men of a company were, and terrible by reason of its iniquities and cruel operations, they could be defeated and eliminated since experience indicated that people like this were of the vile and cowardly nature to pursue those who fled and to make themselves scarce before those who showed their teeth. We perceive that the thief caught in the act loses his nerve and allows himself to be captured by anyone at all; and such is the case with this evil band which forms itself into a company only to rob.[4]

Despite the strong vein of moral condemnation running through this and the subsequent reference to divine aid in securing the expulsion of the Company from Florentine soil, Matteo Villani's analysis of the position is basically psychological. The weakness of the Tuscan cities was exploited by these predatory soldiers of fortune; conversely, their weakness could be exposed by the calling of their bluff with an appropriate show of strength. The line of conduct indicated does not issue from adherence to an exem-

---

[1] III, 89; III, 108–10; IV, 14–16; IV, 23.   [2] III, 110.   [3] VIII, 74.   [4] IX, 31.

plory virtue, but is suggested by certain allegedly observed characteristics of human action. This does not necessarily make Matteo Villani more accurate in his portrayal of events – in fact, as Gerola's study[1] of Fra Moriale's passage through Tuscanny shows, he greatly oversimplifies the reasons which led the other Communes to abandon Florence and make terms with the mercenary captain – but it does mean that he makes a rudimentary if rather unsatisfactory attempt to find a solution to the problem of the companies from an understanding of the motives underlying human behaviour. If he does this crudely, it is at least partly because he is still bound by a view of man in which success is taken to be the reward for virtue and failure the penalty for vice. Thus, if the Communes are heedless of the plight of their neighbours, it must be that they are selfishly and foolishly indifferent to a danger which must ultimately also threaten them – it cannot be that they prefer to buy off Fra Moriale to engaging in a league detrimental to their interests. Equally, if a company retreats before a show of resistance, this must be because the men composing it are cowards, not because they decide that it is not worth their while to undertake a long and profitless siege.

Matteo Villani's realism on a point such as this clearly has its limits; but it still arrives at a method which, though its justification may be ill-founded, is none the less effective and appropriate to the situation. He is not modern in the sense that he explains human behaviour in terms of interests: moral imperatives still bulk large in his view of causal processes; but at least they are absorbed within an interpretation of action in which results proceed from conditions rather than intentions.

It would be misleading perhaps to describe Matteo as more realistic than Giovanni since both chroniclers saw clearly and reported shrewdly what happened around them, while neither was capable of a completely objective analysis of the working of political forces. Yet there is a respect in which Matteo's position does represent an advance on that of his brother: whatever value judgments his conclusions may conceal, he argues not from the authority of traditional models of behaviour but from evidence interpreted in practical terms. He does this not because he is in any way more enlightened than Giovanni Villani but because, unlike the latter, he does not judge experience by reference to pre-established standards that make the end of all exploration of reality the confirmation of certain pre-existing rules, but has to seek to control that reality by exploiting its own intrinsic characteristics.

Matteo Villani's greater naturalism in this direction is a by-product of

---

[1] Gerola, 'Fra Moriale in Toscana', pp. 364 ff.

the weakening of his confidence in authority. Undoubtedly, this issued from the collapse of his assurance in the Church which had been basic to his brother's interpretation of history. The re-orientation of Florentine attitudes to the Papacy struck a crippling blow, not merely at confidence in the Church, but also at the whole basis of the previously conceived world-order, giving rise to the need to find other sources of support in tradition for belief in the historical mission of Florence that the Guelph interpretations of the immediate past had inspired.

There is a clear contrast between the views taken of the Papacy by the two chroniclers. It was of course not unusual for Giovanni Villani to criticise or even condemn popes in the strongest terms, but he seems never to have lost his respect for the institution they embodied or his attachment to what might broadly be called the papal cause. Matteo Villani on the other hand was unambiguously hostile to the Avignon papacy which he represented as corrupt, avaricious and deaf to the pleas of its former allies. His disapproval extended also to the higher clergy in general who were accused of neglecting their pastoral duties and of living in flagrant luxury. Instead of being spiritual shepherds true to the charges given them by Christ over his flock, he complained, they had become rapacious wolves.[1] In order to load their already groaning tables, they left benefices unfilled so that congregations dispersed and 'rapacious wolves' preyed on God's sheep.[2] They lived delicately, squandering money on their relatives and did not care if churches fell into ruin and God's poor died of hunger, being heedless alike of divine wrath and worldly infamy.[3] Their avarice made them misrepresent the terms of an indulgence proclaimed by the pope so as to miss no opportunity of lining their pockets by

remitting sins and vows of all kinds for much money or for little, whichever they could attract; and so as to not deny their greed, they prevailed upon every little old woman and moneyless pauper, in towns, villages and hamlets, to give linen and woollen cloth, household goods, grain and crops; they refused nothing, deceiving people by making good with words what their commission did not endorse...[4]

The animus behind such attacks is far more bitter and pointed than in any of Giovanni Villani's reproofs of the clergy. They clearly indicate a shift in attitude to the Church, now regarded not as the champion of righteousness in the world, but as a corrupt and self-seeking institution, bent only on its own advantage or that of its loose-living members. The popes at the head of it come in, of course, for the severest criticism, both on moral and political grounds. They are not even singled out as indivi-

---

[1] II, I. [2] VIII, 6. [3] VIII, 110. [4] VI, 14.

duals, condemned as Boniface VIII had been by Giovanni Villani, as exceptions to the rule of pious, dedicated occupants of the papal throne. One has the impression that to Matteo Villani all popes were bad. A threat by Innocent VI to take the papal court away from Avignon because some of the cardinals were making a practice of abducting, and publicly living with, the wives of the local citizens was treated with scepticism by the Florentine chronicler because, he held, God would not permit a return of the papal see to Rome until the sins of the prelates had equalled those of previous Italian ones,[1] a remark which certainly did not indicate a very high opinion of popes or churchmen of any period or nationality. Elsewhere, he quotes, with apparent agreement if not approval, a scandalously witty letter reportedly addressed to Pope Clement VI by the devil. (It had mysteriously turned up at a meeting of the consistory and was, so Matteo Villani insisted, read aloud by the pope to the assembled cardinals.) This commended them all for their private and public sins and encouraged them to persevere further in them so that they might deserve in full the grace of his kingdom. It reviled and abused the rule of poverty and the apostolic doctrine which, as his faithful vicars, they hated and held in repugnance, but not as fervently in their teachings as in their works for which he reproved them and admonished them to correct their ways so that they might acquire through merits the highest position in his kingdom. This letter, Matteo Villani commented, 'touched extensively and well upon the vices of our pastors of the church, and for this reason many copies of it were circulated among Christians... But the pope and the cardinals took little notice of it as their later operations indicated.'[2]

It was these operations and the frictions between the Papacy and Florence which anticipated them that were in fact the reason why Matteo Villani took such strong exception to the Church. They revolved basically around the situation, already referred to, which was created by the expansionist designs of Giovanni Visconti, the scheming Archbishop and tyrant of Milan. To contain Milanese incursions into Tuscany and Romagna, the Florentines would have liked, as has already been pointed out,[3] to have relied on their traditional alliance with the Papacy: after all, their city had been a good daughter of the Church, while Giovanni Visconti was an unscrupulous, ungodly despot and a Ghibelline. However, the Papacy at this time was not primarily interested in restraining the Visconti; it was, rather, preoccupied with the problem of the re-conquest of the Papal States and, while it shared with Florence a determination to prevent the Milanese from seizing Bologna, beyond this its aims diverged from those of the

---

[1] IV, 86.   [2] II, 48.   [3] See pages 49–51 above.

Tuscan Commune. Even over Bologna there was, as has been indicated, some mistrust of Florentine intentions on the part of the Church and, when it became clear that the Archbishop of Milan could not be prevented from taking the city, the Papacy preferred to buy him off by conceding its loss to getting involved in a protracted war which could only weaken the Church's position in Romagna even further. To the Florentines and Matteo Villani in particular, this and subsequent papal actions which brought out conflicts of interest between the Papacy and its former Tuscan ally constituted a rank betrayal that could only be explained as the result of clerical irresolution or corruption. 'But he who trusts in matters of war to the appearance given by the initial acts of prelates,' he once ruefully complained, 'and does not consider how the church is prone not to carry through its enterprises will find himself frequently deceived.'[1] Disenchantment in this instance came with the acceptance by the pope of Milanese terms against the advice of the Tuscan ambassadors at his court, something he was led to, in Matteo Villani's view, through bribery and the most sinister forms of influence:

At this time, in winter, the Archbishop of Milan continuously maintained at court solemn ambassadors to secure his reconciliation with the church; and this the King of France urged with the power of the great gifts he made, and continually in his letters pleaded with the pope and the cardinals to pardon the Archbishop who, to be more favoured, sued for peace. The pope's relatives and certain cardinals were so handsomely supplied and so often that they constantly pleaded for him with the pope as the Countess of Turenne never ceased doing, as a result of which the pope forgot the honour and the injuries of the Church. And notwithstanding that he kept the ambassadors of the Tuscan Communes waiting on the proposals they had made, the ambassadors continually recalled in consistory the offences committed by the Archbishop and his predecessors, the injury and violence that he had done and continuously was doing to the Communes of Tuscany, faithful and devoted to the Church. The pope, despite this, favoured beyond all honest measure the cause of the tyrant, for which he was courteously reproved by some cardinals, and those and other cardinals who showed themselves in consistory to be zealous for the honour of the Church were, with the passage of time, silenced thanks to the craft, skill and gifts of the tyrant, as were unloosed the tongues in his favour, so that ultimately he achieved his intention, as we shall show in due course.[2]

After this, nothing was bad enough for Matteo Villani to say about the pope, and in particular Clement VI, whom he described as a squanderer of the wealth of the Church, worldly in his ways, extravagant in his mode of living, over-favourable towards his relatives and above all, much given to the pleasures of the flesh.

[1] I, 70. [2] II, 66.

When he was an Archbishop, he did not abstain from women, but outdid the excesses of the young, lay barons; and, in the papal office, he could neither contain nor conceal himself; but to his rooms great ladies came like prelates; among others a Countess of Turenne was so much to his liking that to her he extended a great share of his favours.[1]

This woman, the pontiff's niece, whom Matteo Villani elsewhere dubbed 'governor of the pope in his temporal needs'[2] and whom Petrarch[3] castigated as Semiramis in some of his vitriolic descriptions of the papal court, seems to have been, in the invective of both, particularly cast for the role of temptress, responsible for drawing Clement VI into his evil ways. The accusations made against her and the pope by both the poet and the chronicler have been dismissed by modern historians such as Mollat;[4] it may well be that they derive from the same source since Matteo Villani could have known Petrarch's Florentine correspondents, Francesco Nelli and Lapo da Castiglionchio (Zanobi da Strada, another member of their circle, is mentioned in his chronicle on the occasion of his coronation as poet laureate in Pisa).[5] Even if he is thus indebted for his information, the motive for his attacks is, however, clearly different from Petrarch's and derives not from personal animosity but from political disillusionment. The Papacy had fallen from grace in his eyes: the very strength of the former attachment of his city to the papal cause sharpened his recriminations. He was consequently intent upon showing up its vices and painting them in the blackest colours in order to emphasise that it no longer stood for the principles it had represented before. Florence was justified in repudiating its lead, was indeed compelled to reject it so as to defend its liberty. Having been abandoned once, it could, and had to turn its back on its formerly prized but now discredited loyalty to the Church. Discussing an appeal by Innocent VI for help against the enemies of the Papacy, he wrote that

it did them little good this time to sound the alarm, for the Commune of Florence, accustomed to keep faith and loyalty, on this occasion closed its ears. Thus it had done before and would do henceforth, for when in the past it undertook lofty and great enterprises, it was left to extricate itself by the governors of the church of Rome whom it had supported; and when the Commune was in need, the church completely abandoned it, to the grave peril of the state.[6]

---

[1] III, 43.   [2] III, 3.

[3] Petrarch *Epistolae sine nomine* 8, 10, 13 in P. Piur, *Petrarcas 'Buch ohne Name' und die päpstliche Kurie* (Halle, 1925), pp. 193–209.

[4] Mollat, *Popes at Avignon*, pp. 42–3.

[5] V, 26. This chapter also includes a reference to Petrarch as another poet of Florentine descent similarly honoured with the laurel crown. Interestingly, Matteo Villani comments that neither had been accorded his due since, delightful though their verses were to the ear, neither had won the favour of the learned.   [6] IX, 100.

The Papacy had not only sacrificed Florence to what, in Matteo Villani's opinion, were unworthy expedients of policy; it had also forfeited the right to act as the champion of those values that seemed to him distinctly Guelph. Having been raised to worldly greatness with the aid of its Tuscan ally, it had gone the way of all proud, earthly powers, forgetting what it had once stood for and so losing its title to the headship of the Church in the true, ideal sense. By resisting it, Florence was not opposing the cause that had once linked it with the Papacy, but only the corrupted men who now pretended falsely to espouse it:

The worldly and temporal state of the Church of Rome having been enhanced and raised to the highest pitch of power in Italy by the force of our Commune, its governors, grown haughty, suppressing all religion and all shame, as men ungrateful and disregardful of benefits received, have sought, according to the laws and customs of wicked tyrants, with plot and treachery, through hidden and covert ways, even to the point of coming out into the open, to purpose our submission to their rule, and deprive us of our liberty; that is why it has been necessary for our Commune to defend its state and justice, to spend millions of florins and, what has been worse, to work against the Church of Rome which gave it its party-emblem, so that it may be said almost against itself; and however much such may be the common cry, the truth has been that the Commune has worked not against the Church, but against wicked and worldly pastors.[1]

This passage indicates a shift in interpretation in more ways than one. Primarily, it distinguishes between the church as a cause and the Papacy as the human instrument by which it is governed: the one can remain good even when the other has become bad. But at a deeper level, there is also a change in the criteria by which this goodness or badness is judged. The pastors of the church are acting like tyrants; they are therefore betraying what has been the aim of Florence's alliance with the Papacy, the preservation of its freedom. The two elements previously fused in the concept of Guelphism, support of the church and the defence of Communal independence against imperial pretensions, have been forced apart by the recognition of a change in papal policy, with the result that the latter displaces the former as the key factor in the combination. To be a Guelph now is to defend civic liberty: if the Papacy has ceased to do so and indeed is working against it, it can have no claim to represent what used to be the Church, understood as a party, as a force in history or politics.

In the twelfth and thirteenth centuries it had suited the Papacy to underwrite the aspirations of the Italian city-states to independence from imperial control; in the fourteenth century the conditions which had

[1] VIII, 103.

caused it to do so no longer held. Yet, accustomed to having an absolute authority, the Church, sanctioning their liberty, citizens of the Communes such as Matteo Villani found it hard to dispense with some justification of it. Hence, on the one hand, bitterness with the Papacy, issuing in protestations that it could no longer claim to be the true voice of the Church, on the other attempts to find in republican traditions an alternative basis for the ideology of civic freedom.

The term 'Guelph' undergoes in the process a modification, if not a transformation. It does not cease to carry overtones of previous association with the cause of the Church, but the Church here signified is an ideal, an historical authority, rather than a reality in the language of contemporary politics. Effectively, it is freedom which comes to be regarded by Matteo Villani as the essence, the distinctive characteristic of Guelphism. In his criticism of the magnates and 'grandi' who, in order to enhance their share of political influence, devised the expedient of 'admonishing' their enemies (that is, debarring them from the exercise of political rights), this is clearly indicated.

Though carried through in the name of the Parte Guelfa, this practice was according to him, 'a means of destroying and degrading its just and sacred title'. The Parte Guelfa, as he put it earlier in the same chapter, 'is the foundation and firm and stable citadel of Italian liberty, and opposed to all tyrannies, so much so that if a Guelph becomes a tyrant, it follows necessarily that he becomes a Ghibelline...'[1] In other words, by acting in a way detrimental to civic liberty, the great families dominating the Parte Guelfa had forfeited their right to champion the principles they pretended to espouse. Their pro-papal political sympathies and the traditional identification of their society with the Guelph cause were irrelevant once they went against the spirit that had inspired it.

The inseparability of Ghibellinism and tyranny which Matteo Villani here took as axiomatic forced upon terms that had previously designated partisans of the Church and Empire the connotation of defenders and opponents of civic freedom. This view of their virtual significance was in fact justified by Matteo Villani on historical grounds. Italy, he wrote, was divided between two parties, the Guelphs or guardians of faith, supporting the Church, and the Ghibellines or *guida belli*, commanders in war, sustaining the imperial cause. (Both words were given a fictitious origin as verbal distortions of their allegedly original forms.) Originally, cities subject to both factions had enjoyed free republican institutions. But the German Emperors who, in their incursions into Italy, were naturally

---

[1] VIII, 24.

favourable to the Ghibellines had, by placing vicars over the places loyal to them, promoted tyranny, for no sooner had they left or died than their regents became in effect despots. Furthermore, lacking the sophistication to rule Italians either through wisdom or power, they fostered dissensions so as to be able to control through their divisions those whom they could not master through skill or an understanding of their way of life. This meant that those cities which were Ghibelline and received the Emperor underwent a change in government culminating in tyranny.[1]

Thus, either by one route or the other, Ghibellinism issued in the loss of free institutions with which it became synonymous.

By contrast, the Guelphs were those who had maintained their liberty. Clearly, in the light of the above argument, they owed this only in the most indirect sense to the Church in so far as, being its supporters, they were disloyal to the Emperor and therefore were saved from the consequences of submission to him. Their adherence to the cause of liberty which was now the crucial distinguishing mark of their Guelphism was something they had inherited not from their alliance with the Church but from their traditions of communal freedom. In the chapter of his chronicle immediately preceding that in which Matteo Villani established what to his mind was the connection between tyranny and Ghibellinism, he outlined a theory of the delegation of authority to the Emperors from the Roman people (among whom he included the inhabitants of the Tuscan towns), a delegation which was, by implication, provisional so that the liberty the Italian city-states enjoyed was theirs by right and did not flow as a concession from imperial favour:

with the Roman people the Communes of Italy, and particularly the Tuscans, under their sovereignty shared the citizenship and liberty of that people, whose authority created the Emperors: and this same people, not of itself, but the Church acting on its behalf, by way of faithful Christians' tribute, conceded the election of the Emperor to seven German princes. From which it is manifest – it happens very many ancient histories show it – that the above-mentioned people made the Emperors, and for their misdemeanours sometimes overthrew them, and the liberty of the Roman people was in no way subordinate to the liberty of the Empire, nor tributary to it like other nations which were subject to the Roman people, and to the Senate and the Commune of Rome, and through this Commune to the Emperor; and our Communes of Tuscany, having maintained the ancient freedom handed down to them from the civic heritage [*civiltà*] of the Roman people, it is very clear that the majesty of that people was outraged by the free submission made to the Emperor by the Communes of Pisa, Siena, Volterra and San Miniato and the freedom of Tuscans vilely abused, due to the envy which one Commune bore the other rather than any other reason.[2]

[1] IV, 78.   [2] IV, 77.

This passage, which has been singled out for notice by Capponi[1] and Rubinstein[2] as an indication of changing attitudes to liberty in mid-fourteenth century Florence, has an importance transcending its immediate pretext – Matteo Villani's wish to defend his city for not making submission to the Emperor Charles IV by condemning the formal acts of homage of the other Tuscan Communes. Its significance lies both in its appeal to a classical tradition to justify Florentine claims to freedom and in its ingenious attribution of the source of imperial authority not to the Roman Empire but to the Roman people whose rights are then considered to have been transferred to their supposed Tuscan descendants. Liberty comes, in this context, to be regarded not as something sanctioned by God through the Church or accorded by a superior power, but as an inheritance of which, by the historical anomaly of the 'translatio imperii', those legitimately entitled to it have (at least formally) been deprived. The displacement of the centre of the Empire to Germany and the conferring of the right of imperial election to seven German princes are seen as aberrations from a proper and originally intended procedure of government of which the rise of tyranny in Italy is a natural by-product. In 'the adverse times of the misguided Empire,'[3] as Matteo Villani elsewhere described it, the inappropriateness of a German occupancy of the imperial throne[4] created a distortion in the political situation in Italy which was compensated for only by the resistance of the Church and the Guelph party to Ghibelline influence.

This enabled liberty to survive but only, as it were, accidentally: its true roots lay in the Roman past, the seeds of which the Church had not so much nurtured as fortuitously prevented from being destroyed.

The pattern of historical interpretation here outlined has a formal resemblance to that propagated later by the humanists: in both cases, the source of what is natural and right is placed in antiquity and its absence from the medieval world is explained by a deviation from, or misunderstanding of, the rules governing the order that had permitted it to flourish. For Matteo Villani, it was a question only of liberty; for the humanists it was a matter of art, style and scholarship; but underlying this difference there is the same idea of a history shaped as a sequence of authoritative achievement, decline and revival through a recognition of that decline and a return to the norms of the classical era.

[1] G. Capponi, *Storia della repubblica di Firenze* (3 vols., Florence, 1876), I, 275; 407–8.
[2] N. Rubinstein, 'Florence and the Despots: Some aspects of Florentine Diplomacy in the Fourteenth Century', *Transactions of the Royal Historical Society*, Ser. v 2 (1952), 31–2.
[3] III, I.
[4] This point, central to the argument of IV, 78, is re-iterated in v, I.

Matteo Villani's motive for the development of this view of the role of the Romas tradition was not, like Petrarch's, an affinity with the outlook of Latin authors, but the exigencies of a historical situation in which it was possible to discover a political ideal neither in the exhausted Guelph cause, nor in a universalist imperialism like Dante's. In his eyes, the Church was discredited, the Empire weak. Liberty, his prime preoccupation in an age of tyranny and of threats to Florentine independence, had to be given another basis. This was naturally found in the continuing tradition of the Italian city-state which could trace its origins back to a Rome that, by its civilisation, had a title to respect as worthy as, in many ways worthier than, that of those now fading twin-luminaries of the medieval political firmament, the Empire and the Papacy. The direction in which Matteo Villani's thought moved, while it points towards the Renaissance, is determined not by the values that later come to characterise that movement but by a loss of faith in existing institutions. It derives, like his tendency towards a greater naturalism and more humanitarian standards of judgment, from his basically negative response to the political and social realities of his age. His reactions differ from those of earlier writers such as Dante because nothing seems to him dependable except what one has and, since even that is precarious, nothing is worth fighting for except its retention. The great Florentine poet had in his day been even more cruelly disillusioned with the Papacy than Matteo Villani was to be; but his rejection of it only made him believe all the more strongly in the historical mission of its rival and alternative, the Empire. Like Dante, Matteo Villani could trace back the evils of his lifetime such as tyranny to a deflection of the proper course of history through the arrogation of power by those not intended to exercise it; but this did not bring him to an ideal solution of the world's ills in terms of a restoration of what had been wrongly removed. All it did was to make him re-inforce and justify that liberty which seemed to him the essence of a way of life now endangered by forces inimical to its survival and bereft, through the rift between Florence and the Papacy, of its previous philosophical supports. To him, the identification of the Florentine with the Roman people was a form of ideological re-insurance, a means of buttressing by reference to a still venerated and enduring authority what otherwise would have seemed tenuous and fragile in a shifting world.

His strengths as a chronicler and observer of his times do not issue, as do his brother's, from his certainties, but rather from an honest, if sometimes excessive recognition of the instability and harshness of his age, and his willingness, in an effort to preserve for life some of the meaning Giovanni Villani had found in it, to adapt his standards to absorb even strife and adversity within a vision of things expressive of a concern for morality and human values. For him, history ceased to be structure and became the endurance by man of the penalty of his failings. Its lesson was to avoid greed, violence, ambition which, directly in their immediate effects, indirectly as pretexts for divine retribution, kept the world in ceaseless turbulence and suffering, eroding liberty and social order. *Anime tribolate, se potete, datevi in viaggio pace e buon piacere* – 'Afflicted souls, if you can, give yourself in your journey peace and good comfort'[1] – such was his exhortation to his readers. If he concentrated upon the vices of men and the evils of life, it was as he himself said, so that the works of the wicked might be exposed and the rulers of the state cautioned against the pitfalls of government.[2] The aim he set himself was modest and practical; yet, in combination with the world picture which he had inherited, it could not but produce interesting and, in the long run perhaps, fruitful distortions of traditional patterns of thought. To Giovanni Villani, the order which history disclosed was a reflection of a cosmic design interweaving natural and supernatural forces in a single, harmonious whole. To his brother, the values which this system had generated were still real, but as they broke loose from the structure which had given them their original meaning, their significance changed. They came to reflect not a conception of life as struggle between forces of right and wrong, clearly identified in the actual protagonists of political conflict, but the judgment of actions in terms of their perceptible effects. Experience to which Giovanni Villani had resorted to discover confirmation of his interpretation of history thus began subtly to modify the essential nature of that interpretation as taken over by his brother and applied to the altering political context of his age. In this way, Matteo Villani arrived, despite himself, at a position that implied distinctively new standards as a result merely of trying to preserve what he had borrowed by the very means he had inherited.

[1] XI, I.   [2] VIII, 103.

3

THE FLORENTINE CHRONICLES
OF THE LATER FOURTEENTH
CENTURY

MILLARD MEISS, in his study of painting in Florence and Siena after the Black Death, remarks on the contrast between the tone of Tuscan art before and after 1350:

The great styles that succeeded one another during the preceding fifty years... constitute a rather orderly development, the younger painter in each instance developing one or another aspect of the older master's style. Around 1350 this continuity seems interrupted. Though the influence of the earlier tradition persists, many of its fundamental elements were rejected, and others were combined in a new and wholly different way...[1]

He sees in the art of the latter half of the fourteenth century a return to a more conservative conception of space and choice of subject-matter, revealing a renewed emphasis upon the divine at the expense of the human. If one accepts this thesis in so far as it applies to painting and searches for signs of a similar tendency in the outlook of the chroniclers of the period, one discovers little unambiguous evidence of the exaltation of the supernatural which, for Meiss, is central to the intentions of the artists he discusses. However, the process he describes has its parallel in the work of the chroniclers in the dissociation of the natural from its previous conceptual framework. That the middle of the century marked a significant turning-point in view of the relationship between the physical and human worlds, the chronicles confirm. But it seems (if Meiss is accurate in his analysis) that this change manifested itself in one way in painting and in a rather different one in the writings of chroniclers such as Matteo Villani. The recoil from the sensory which Meiss discovered in Orcagna, Andrea da Firenze and others had its counterpart in Matteo Villani's pessimism and his distrust of man's capacity to redeem himself. But there is a dimension of his outlook which was evidently lacking in that of the painters who were

[1] Millard Meiss, *Painting in Florence and Siena after the Black Death* (Princeton, 1951), p. 2.

his contemporaries: simply because he cut loose from a unifying scheme of historical interpretation that reconciled the human with the divine, he was incidentally drawn towards a rudimentary naturalism that reflected his essentially practical approach to the problems of his age. It would seem that the predicament facing both painter and historian in Florence and the rest of Tuscany in the mid-fourteenth century which Meiss has described with reference both to the Black Death and the social conditions of the time gave rise to two contrary tendencies: on the one hand, to a renewed emphasis on faith and a repudiation of the values of the here and now, on the other to a willingness to accept the natural world, in so far as it had to be accepted, on its own terms.

In the Florentine chronicles of the latter half of the fourteenth century and the first years of the fifteenth century, in other works of the period immediately following the readjustment of attitudes to conditions that took place around 1350, it is the latter trend that manifests itself most clearly, at least in the larger historical works that continue the tradition established by the Villanis. In the smaller chronicles, or *ricordanze* of the same time, which are concerned less with the description of public events than with personal recollections and the tracing back of family origins, the more intimate nature of the subject-matter does, however, permit some of the religious preoccupations of their middle-class authors to reveal themselves. Christian Bec, in a recent study,[1] has examined the outlook and values of a number of these writers who found themselves torn between the demands of religion and morality on the one hand and of hard-headed business sense on the other to an extent that had been unusual in the first half of the fourteenth century. It is significant that, at this period, these smaller, less ambitious works of the family-chronicle type are produced more frequently than before: it seems as though something of the general uneasiness characteristic of the times is reflected in the urge to tap the accumulated experience of a man's life or the history of a family so as to forearm descendants against the pitfalls of the future. Also illuminating of the quality of the age is the uncertain balance which prevails in these writings between the real world, depicted usually as unreliable, adverse, treacherous, and the spiritual cravings of the men who composed them which tend to flare up with unexpected intensity at moments of crisis, but which seem otherwise to have little relation to their everyday existences.

A characteristic illustration of this can be found in the *Ricordi* of Giovanni di Pagolo Morelli, one of the authors with whom Bec deals, though

---

[1] C. Bec, *Les Marchands écrivains: affaires et humanisme à Florence 1375–1434* (Paris–the Hague, 1967).

from a point of view which leads him to emphasize other aspects of this writer's work.[1] Morelli, in these recollections, is mainly interested in setting down the kind of information which will prove the antiquity and worth of his family. He traces back its genealogy, describes the lives and characters of those of his relatives whom he has known or of whom he has indirectly had knowledge and then goes on to an account of his own life, interspersed with occasional references to political events. Yet, at the same time, his *Ricordi* are a record of his personal experiences, of the moral lessons he has drawn from them and of the feelings they have inspired in him. Most of these are mundane enough – the usual business dealings of a merchant's life, the financial gains and losses, the marriages, the births and deaths of children, the enmities encountered and friendships made, with their accompaniment of insistently professed moral sentiments and self-justifications one would expect of a man of Morelli's time, class and background. But, towards the end of his book, a new dimension is added to the whole conception of the work by an allegorical passage which draws together its unrelated threads and endows the whole with a transcendental meaning the expression of which its foregoing text hardly leads one to anticipate. This describes the author's grief at the death of his eldest son and relates how he tried to console himself for it by prayer and the contemplation, how he was then tempted by the devil who assailed him with thoughts of the futility and meaninglessness of his life and how finally, in a dream, a mystic vision of St Catherine and of his dead son comforted him and placed his sufferings in their true, religious perspective. Although this was written in 1407 or later, it shares the prevailing temper of much late fourteenth century Florentine writing. Life is seen as tribulation and failure for which the only compensation is spiritual. At the same time, there is a telling worldliness in the devil's advocacy of a more hedonist response to the adversities of the times. Urging that Morelli has been much abused by fortune, he insinuated the thought that for this there is no remedy but reprisal: . . . 'if she deprives you of a hundred florins, steal as many: if she gives you sickness act when you are well so that you break every law, satisfy your every wish and scorn everything else'.[2] Subconsciously, the urge to defy all moral standards, here represented as a diabolical prompting, contends with the religiosity of an emotional recourse to the supernatural

[1] *Ibid.* pp. 53–75. Bec is essentially concerned with presenting a composite picture of the attitudes of the late fourteenth-early fifteenth century Florentine merchants as revealed in their chronicles, memoirs and letters. He therefore concentrates upon their views on trade, usury, social conventions, family responsibilities, rules of conduct and action, and only brings in their response to religion when it bears upon their practical preoccupations with money making and prudent and upright behaviour.

[2] Giovanni di Pagolo Morelli, *Ricordi*, ed. V. Branca (Florence, 1956), p. 493.

to right the wrongs, absolve the sins of this life. The conflict is of course resolved in favour of the forces of light, but the shadows define themselves with revealing sharpness, and, even in the final evocation of the symbolic spiritual figures of a mythical bird, the pure virginal saint and the departed and now transfigured son, set against the idyllic, idealised background of the Mugello, leaves the impression less of an assurance in faith than of a conjuring away of deep disillusionment through the wish-fulfilment of an edifying fantasy.

Digressions indicative of intense personal feeling, implying in this case a flight from an unacceptable reality into mysticism, can have a place in art and in the record of individual experience but do not belong with the recital of historical events. Hence, in the chronicles proper of the period, this kind of recourse to the spiritual is notably absent. The relevance of its occurrence in the more intimate family chronicle to the larger, more impersonal works of those who set themselves the task of recording history is that it indicates the relegation of the sense of the supernatural to private, subjective experience and, by implication, the weakening of its applicability to the objective world of public action. It is not surprising, in the light of this, that the political chronicles of late fourteenth-century Florence make little reference to spiritual forces in history, in contrast to that of Giovanni Villani which had been so extensively preoccupied with them. It is equally interesting that these chronicles are at the same time less personal in tone: with the decline of belief in the materialisation of the supernatural in history, there seems to go a growing awareness of the divergence between the external reality of the political world and the inward reality of personal experience, the one the subject of detached observation, the other of emotional involvement. Essentially, these chronicles are specialised descriptions of events, unconcerned with placing them within a comprehensive word-picture and therefore, as it were by default, inclined to a more pragmatic approach to political problems. Their naturalism, in so far as one can describe it as such, proceeds from an acceptance of the disjunction between the supernatural and the everyday realities of this life.

There are two large, extensive chronicles written in Florence in the latter half of the fourteenth century, in addition to that of Matteo Villani. They are by Marchionne di Coppo Stefani (or Bonaiuti as he ought properly to be called)[1] and by an anonymous author formerly identified, in the Tartini supplement to the old edition of Muratori, with Piero Minerbetti.[2]

[1] A. Panella, 'Per la biografia del Cronista Marchionne', *Archivio Storico Italiano*, Ser. VII 14 (1930), 241–62.

[2] G. M. Tartini, *Rerum Italicarum Scriptores* (Volumes supplementary to those edited by L. A. Muratori) (Florence, 1770), II.

Both works are on a scale which, though slightly inferior to that of the two Villani chronicles, is equalled round about this time in Tuscany only by the chronicles of Giovanni Sercambi of Lucca. They are, however, more modest in their intentions than the universal history of Giovanni Villani. Though Marchionne does, in imitation of that work, go back to the origins, not merely of Florence but of mankind, this represents no more than a perfunctory concession to an accepted convention. His true subject is Florentine politics in the fourteenth century, particularly in its internal aspects. The culminating incidents of his narrative, the factional strife of the 1360s and 1370s, the War of the Eight Saints and the Tumult of the Ciompi, clearly provide the inspiration of his chronicle which, being predominantly political in its preoccupations, is narrower in focus than that of Giovanni Villani. Even though Marchionne is not immune from the habit of moralising, endemic to Italian middle-class writers of this period, and even though he follows the usual custom of noting down astrological indications, the character of his work is markedly secular. It is significant that where, in the early part of his history, he derives material from Giovanni Villani, he tones down the element of the supernatural in what he borrows.

The anonymous chronicler is even more clearly a recorder of events undistorted by interpretation or judgment. As he himself naively admits, his motive for writing is simply that his memory is failing and he finds it embarrassing not to be able to recall happenings of a year or two back: hence he has resolved to set them down – 'to take note purely for my own sake' (as he puts it himself), 'of things that I hear are being done in many places...so as at least to be able to read those things which I cannot remember on hearing them said to others'.[1] With such intentions, it is hardly surprising that he achieves a degree of objectivity. What is remarkable, however, is that his chronicle is not a mere list of incidents, but does have considerable descriptive interest. The period it covers, between 1385 and 1409, is one distinguished by the dramatic events surrounding Giangaleazzo Visconti's attempts to subjugate Lombardy and Tuscany. These are fully recorded as are other details of the turbulent Italian history of the time which, in themselves and in this author's reaction to them, give the work a distinctive colouring. One has the impression, reading it, of a world ruled by fraud and violence, viewed with a detachment that seems almost to imply consent, or at least acquiescence in the morality of action it displays. It stands at the opposite pole from the insistently moralising, didactic chronicle of Giovanni Villani.

---

[1] 'Cronica volgare di anonimo fiorentino dall' anno 1385 al 1409 già attribuita a Piero di Giovanni Minerbetti', ed. E. Bellondi, *Rerum Italicarum Scriptores*, n. ed., XXVII, part 2.

The works of the two Villani, Marchionne di Coppo Bonaiuti and of the anonymous chronicler, each describing (insofar as these writers deal with their own immediate experience) successive periods of Florentine history from the last decade of the thirteenth to the first decade of the fifteenth century, also reflect a progressive weakening of the sense of historical structure and, with it, of preconceptions as to the necessary moral significance and transcendental implications of the course of events. The two decline together, not through any growth in scepticism but because religion ceases to have relevance to the area of public action with which the chronicles unavoidably deal. No longer conceived as forming part of a coherent connected process, history fragments into a collection of independent facts susceptible to interpretation only in terms of the natural world; thus, a kind of objectivity is created although it does not in any way imply a modern historical method. It signifies perhaps the removal of one obstacle to the development of such a method but in itself it indicates the persistence merely of an old technique of historical reporting which, enhanced though it is by the realism and commonsense of the practical men who used it, is still limited by the narrowness of essentially descriptive intentions.

The authors whose works effectively continue the coverage of fourteenth-century Florentine history where the Villani left off had the same predispositions and, so far as one can tell, the same social background as the two earlier, more famous chroniclers. Marchionne, though he does not appear to have practiced a trade, came of a merchant family, well-connected in Florentine society but not of aristocratic rank. Like the Villani, he was active in civic affairs. He belonged, however, to a much later generation. Born in 1336,[1] he did not become involved in Florentine politics until the late 1360s and held his first important office, as one of the Dieci di Libertà, only in 1372.[2]

His formative experience came consequently not at a relatively stable period in the internal history of the city but in the strife-torn sixties, seventies and eighties of the century. Inevitably he was compelled to identify himself far more unambiguously with regimes and parties than Giovanni Villani and he was, on the other hand, far more prominent than Matteo Villani as a supporter of them. During the War of the Eight Saints, he went as an emissary to the Commune of Bologna[3] to enlist its aid against the Papacy. He was also, during the same conflict, one of the

---

[1] Rodolico's introduction to Stefani's *Cronaca fiorentina*, in *Rerum Italicarum Scriptores*, XXX, part I, p. ciii.

[2] *Ibid.* p. cix. [3] *Ibid.* p. cx.

commissioners charged with the confiscation of church property.[1] He came thus to be closely associated with both the internal and external policies of the 'Eight Saints'. After the Tumult of the Ciompi, his continued willingness to serve the Commune linked him with the relatively democratic interlude in Florentine politics that followed, even though he was active as a prior only in 1379 after the revolutionary excesses of popular revolt had subsided and the city was in effect ruled by a coalition of lesser and greater guilds. He carried out a number of commissions for the Florentine government at this time, including embassies to Milan and to the imperial court in Germany;[2] but after 1381 ceased to play an active part in politics owing largely to the reassertion in 1382 of the power of the oligarchy of great families hostile to him. His chronicle was presumably written between his withdrawal from public life and his death in 1385, or possibly 1386.[3] Like Giovanni Villani's later books it was thus almost certainly composed in the shadow of disappointment.

The absence of biographical information on the anonymous chronicler means that it is possible only to speculate as to his social status and political experience from the internal evidence of his book. This does, however, reveal a degree of familiarity with internal and external developments that suggests participation, at some time or other, in active political life. The style and tone of the work and what can be inferred from the rare comments it contains are, further, consistent with the attribution of it to a member of an upper middle class family of mercantile origin. On points of manner of writing and approach to political problems, there is very little to distinguish it from the chronicles of the Villani and of Marchionne di Coppo Bonaiuti. Its differences, like the differences between Marchionne's work and those of the Villani, where they are not personal, reflect changes in time, viewpoint and emphasis rather than of basic outlook and method.

In Marchionne's chronicle, it is the preoccupation with civil strife that sets the keynote of the work right from its preamble and, by focusing attention on the domestic history of Florence, at once narrows the scope of the work and renders redundant traditional trappings of interpretation intended to place the detail of historical events within a universally meaningful scheme. Although he begins his justification for undertaking his labours with the customary profession of his desire to glorify Florence, this is quickly followed by a statement of his intention also to show the other side of the medal:

[1] M. Becker, 'Un avvenimento riguardante il cronista Marchionne di Coppo Stefani', *Archivio Storico Italiano*, An. 117 (1959), 137–8.

[2] Rodolico, Introduction to Stefani's *Cronaca Fiorentina*, pp. cxv–cxvii.

[3] Panella, 'Per la biografia del cronista Marchionne', p. 250.

And thinking how magnificent that city is in our time, we will set down in our present writings the magnificent and virtuous works, the magnanimous exploits, the just ordinances and laws, its exaltation, the sublime victories, the sophisticated subterfuges and the moving of minds to achieve great enterprises and alliances, of victorious citizens and valiant knights to abide by and magnify its rule and magistracy; and on the other hand its enemies and perverse citizens and their cruel machinations in seeking to usurp the state, overcome it, go against it and oppose it, to generate in it divisions, factions, plots, parties, tumults, strife and slaughter and purely for their own interest and honour to seek to reduce it to their power.[1]

From the very beginning of the work, the reader's notice is drawn to that besetting evil of Florentine politics, factional conflict, here singled out as no less deserving of the chronicler's attention than the great achievements of the Commune. An awareness of its continued and ineradicable presence appears to pervade every reference to it. For instance, in discussing the original emergence of the Guelph and Ghibelline factions early in the thirteenth century, Marchionne remarks that their names

have been the scourge of Christendom and especially has this been, is and please God may it not be so in Florence, of which however I see as yet no sign, Florence standing, what with parties and factions, in tribulation, and the Guelph and Ghibelline parties adding so much fuel to the fire that, no matter how large it is, it goes on growing greater every day anew.[2]

Marchionne's embitterment with the Parte Guelfa of his own day, his brushes with at least one member of which Becker[3] has documented, here breaks through to inject a note of almost personal venom into his otherwise calm historical narrative. It is the same with allusions to his other governing obsession, competition for offices, which he saw as the great, indeed virtually the only cause of civil strife. He could not write of the dissensions of the 1290s, for example, without using them as a pretext for airing complaints inspired by his own political experience:

As we have previously said in several places, ambition for offices and for government had grown so much that everyone wanted and sought after the government ...and please God that those ambitions might have prevailed then and been absent today; for how they were then I have not seen but heard; but in these days I have seen and heard so much of requests for offices and the hostility of whoever does not get what he asked for that God could not bear it; for surely it is a marvellous thing that pleas outrage all honesty for I have been asked sometimes so that I myself have been ashamed for the supplicant and for the office or the

---

[1] Stefani, Preamble, p. 1. [2] R. 82, p. 34.
[3] Becker, *Archivio Storico Italiano*, An. 117 (1959), 140.

7-2

ballot to be gained; and certainly all the maledictions which the city of Florence has had in my time have been only on account of offices.[1]

The use of an identical formula of expression, indeed of almost identical language, in these two separate digressions points to a fixed thought pattern, which made Marchionne interpret the past in terms of his own immediate political experience. The impulse to seek offices and form parties which he has deduced in his own day to be the dominant motive in political behaviour becomes the key factor in similar situations in history. His fixation with the jealousies and ambitions that prompt rivalry for power reflects, up to a point, an inference from observation. Yet it arises equally from an adaptation of the traditional view that the passions of men make peace and stability impossible of achievement: like Giovanni Villani and in almost the same terms, Marchionne held that times of amity and prosperity in the city engendered strife by arousing covetousness. Florence, he remarked once, echoing Villani, 'being at peace and magnified by victories, strife arose between the Adimari and the Donati'.[2] Or, as he put it elsewhere in explaining the tension between classes in Florentine society in the period immediately following the expulsion of the Duke of Athens in 1343,

...as the saying goes that men always suffer evil better than good, the city standing so much at rest, in harmony and happiness from having returned to liberty, they did not know how to enjoy the good they had...either because pride would not be quieted, or that it was destined that Mars, designator of the city of Florence, and the sign of Leo which was in the ascendant at sunrise at the birth of our city, gave it the tendency never to be at rest, whatever the reason was, scandals in so sweet a city and concord brought in their train the malicious and old serpents, enemies of the human race, for the Grandi began in the city and in the *contado* to use force and extortion through the license afforded them by the offices they had.[3]

Stability, in this view of things, in itself prompted change and that change, Marchionne concluded with characteristic pessimism, could only be bad. 'It always seems,' he once wrote, 'that when things are transformed in their being, nothing either useful or decent ensues.'[4] In the light of this, Marchionne's strictures against his fellow citizens for their ambition and party-spirit fit with the stereotypes of an older outlook: men's desires are evil and do violence to the principle of rest that is the essence of order; yet being what they are they are driven to act for their own private interests against the good of all; hence political life is a constant ferment of rivalry,

---

[1] Stefani, R. 196, p. 70. For other expressions of the same idea, see R. 228, p. 85.
[2] R. 152, p. 56.   [3] R. 588, p. 211.   [4] R. 495, p. 173.

animosity and strife. The ideals of peace and stability can be only transiently realised since the impulses of human nature are inimical to them.

These basic presumptions Marchionne has clearly taken over from the past to build with them his own view of Florentine politics. Where this differs from, say, that of Giovanni Villani is not in its preoccupation with civic dissensions, though this is more prominent in Marchionne's interpretation than in that of the Villani, but in its greater consciousness of what one might describe as the mechanics of factional strife. For the Villani, the divisions in Florentine society issued from the rift in the original composition in the city's population and, of course, from the basic sinfulness of men. Clashes between parties and families illustrated a disposition either of human nature or of the Florentine people. Marchionne, of course, also acknowledged this, but he went on to distinguish the motives for conflict more precisely, particularly in class terms. The world in which he lived was not only one of factions, but of 'grandi', 'magnati', 'popolani grassi' and of the 'popolo minuto'. The lower classes had, of course, figured in the chronicles of the Villani; but essentially they were regarded as intruders upon the political scene. The real issues were those between the Guelphs and the Ghibellines, the Blacks and the Whites, the Albizzi and the Ricci, each as it were playing out in their mutual antagonism the legendary roles of the Romans and Fiesolans whose intermingling had allegedly sown the seeds of discord in the city. Marchionne, by contrast, found the causes of enmity either in the aspirations of the lower orders for more power in the state or in the resentment of the great at the competition for offices of those they considered socially beneath them. The springs of politics still lay in human passions but the pretext for these was less family or factional rivalry than tensions between different strata of the Florentine community.

Marchionne's pre-occupation with class distinction and conflict undoubtedly arose from the predicament which he shared with others of his social group in his lifetime: not admitted to the tight, oligarchic cliques of the 'Grandi', such men were equally distrustful of the growing political influence of those of lesser social rank than themselves. Conditioned to the view that only citizens of old burgher stock had the experience to deal competently with the business of government, yet also affronted by the even more exclusive pretensions of the great patrician families, Marchionne was sensitive to the bearing of class and status on political action to an extent unusual in his predecessors. Manifesting itself in a hostility towards, and disparagement of, the forms of pressure exerted by both those above and below him in the social scale, his reaction to the tussles for power which he witnessed reveals, despite his prejudices, an understanding of the objective factors underlying the fluctuations of politics. Whereas for Giovanni Villani, change appeared to arise from basic flaws in the constitution of things – from evil, from excess, from violation of the natural order, in accordance with a time-honoured formula that veiled with Christian morality the ancient notions of measure and fortune – for Marchionne (writing admittedly of the far more limited sphere of Florentine politics), it sprang from the inability of forms of government to satisfy the demands of all social groups. The political pendulum was constantly swinging, not because of the cycle of sin and retribution, but because every regime excluded some section or other of the politically active population from the influence to which it felt entitled. Its existence became therefore precarious since at no point could it achieve a balance of representation that would command the acquiescence of the whole city. This situation Marchionne judged in moral terms by attributing the resultant instability to the selfishness, inexperience or folly of those whose political prominence he had cause to resent, but he explained it naturally with reference to the jealousies and animosities that each short-lived ascendancy excited.

The interpretation he gave to events in Florence from the 1340s on did not pre-suppose or suggest any idea of structured historical development. It did, however, give an impression of the nature of political forces as they operated in the peculiar conditions of Florentine society. Marchionne was always careful to show how each level of the community reacted or contributed to the developments he described and how these developments were the outcome of a particular combination of the factors acting at the time. In explaining the willingness of the lower and middle classes to support the Grandi in their invitation to the Duke of Athens to assume power in the city, he pointed out that, at this stage, despite the advantage of greater numbers, these subordinate elements in the population had neither the initiative nor the organisation to express their wishes and so followed meekly the lead of their social betters.

The populace and even the middling sort of men (*mezzani*) who live without any order and, since they are too numerous to assemble or come to an agreement among themselves, are suborned by ear or by a tap on the shoulders and, given present blandishments, without any thought for the future on their part, unless there is someone to disclose it to them, they agree with whoever talks to them, and believe; the Grandi with their sense, gentility, order and their lineage, or the few, seldom acquiesce and discuss their business and see what is best – I do not say the best of their desires always, but what they wish of their desires they rather decide, be it good or evil that they choose, because they have fewer to consult and to assemble; among peoples, as has been said, this is impossible. And thus it was soon agreed to grant the Duke of Athens the abovementioned offices and household.[1]

In this passage, in its way remarkable for its psychological penetration, Marchionne defines the starting-point of a series of political vicissitudes that form the main thread of his account of events over the next forty years. He describes a situation which may in a sense be considered as stable: the lower classes are still submissive; the Grandi can cajole and man-oeuvre them into accepting what they want. But this state of affairs is not presented, despite its apparent equilibrium, as in any way ideal. It is indeed blamed for the decision that to any late fourteenth-century Florentine must have seemed particularly unfortunate for the Commune, namely the choice of the Duke of Athens as its ruler. The partisan spirit of the Grandi and the political passivity of the lower classes combined to produce a result that was to show up the dangers inherent in each of these dispositions. The Duke of Athens, having been hoisted into office with the aid of the great families, spurned their support for that of the 'popolo minuto' once he had established his authority for, as Marchionne explained, 'one rarely sees a lord or tyrant who does not abase as much as he can whoever gives him power, for he says "As they have given it to me, so they may take it from me."'[2] As a result the Grandi, disappointed in the man they had originally welcomed with enthusiasm, began to plot against him, while the previously docile populace, feeling itself courted, grew bolder and more demanding. The tyrant's reliance on the lower classes Marchionne regarded askance, partly because he considered it ill-advised to trust the fickle people, partly because of his own prejudices against giving the mean and lowly ideas above their station and so encouraging them to murmur against the social order. The Duke, he remarked, in aligning himself with the people, forgot '. . . that they had crucified Christ, crying "Let him die, let him die." Well should he have remembered that they would not act towards him any better than they had done to Christ, who was just a Lord.'[3] As for currying the favour of the mob and allowing his French retainers to mix with the lowest dregs of the population, this was to undermine social discipline and, as the introduction into the Florentine vocabulary of the ominous word 'Ciompi' was symbolically to suggest, to spread disaffection among the people.

While old and honoured citizens were thrust aside, Marchionne complained, the Duke's men drank and associated with working men whom they addressed as 'Compar' or 'Companion' which (so the chronicler insisted) became corrupted in the Tuscan pronunciation to 'ciompi', so

---

[1] R. 553, p. 194.   [2] R. 565, p. 199.   [3] R. 564, p. 199.

that the lower classes began to describe and think of themselves as Ciompi or companions of the rulers of the city.[1] Offended by such unseemly fraternisation with the lesser orders and by the other excesses of the Duke's government, the politically active population began to work for his over-throw. When he was expelled, social harmony reigned for a brief spell, the working classes having promptly deserted his cause and animosities between other social groups being temporarily quieted. Rejoicing in recovered liberty did not, however, last long and soon the Grandi, 'popo-lani grassi' and artisans were falling out over the share of offices which each section in Florentine society was to enjoy. Eventually the Grandi found themselves isolated and, unable to prevent the institution of a relatively democratic regime, nursed their resentment and strove to exacerbate social tensions in order to upset the *status quo*. The scene was thus set for the classic situation that was to prevail in Florence for the next half-century in which every precariously achieved state of political equilibrium was im-mediately challenged by those who felt it denied them their proper share of power and in which rumblings of discontent from the disenfranchised but now unsubmissive lower classes produced a ground swell of barely re-strained popular disturbance and violence.

Marchionne, in his account of these years, highlighted the sequence of quarrels, plots, street battles and riots. First the Grandi and the 'popolani grassi' came to blows and the house of the Bardi was burnt down;[2] then some 1300 textile workers rose and looted the city, justifying themselves according to Marchionne with the claim 'We shall magnify ourselves so much that we will have great riches, so that the poor shall be rich;'[3] later, after the Black Death, the Albizzi and the Ricci, the Bordoni and the Mangioni divided Florence with their family feuds from which ensued, as a convenient means of political assassination, the practice of 'admonishing' as Ghibellines those who lost out in such faction fights.[4] The captains of the Parte Guelfa, who administered this ingenious system, used it not only as a means of excluding their personal enemies from civic office but also virtually as a class weapon to ensure that anyone who challenged the position of the great families dominant in the Parte was politically neutralised. Marchionne recorded that one captain would say to another: 'Have you an enemy? Grant me my way with mine and you can have your way with yours...'[5] Effectively, this device became a counterpoise in Florentine

---

[1] R. 575, p. 203. There is no other evidence for this explanation of the origin of the term 'Ciompi' and no modern authority accepts it.

[2] R. 592, pp. 213–15. [3] R. 593, pp. 215–16.

[4] R. 663–5, pp. 245–7. For a description of this system and an account of its institution, see also Matteo Villani, *Cronica* VIII, 24, 31–2. [5] R. 674, p. 251.

politics to the prevailing tendency for a wider participation in government by which a certain section of the patriciate sought to reassert its influence. If a measure supported by the Parte encountered opposition in the communal councils, its captains would, according to Marchionne, threaten to 'admonish' any one who voted against it.[1] In this way, a considerable degree of indirect power could be wielded by a small, aristocratic group. Such tactics, however, were bound in time to excite the hostility not only of the broad mass of the Florentine middle class but of rival great families whose favourite resource in such situations was conspiracy. In the ensuing years, plots multiplied, as did condemnations of those suspected of hatching them. In the general climate of political turbulence, exacerbated by the passions aroused by the War of the Eight Saints, bitterness against the Parte Guelfa mounted to the point of arousing open revolt. The use of the practice of 'admonition' was by this time so widespread that, Marchionne noted, none felt secure:[2] even members of the highest councils of the republic, such as the *Otto della Balìa*[3] could not escape it. It seemed, to Marchionne at least, as if the Parte were on the verge, in effect, of controlling the appointment to all key positions in the Commune by 'admonishing' and so excluding from them all who did not fall in with its wishes.[4]

In these circumstances, there occurred Salvestro de' Medici's challenge to its power that unleashed the Tumult of the Ciompi and threw the whole political future of Florence into the melting pot. To Marchionne, this represented a providential deliverance from the stranglehold of an oppressive clique: the ways of God, elsewhere in his chronicle conceded little place in his interpretation of history, were seen at this juncture as mysteriously fulfilled in the sudden termination of the ascendancy of the Parte Guelfa.

When God indeed no longer wishes to suffer iniquities, he does his work as a just Lord, and thus he did with these, since he devised such a remedy that those who put part of it into effect, did not believe that things would turn out as they saw them do...And so it came about as the proverb says 'To him who does what he should not there happens what he does not anticipate'.[5]

Even in the burning of the houses of the supporters of the old order Marchionne strained to discover the finger of God. Speaking of the choice of the places which the mob attacked, he remarked

some said that the people moved of its own accord, and some said that there came instructions from the palace on which were written those that should be burnt. But I believe that it was a true divine judgement that none other than the undermentioned were either burnt out, or touched, or robbed.[6]

---

[1] R. 730, p. 280.   [2] R. 781, p. 315.   [3] R. 781, p. 311.
[4] R. 788, pp. 315–16.   [5] *Ibid.*   [6] R. 792, p. 319.

His anger against the Parte Guelfa made him here revert to an earlier, more primitive style of interpretation by which any sudden, unexpected reverse to those who were felt to be bad was immediately put down to divine intervention, working through the very actions of those who were to be punished by it. This was, however, only to be a momentary regression. In his account of the events that followed Salvestro de' Medici's *coup* and the Tumult of the Ciompi, he adopted his usual, more neutral, descriptive technique of presentation. Even though he made clear his disapproval of those who, in this troubled phase of Florentine history, sought either to suppress completely, or secure the uncontested dominance of, popular influence in the city's government, his strictures against both political extremes had the mildness of irony rather than the sharp edge of the bitterness that had characterised his condemnation of the men who had tried, before 1378, to restrict his exercise of civic rights. His attitude was no doubt governed by his own association with the regime and his consequent tendency to see the dissatisfaction with it of one or other element in Florentine society in terms of contending pressures upon it rather than as forces detrimental to the survival of civic liberties as such. His narrative continues to centre on the swinging balance of power with the 'popolo minuto' now at one extreme of the political spectrum and their disgruntled, intransigent opponents at the other. A succession of riots, plots and switches in the composition of the government and its policy is shown to reflect the instability of a situation in which popular violence within, and the conspiracies of exiles without, alternately challenge the prevailing regime depending on whether it falls, or appears to fall, under more conservative or more popular influences. If not viewed with anything approaching approval, the eruption of the lower class into politics is dismissed with patronising tolerance: the 'popolo minuto', naive, wild, childish, burst periodically upon the historical scene to be treated by Marchionne with a gentle sarcasm, in mockery of their pretensions to be 'the people of God' or elswhere 'the people of their God'.[1] The artisans, as a more serious political force and therefore a graver threat, receive shorter shift from him. The pressure they exerted to lower the value of the florin, thus raising that of the *soldi* in which they were paid, Marchionne heartily deplored:

But such was the power of the artisans that in every matter under discussion they passed in the councils what they wanted passed since there are in the councils twenty-three guilds of which sixteen are minor ones, and in every consulate, the minor have more consuls than the major. And so it goes the way of those who

---

[1] R. 801, p. 330; R. 803, p. 352.

have most pull notwithstanding whether it is to the good or advantage of the city, and everyone draws water to his own mill, as he sees best to do it; neither law nor ordinance avails in things...[1]

The pretensions of the dyers, previously subject to supervision by the wool guild, to regulate themselves struck Marchionne as an equally irregular inversion of the proper order of things, particularly since it meant that the workers and apprentices could dominate the masters.

in this it came about that the apprentices (*discipoli*) were the consuls and not the masters and, if they were masters, they were their boon companions; and things went so far that through fear the workshops gave in to the apprentices. This was a detestable thing because the city was weak from events outside so that confidence in the Priors needed to be restored...and the city was almost under arms. But afterwards it was settled to the detriment of the wool-merchants and the rich and the poor acquired jurisdiction and prestige.[2]

The sectional interests of the lower middle class and of the artisans in particular were to Marchionne merely divisive factors, weakening the city both internally and externally. It was his constant lament that no social group considered the welfare of Florence as a whole. Each strove for its own pre-eminence and advantage. The greater the liberty accorded to the various sections of the community, the more precarious the survival of the government and of the state became. The reaction when it occurred in the form of a restoration of oligarchic predominance was, for Marchionne, a consequence and manifestation of the endless striving for offices that reflected the inability of any group in Florentine society to rest content until it had a ruling voice in the government of the city. Commenting on the events of 1382 that brought to an end the phase of relatively democratic rule which had prevailed during the previous four years, he once again harped upon this point in explaining both the inner turmoil and diplomatic impotence of Florence. All that had ever gone wrong in the city, he asserted, had arisen from the desire for offices and for the exclusion of everyone else from them, '...each one wanting them all for himself and ousting his companion, as the hedgehog did when he flattered the serpent in the hole'. As a consequence, 'companies or lords or tyrants' could devastate Florentine territory and 'where four years before the city of Florence was dreaded and feared by pope, emperor and every ruler, it was now in so low and vile a state that a few lances shamed the city through the divisions in the city among citizens'.[3] To the very end of his chronicle, even after his withdrawal from active participation in politics, Marchionne was persistently preoccupied with the single issue of civic strife. The last sentence of his

---

[1] R. 877, p. 382.   [2] R. 887, p. 386.   [3] R. 923, p. 413.

political narrative, appropriately, read: 'And so with these contests our city remained not in a good state but in conflict between one side and the other, both with evil ends.'[1]

Although he did not, in his observations on it, arrive at a realistic analysis of the struggles for power he had witnessed, in his moralising way he did present a view of politics as a self-generating process of change of which the motive force was human passion. The division of society into classes or groups created a condition of irresolvable conflict in that no layer of the social pyramid was satisfied with less than dominance and none was prepared to accept subjection to any other. In a sense this proceeded from men's sinfulness but the resultant instability was a direct, natural consequence of their action and not a form of retribution. Something like the classic cycle of Aristotle and Polybius issued in the alternation of regimes, none of which could last because none could meet all the demands made upon it. Marchionne did not, of course, draw any such explicit conclusion from his account of events but such a pattern is to some extent inherent in it and is underlined by the emphasis he puts on sectionalism as the root of discord and so the cause of change.

The derivation of a cyclic pattern of events from natural processes inherent in human action, though it might have masked unconscious acceptance of older fatalistic notions, also divorced them from the cosmically organic view of the world of which they had formed part. Its trappings, such as the supernatural and astrological indications of the coming shape of events, were no longer needed. Custom might dictate acknowledgment of them, but now only as largely irrelevant curiosities of history, perhaps occasionally reinforcing with their traditional authority the judgments of prejudice, but effectively immaterial to the texture of interpretation.

A comparison of the earlier parts of Marchionne's chronicle with that of Giovanni Villani which was its principal source reveals a consistent elimination or qualification of the element of the supernatural in passages from the one work incorporated into the other. In reporting the outbreak of fires in Florence in March 1115 which Giovanni Villani had ascribed to the prevalence of heresy in the city,[2] Marchionne merely noted that they did great damage.[3] Other fires in 1177 which, according to the older chronicler were '...a judgment of God, since the Florentines had become very proud because of the victories won over their neighbours, and among themselves very ungrateful to God and tainted with other dishonest sins',[4] Marchionne

---

[1] R. 995, p. 442.
[3] Stefani, R. 40, p. 22.
[2] Giovanni Villani, *Cronica* IV, 30.
[4] Giovanni Villani, V, 8.

similarly recorded with no comment except for a reference to the damage they had caused to merchandise, houses and shops.[1]

Astrological indications were also as a rule shorn by Marchionne of the significance Giovanni Villani had seen in them. For instance, an eclipse of the moon in July 1330 which had been linked in Villani's chronicle with a decline in the fortunes of Lucca[2] elicited from Marchionne only the remark that '...many spoke variously of the signs that should come to pass through it, as it is the practice always to speak of this, but we will remain silent on it'.[3] The triple conjunction of 1345 with which Giovanni Villani had dealt at great length[4] drew briefer and rather more non-committal comment from Marchionne. Characteristically, he began his digression on its significance by apologising for writing of it at all: 'But even though it is not to the point of our subject, there is still reason for us to say something of it because it induced some of its effects in our climate.' Then, after a brief allusion to the twenty-year cycle of conjunctions of Saturn, he conceded that it presaged '...death and the appearance of rulers and changes and factions...and rains and plague...According to astrology this signified more in Italy than almost anywhere else.'[5] This was the furthest Marchionne was prepared to go in his chronicle in attributing effects to astrological phenomena. In his other reference to them, he either vaguely stated, as he did in connection with another eclipse of the moon in 1330, that it 'signified very many and bad things'[6] or he left it up to the reader to determine the appropriate consequence of a celestial sign as he did with another conjunction of Saturn and Jupiter which occurred together with an eclipse of the moon in 1385: '...its effects we will await, so as not to draw things out for they are of not much consequence; and whoever wishes to find them may search if he has the conviction'.[7] The importance the particular conjunction of 1345 had for Giovanni Villani doubtless influenced Marchionne to depart from his usual practice to the point of ascribing explicit effects to it. The later conjunction of 1385 which he dutifully noted, faithful to the habit he had inherited from Giovanni Villani of recording such events, he could, however, dismiss with less elaboration, especially since he himself was all too well aware of the irrelevance of such phenomena to his basically political narrative. Half-indifferent, half-sceptical, he could, now that he was on his own historical ground and needed to pay no deference to a previous source, leave it to those who had an interest in such matters to make what they could of the information he provided.

[1] Stefani, R. 47, pp. 24–5. [2] Giovanni Villani, X, 157. [3] Stefani, R. 469, p. 166.
[4] See pp. 31–2 above and Giovanni Villani, XII, 41.
[5] Stefani, R. 615, pp. 222–3. [6] R. 473, p. 167. [7] R. 996, p. 442.

The contrast between his attitude to astrology and that of Giovanni Villani is further brought out in their treatment of the case of Cecco d'Ascoli. Marchionne would have relied principally for his knowledge of this upon Villani, but he also had access either to other written accounts of it[1] or to oral traditions that enabled him to present an interpretation of it more in line with his own more matter-of-fact view of such things. For Giovanni Villani, Cecco d'Ascoli was a skilful practitioner of the science of prediction by the stars whose prophesies had frequently been verified but who over-reached himself by writing the treatise *La Sfera* in which he argued in favour of a determinist interpretation of the power of stellar influences.[2]

His execution was therefore the merited punishment of a heretic who had held, among other things, that even the incarnation and crucifixion of Christ had been decreed by the course of the heavens. For Marchionne, on the other hand, these charges were pretexts and the accusations brought against Cecco were prompted rather by personal malice:

A Master Cecco d'Ascoli...was a most skilful man in astrology, and it was said that he said things against the faith; but he never admitted it. But even so they had him burnt for something that he had written in one of his books...; but it was said that the reason why he was burnt was that he said that Madonna Giovanna, daughter of the Duke [of Calabria] was born at a point compelling her to live in disordinate lust. From which it seemed there was an offence to the Duke, for it would not have been decided that such a man should die for the sake of a book. And many were inclined to say that he was the enemy of that Franciscan Inquisitor and Archbishop of Cozenza, for the Franciscans were very much his enemies.[3]

The tone in which Marchionne dealt with this incident was markedly different from that adopted by Giovanni Villani not only in the indifference he showed to the question of the compatibility of astrology and Christian faith which had so much preoccupied the older chronicler, but also in the general levity of his approach to the problem of Cecco's condemnation.

[1] I. von Döllinger in the Documents appended to his *Beitrage zur Sektengeschichte des Mittelalters* (Munich, 1890), II, 597, printed an addendum, written in a different hand, to the Inquisitor's Report on Cecco's condemnation (Magliabech. Cod. 459) which contains a sentence virtually identical to that in Marchionne's account of this incident. It is not, however, clear whether this was, in part, the chronicler's source or whether the comments subsequently appended to the official summary of the trial derive from Marchionne's work. The latter seems the more plausible possibility judging by the greater consistency with the tone of the remainder of Marchionne's text of the sentence the two passages have in common. Assuming this to be so, Marchionne probably owed his rather more cynical explanations of the death of Cecco d'Ascoli to rumour or oral tradition.

[2] Giovanni Villani, x, 40. See page 33 above where this case is discussed in relation to Giovanni Villani's view of astrology.   [3] Stefani, R. 435, p. 154.

The idea that this could have been due to what he had written in a book is brushed aside and instead other ulterior motives are introduced to explain the astrologer's conviction on a charge of heresy. The situation is extracted from the context in which Giovanni Villani had placed it, one in which it was taken for granted that the stars did determine men's destinies and that therefore the relationship of their action to the will of God was a question of utmost concern, to one in which the whole subject of astrology became a mere matter of opinion, disagreements about which were too trifling to be taken seriously as the possible cause of a man's death.

Marchionnne's views in this respect seem to go considerably further than even those of Matteo Villani who did something to re-interpret the effect of the stars on the world in natural terms but who did not exclude their influence as a major force in human life as Marchionne tended to do. Even though Matteo Villani did not involve astrological phenomena in the intimate relation with historical events in which his brother had placed them, one can still detect in his reference to them belief in the power of heavenly emanations. Of this, there is no trace in Marchionne's work. Such allusion as he makes to the stars is, except on the one occasion when he follows Giovanni Villani half-heartedly in attributing a range of effects to the triple conjunction of 1345, no more than a perfunctory gesture to an accepted but now purely formal convention.

The same tendency towards a growing disregard of astrological signs is evident in the work of the anonymous chronicler formerly identified with Minerbetti. Like Marchionne, he did not explicitly reject their validity and occasionally brought them into his narrative in deference to accepted practice, yet without any evident conviction in their historical significance. At one point in his work he did mention, after reporting the conquest of Albania by the Turks, that '...many astrologers, and particularly Master Paolo, had said that in these times Christians should be oppressed in many places by the Infidels and enemies of Christ'.[1] On the other hand, in discussing the outbreak of the plague in 1390, he dismissed the opinion that its ravages waxed and waned with the phases of the moon.[2] In other words, he recorded the prognostications of the astrologers and, where they corresponded with what actually happened, noted this fact; when they did not, however, he was prepared to be critical and question the connection between the relevant celestial phenomenon and its alleged earthly effects. He did not go out of his way to link astral signs with particular political events. His only comment on the comet of 1401 was '...it was said it

---

[1] *Cronica volgare di anonimo fiorentino* 1387, 50, in *Rerum Italicarum Scriptores, ed.* Bellondi: XXVII. [2] *Ibid.* 1390, 36.

signified that many things should come about'.[1] Yet it preceded the death of Giangaleazzo Visconti with which it would have been natural to connect it since traditionally comets had long been regarded as omens of mortality, change and the passing of great men. The vagueness of the anonymous chronicler on this point undoubtedly reflects an indifference to the precise bearing of astrological indications on historical events.

Other kinds of portents, or phenomena which might earlier have been construed as such, he sometimes recorded, but in the same non-committal way. In reporting the killing in Florence of a lioness, he mentioned that this had been thought by many to augur the civic dissensions that broke out two years later.[2] The snapping in a high wind of a flagstaff bearing the Florentine banner was, according to him, also viewed as an unfavourable omen.[3] In both these instances, it is noteworthy that what is stated is the current opinion on the question, not the existence in reality of the correspondence between sign and event which it postulated. Where rumour made no reference to the possible effects of untoward happenings, the anonymous chronicler refrained from speculating as to their significance. He was content to note without comment the appearance of 'fires in the sky'[4] which had in the past been usually considered portents of great changes. More remarkably still, he drew no inference from a striking series of evidently inauspicious incidents which had accompanied the departure of Urban VI from Lucca, despite his frequently stated hostility to that pope. The pontiff's horse had bolted immediately he had mounted it, his mitre had fallen on the ground and been broken and, when he had finally got away, ignominiously seated on a mule, his standard-bearer had had great difficulty in getting the papal banner through the town gate.[5] Singular though these events were, fateful though the smashing of the papal tiara might appear, the anonymous chronicler left their significance open and drew no conclusions.

That he mentioned them at all no doubt indicates a lingering consciousness of the possible meaningfulness of the abnormal and freakish. But his failure to interpret them in any way is none the less revealing of his disinterest in their bearing on history.

Like Marchionne, the anonymous chronicler showed no inclination to work the supernatural into the texture of his interpretation. Unlike him, he did not colour it with moral judgments. Despite the depravity of the political world he depicted in his narrative, he did not, like his older contemporary, deplore factional strife nor exhort his fellow citizens to pursue

[1] *Ibid.* 1401, 20.   [2] *Ibid.* 1392, 32.   [3] *Ibid.* 1395, 13.
[4] *Ibid.* 1387, 41.   [5] *Ibid.* 1387, 27.

the common good. His objectivity in this respect is quite remarkable in view of the reversion to a more moralistic viewpoint by later chroniclers such as Goro Dati. It sprang basically from the absence of a structured conception of history and of a consequent incuriosity about the causes of events beyond the circumstances which immediately precipitated them. That things happened was for him the result of conditions and motives, not of basic tendencies of human behaviour between which one could choose (such as vice and virtue) or of forces inherent in the substance of history itself (such as divine providence). Insofar as any rationale of explanation is present in his account of events it is one which assumes that men's action will be governed by their interests uninfluenced by scruples or moral reservations. It is not altogether inappropriate that Machiavelli[1] should have used it as a source for his *Florentine Histories*: while it entirely lacks the analytical qualities that later distinguished the work of the leading Florentine political thinker, it does display a neutrality of observation and suspension of moral judgment that seem to anticipate Machiavelli. Also, there is in his treatment of the incidents to which the anonymous chronicler devotes the fullest attention something of that expectation of treachery and barbarity that was to colour Machiavelli's view of politics. The sphere of human action was to him such that those who put their faith in the trust-worthiness of men were doomed to betrayal. No favour of generosity could overcome, it would seem, the inherent envy and perversity of human nature. Recounting the murder of Rinaldo Orsino in Aquila, the anonymous chronicler made a point of mentioning that this ruler had always walked unarmed in that town because he had had greater confidence in its inhabitants than in any of his other subjects. He felt sure of them for he had made great and powerful nearly all those who lived in that city and banished all of their enemies. Yet, despite this, he fell victim to a conspiracy led by the very man to whom he had given his daughter in marriage.[2] Similar treachery and ingratitude were shown by Jacopo d'Appiano to Piero Gambacorta in Pisa. Piero had brought up Jacopo, been as a father to him, given him an education, showered benefits and honours on him. His reward was to see his adopted son plot against him, divide the city and, after feigning renewed friendship, use the meeting at which they were to be reconciled to kill him.[3]

The urge to power clearly neutralised all human ties. No-one's word was to be trusted because a promise became, in the political jungle which the anonymous chronicler described, no more than a device for luring a pros-

---

[1] See Bellondi's introduction to *Cronica volgare di anonimo fiorentino*, p. iv.
[2] *Cronica volgare di anonimo fiorentino* 1390, 7.   [3] *Ibid.* 1392, 51.

pective victim into a pre-arranged trap. It was so used by the Marquis of Ferrara who got Otto Buonterzo into his hands by proposing negotiations, persuading his enemy to come unarmed to discuss peace terms and then violating the safe-conduct that he had given him.[1] Even more elaborate deceptions were employed by a young man who schemed to kill the Patriarch of Aquileia in order to revenge his father. The Patriarch, fearful of the vendetta, avoided Udine where the young man lived. When, however, this youth killed the Bishop of Concordia who had also been implicated in his father's murder and who had subsequently fallen out with the Patriarch, the latter was taken in by the young man's protestations of friendship and forgiveness.

The Patriarch, having persuaded himself that the young man had freely forgiven him, was emboldened to come to Udine and did not take precautions, all the less so since, after he came to the city, the young man repeatedly went to him and with great reverence asked him for many favours, all of which he was granted. Then one morning, he came up to him in his hall with twelve armed companions and there killed the Patriarch...At this time, this young man was perhaps twenty years old, so that it seems he was very young to do such treachery.[2]

The last sentence is revealing of the casualness of the chronicler's reaction. It is a matter of surprise, almost one feels of a grudging admiration, that one so young should practise such consistent deception. That he killed two men is, however, passed over without comment. There is no suggestion of moral disapprobation, no hint that such violent and treacherous deeds might bring some form of retribution. The tone in which the incident is related seems indeed to reveal an indifference not merely to morality but to human life itself.

There is a quality of detachment about this that comes out more strongly still in the anonymous chronicler's account of another episode, even more bizarre and macabre than that involving the Patriarch's assassin. It concerns the *condottiere* Giovanni da Barbiano and Azzo d'Este, tyrant of Ferrara. One of Azzo's relatives, Niccolò, wanted him out of the way and bribed Giovanni da Barbiano to kill him. Giovanni was loth to carry out this commission but equally did not wish to forgo the huge sum he had been offered for murdering Azzo. So, in collusion with his ostensible victim, he arranged for a substitute to be killed in place of him. A German 'who closely resembled Azzo' was persuaded with 'feigned blandishments' to allow himself to be disguised as the tyrant and, two hours after nightfall, led into the semi-obscurity of the hall of Azzo's palace. Immediately he appeared, Giovanni and his associates stabbed him, being careful to dis-

[1] *Ibid.* 1409, 10.   [2] *Ibid.* 1394, 12.

figure his face so that no one should realise he was not in fact Azzo. The palace servants were arrested as a precautionary measure to ensure that none of them discovered and betrayed the secret of the murdered man's true identity. The members of Azzo's household, believing their Lord to be dead, gave themselves up to lamentation and Niccolò's envoy who had been concealed in the building to witness the assassination was convinced both from what he had seen and from the appearance of the mutilated corpse that Azzo had been killed. He reported accordingly to his master who duly paid Giovanni da Barbiano the promised sum of money. Once this had been delivered, Azzo suddenly emerged from hiding and Giovanni exposed the ingenious fraud he had perpetrated.

On this skilfully contrived piece of villainy, the anonymous chronicler's only comment was: 'Count Giovanni da Barbiano was a real Romagnuole and a master of treachery which he knew admirably how to carry out.'[1]

The fate of the unlucky German, sacrificed to the Count's greed and Azzo's safety, evoked no compassion; his death was no more than a necessary incident in a plot otherwise admirable and remarkable for its virtuosity. The values by which such actions were judged were no longer either moral or humane but took account only of skill, of ingenuity of deception, of the dexterity with which politics could be mastered as a ruthless and irresponsible game. In recording how the papal legate at Bologna had first induced Astore of Faenza to surrender his city in return for the promise that his life would be spared and then, when he was in power, had had him beheaded, the anonymous chronicler did not, as earlier writers might have done, deplore such treachery in a prince of the Church. Instead, he paid him the compliment of having tricked an opponent who had himself tricked so many others: 'So the Romagnuole Astore ended his life, having it taken from him by an Apulian. This Astore was a master of deceptions and betrayals and many he had come to do in his life; but the Apulian outwitted him this time.'[2]

Clearly the standard which held here was one which admitted no limits to the demands of expediency. Statecraft was an art of deception, and he was most excellent at it who could most effectively deceive the deceivers. The killing of one's enemies and the breaking of one's word were among its normal procedures and as such excited no reproaches. Wanton murder, uncalled for by the needs of the situation, was however to be deplored: in discussing the poisoning by the Venetians of Jacopo and Francesco da Carrara, the anonymous chronicler remarked that many had expressed strong disapproval at

[1] *Ibid.* 1394, 14.   [2] *Ibid.* 1405, 20.

...so great a cruelty done by the Venetians towards those of Carrara,...for the said lord of Padua freely betook himself to their camp to surrender the city of Padua to them; and he and his sons would have gone elsewhere to live wherever the Venetians wanted or it would have pleased them to send him.[1]

No objection had been raised either by the anonymous chronicler or by the current opinion he repeated to the trickery by which the Venetians had got Jacopo da Carrara into their hands through the standard device of offering him a safe-conduct which they later violated.[2] However, the further, needless barbarity of killing him and the other members of his family could not be justified by reasons of state and stood condemned on humanitarian grounds.

Objectivity of outlook could hardly go further than this. With the collapse of any sense of structural unity in history, morality had reduced itself to the defence of what little could be spared from the demands of *Realpolitik*. Men should not be made to suffer more than was unavoidable in a necessarily brutal and treacherous world. Yet within the sphere of action, brutality and treachery were at least to be condoned if not admired provided they were exercised with the requisite skill. Considerations of economy rather than justice were to govern their use. Those who killed or tricked more than they needed were to be blamed.

The cynicism inherent in such detachment of political judgment from moral standards is clearly Machiavellian. Yet, as has already been stated, it would be a mistake to see in the anonymous chronicler's work an anticipation of the thought of the later Florentine political thinker. Its author was no advocate of an a-moral realism but a mere dispassionate witness of the cruelty and treachery of his times. If he allowed his account of events to leave the impression that in history effectiveness was all that counted, it was precisely because he made no sustained attempt to square what he recorded with a systematic set of convictions. Unable to work history into clear-cut patterns of significance, he judged actions only by their effects. His chronicle marks the last stage in the loosening of the links by which the traditional interpretation of history had formerly given a moral sense to events by relating them to a reality, whether religious or ethical, higher than themselves. To the anonymous chronicler, such a reality, though he made no effort to question or deny it, had no evident bearing on their course which could therefore be judged and recorded neutrally. The trend this represented was not, however, irreversible. When the uncertain mood of late fourteenth-century Florentine politics gave way before a renewed

---

[1] *Ibid.* 1405, 21. [2] *Ibid.* 1405, 6.

sense of civic mission and destiny, it was to be expected that history would again knit together for his compatriots into a meaningful and morally edifying form. But when it did so it was also to be anticipated that the changes in outlook that had occurred since the confident early decades of the fourteenth century would leave their mark on the reconstituted synthesis. The pragmatic attitude that had become dominant in Florentine historical thinking in the late Trecento would necessarily be basic to any new interpretation. It would be through man and through society, rather than directly through God and the intervention of the forces of the other world, that political issues would resolve themselves.

4

GORO DATI

GORO DATI's *Istoria di Firenze* covers much the same time-span as the chronicle of the anonymous Florentine (it deals with the years 1380 to 1405 as against those from 1385 to 1409 recorded in the latter work); yet despite this it is in effect the product of a slightly later period, having been commenced probably in 1409.[1] It therefore reflects quite a different climate of opinion from that which prevailed in the 1380s when the anonymous chronicler began his account of events. Unlike earlier Florentine chronicles, it is a retrospective history, not a year by year description of noteworthy incidents. It was clearly inspired by the resolution in favour of Florence of the conflict between that city and Giangaleazzo Visconti of Milan and has the war between the Commune and the tyrant as its unifying theme. While it is set out in the conventional books and chapters of earlier historical narratives, it departs from their customary indiscriminate selection of material and in fact largely assumes the form of a dialogue in which questions are asked and answered about the reasons why events turned out as they did. In approach, it is transitional between a true chronicle, concerned merely with recording what happened, and a history aimed at the coherent presentation and explanation of developments.

By background and mentality, Goro Dati belonged to the same group as the fourteenth-century Florentine chroniclers. Born in 1362,[2] he came of a reasonably well-to-do burgher family, was apprenticed at the age of thirteen in the silk trade[3] which he followed for the rest of his life, achieving the dignity of Consul of the Arte di Por San Maria, the Silk Guild, no less than eleven times.[4] He was associated, through a number of partnerships,

---

[1] L. Pratesi in the introduction to his edition of Dati's *Istoria di Firenze*, argues that this work was written around 1410 (p. xiii). Hans Baron in 1955 in his *Humanistic and Political Literature in Florence and Venice at the Beginning of the Quattrocento* (Cambridge, Mass., 1955), pp. 62–8 brought forward its date of composition to 1407–8, but has more recently (1968) in *From Petrarch to Bruni* (pp. 138–50) come to the conclusion that it was produced in the first half of 1409. Since Dati was in Spain between 1408 and 1410 (G. Dati, *Libro Segreto*, ed. C. Gargiolli, Bologna, 1879, pp. 80–1) this entails supposing it was written abroad, a possibility which Baron suggests is supported by the explanatory tone of Dati's *Istoria* which is consistent with it having been written for a non-Florentine audience. (*From Petrarch to Bruni*, p. 147.)   [2] Dati, *Libro segreto*, p. 113.   [3] *Ibid.* p. 14.
[4] *Ibid.* p. 79; pp. 80–1; p. 82; pp. 94–5; p. 105; p. 107; p. 109; p. 111.

with a company that had commercial dealings with Spain, a circumstance that occasioned his residence in Valencia in 1390–2 and again in 1408–10.[1] Like Giovanni Villani who had been an agent of the Peruzzi in Bruges, he conformed to the type of the Florentine merchant whose early years were taken up with the building up of a business enterprise and the representation of its interests abroad and whose middle and old age were distinguished by an active participation in civic government. From 1412 when he was chosen as *Gonfaloniere di Compagnia* for the first time,[2] he filled a succession of offices: *Ufficiale delle nuove Gabelle* in 1413,[3] one of the *Dodici Buoni Uomini* in 1421,[4] Prior in 1424,[5] *Gonfaloniere di Giustizia* in 1428,[6] *Gonfaloniere di Compagnia* for a second term in 1430,[7] and one of the *Sei di Mercanzìa* in 1433.[8]

In the last twenty odd years of his life (he died in 1435), his political experience was thus quite extensive. This did not, however, indicate in his case particular eminence either in wealth or social position.[9] Although one of his marriages was to the widow of Giuliano Brancacci and another to one of the Guicciardini, he was not of patrician rank and his own *Libro Segreto* bears witness to the financial embarrassment into which his business affairs brought him from 1408 onwards.[10] His education was limited to commercial training and he does not appear to have been, like his richer, young contemporaries Palla Strozzi and Cosimo de' Medici, influenced in any way by the teaching of the humanists. His only contact with the world of learning seems to have been through his brother Leonardo, the author of *La Sfera* and General of the Dominican Order from 1414 to 1424, in other words, in early fifteenth century terms, with the more conservative tradition of scholasticism rather than with the new currents of Renaissance thought.

There was nothing in the outlook and background of Goro Dati to distinguish him from his predecessors, the great Trecento vernacular chroniclers. Despite this, his work does represent an advance upon theirs. Hans Baron, in his *Crisis of the Early Italian Renaissance*,[11] was the first to recognise its importance and since the first edition of that book in 1955, other scholars, notably Claudio Varese[12] and Christian Bec,[13] have given

---

[1] *Ibid.* pp. 18–19; pp. 80–1.   [2] *Ibid.* p. 82.   [3] *Ibid.* p. 83.
[4] *Ibid.* p. 97.   [5] *Ibid.* p. 105.   [6] *Ibid.* p. 110.   [7] *Ibid.* p. 111.   [8] *Ibid.* p. 112.
[9] Bec, *Les Marchands écrivains*, p. 152 discusses the relationship between Dati's relatively modest social position and his rather exaggerated pride in his city, its institutions and, of course, his own participation as a civic official in its government.
[10] *Libro segreto*, pp. 116–19.
[11] H. Baron, *The Crisis of the Early Italian Renaissance* (Princeton, 1955–66). In the second 1966 edition the chapter on Dati occupies pp. 167–88.
[12] C. Varese, 'Una "Laudatio Florentinae urbis": La Istoria de Firenze di Goro Dati', *Rassegna della letteratura italiana*, LXIII (1959), 373–89.
[13] Bec, *Les Marchands écrivains*, pp. 151–73.

Dati the attention he merits in the studies they have made of late fourteenth and early fifteenth century writers and memorialists. Essentially, it may be said that what distinguishes Dati's *Istoria* from the chronicles that had preceded it is, besides a tighter, more organic form, its author's more self-conscious approach to history and his sub-ordination of the descriptive intentions formerly characteristic of Florentine historical writing to the aim of analysing the course of events so as to arrive at the underlying reasons for political success and failure. While earlier accounts of Florentine history had been concerned to draw morals from historical occurrences or, more broadly, to show the consistency between what had happened and what ought to have, Dati sought to explain, in what more ostensibly objective terms, the final victory of Florence over the tyrannical power of Milan. His preoccupation with a single problem at once gave his work a more unitary and coherent structure and made it possible for him to present as generally valid historical or political principles what were in reality the inferences drawn retrospectively from one set of events.

The anonymous chronicler had, of course, lived through the same dramatic events that gave Dati his unifying perspective upon the history of his times; but, writing while they were happening and belonging to an older generation formed by different conditions, he had not seen them in the same light. The significance they had for Dati was at least in part the result of hindsight which projected upon them a meaning they only subsequently acquired through their association with the successful outcome of the conflict with Milan. His was a simplified view, more consistent yet at the same time perhaps less faithful to the actual confused texture of events than that of the anonymous chronicler.

His purpose being also more limited, he came closer to the modern historian's understanding of the function of history. To the medieval chronicler, information in itself had a positive virtue since he thought in terms of a world-view in which everything might have value or relevance; all was part of creation and therefore, understood aright, significant. For Goro Dati, however, as for the humanists, history was a source of moral edification, a means of inferring right and proper rules of conduct from a study of the past and was therefore necessarily selective – in as much as only some of the material which it contained was relevant to the demonstration of the kinds of general principles it was the historian's task to illuminate. In explaining how he came to compose his *Istoria*, Dati intimated at the very opening of his work that he had done it first in answer to the request of his imaginary listener who wished 'to avoid the idleness and sleep of the hours of the afternoon' by discussing 'some useful as well as diverting subject', then that he had chosen history as the most suitable material for this purpose since 'memory made more a habit of it than any other' and in particular since he proposed to deal with 'the long and very great war that was in these our days between the tyrant of Lombardy, the Duke of Milan, and the magnificent Commune of Florence,' this being 'more worthy of recollection than any other from a great time since until now and full of fine and useful examples for those to come because in it fortune disclosed its judgment very marvellously'.[1]

Dati thus revealed his purpose in writing as the explanation and analysis, for future guidance, the operation of 'fortune' or circumstance. His object was not merely to celebrate the greatness of Florence as Giovanni Villani had aimed to do, nor to expose the perversity of man as Matteo Villani had done, nor to show the ill-effects of the civic dissensions that had pre-occupied Marchionne, but to discern a quality or tendency of action, the knowledge of which would be of advantage to his readers or hearers. To this extent, his approach was more practical as, in its way, was the pretext he alleged for embarking on his task, the desire to make profitable the use of hours otherwise lost to sleep. Dati's concern with overcoming waste of time by some useful and edifying labour may well be connected with the resolution expressed in his *Libro Segreto* on New Year's Day, 1403, to make good the misspent first forty years of his life in the eyes of God by fulfilling certain vows – not to work on feast-days or permit any of his employees to do so, to observe chastity on Fridays, not to allow any day to pass without either giving alms or praying or doing some other work of piety, not to accept an office that gave power to judge and condemn offenders in life and limb.[2] As he entered his forties, the decade of his life in which his *Istoria di Firenze* was written, he obviously felt the need to remedy the omissions of the past by losing no opportunity of putting the remainder of his time to valuable employment. Self-restraint would bring religious benefits; working at some commendable enterprise while others rested would be otherwise gainful. At this stage Dati had not, except for occupying minor offices such as that of consul of his guild, become absorbed in his later, distinguished public career. It may be that he saw in the writing of his history a form of service to his city, a substitute for or complement to office-holding which, as he admitted in his *Libro Segreto*, he desired for his own honour and that of his descendants.[3]

Whatever the exact relationship between Dati's misgivings about his spiritual worth and the inspiration of his *Istoria*, there can be no doubt that not long before writing it he had been preoccupied by a sense of the

[1] Dati, *Istoria di Firenze*, i, p. 11.　[2] Dati, *Libro segreto*, pp. 68–73.　[3] *Ibid.* p. 71.

inadequacy of his life and had sought means of justifying it by dedication to laudable commitments. The recent conclusion of the war between Milan and Florence in the latter's favour would, in these circumstances, have provided a fitting theme for a work, praiseworthy both for its patriotism and its value in elucidating the lessons to be learnt from the experience of that conflict.

That he should have seen these in terms of the unravelling of the workings of fortune is indicative of the at once practical and didactic nature of his aims. Fortune operated through natural channels; yet at the same time conveyed the idea of a destined decline of earthly power. Hence it was something the effects of which could be directly deduced from political action but which at the same time showed that history was consistent with morality by working towards the necessary elimination of the forces of evil. Dati's use of the concept of fortune for drawing moral conclusions from his study of events made of it, in his interpretation, a far more predictable tendency than it had been to earlier Florentine chroniclers or was to be to later, Renaissance historical theorists such as Machiavelli. It was no longer merely the wheel of power, as Giovanni Villani had seen it, bearing good and bad first to the pinnacle of success and then, by its irresistible motion, down to the depths of a failure proportional to the heights it had previously lifted up those it now cast down. Nor was it, as Matteo Villani had understood it and as Machiavelli was to interpret it, just the element of chance in human affairs that it was the duty of effective statecraft to keep within its proper limits.[1] Instead, it became a force comparable to providence in Giovanni Villani's conception of history, the action of which was, on the one hand, historically demonstrable, while on the other it restored the balance of right and wrong in the world when human transgressions upset it.

The novelty of the meaning which Dati ascribed to fortune is evident from the way he personifies it not as the blind, inscrutable diety of the Middle Ages, but as a purposeful and morally directed determinant of the course of events. Using the defeat of King John of France by Edward III of England as an example to illustrate surprising switches of fortune, Dati merged the notions of retribution and fatality.

Doubt not in the least that it is an infallible sentence that the possession that comes by an evil means serves to lead man into evil ways; and also true is the sentence that says that fortune raises some very high to make them fall with the

---

[1] For a comparison of Giovanni and Matteo Villani's views of fortune see pp. 56–8 above. See also A. Doren, 'Fortuna im Mittelalter und in der Renaissance', *Bibliotek Warburg Vorträge*, II (1923), 71–144, which deals more fully with the general medieval conception.

greater impact and well can one take as a good example of this King John of France of whom you ask me and about whom I answer you that, he and his kingdom being in such peace and tranquility as his predecessor was never in, he was entirely intent in mind and action upon gathering treasure and making money in every way; fortune withdrew her hand and he was struck down by King Edward of England, whom the King of France by virtue of his own greatness held almost in contempt, not fearing threats and having already laid plans to set his hands on his gold; when it came to a battle, the French with four times as many men, were miraculously defeated and the said King John, the Duke of Anjou his son, and many barons captured.[1]

Dati's reference to this historical incident, although it falls beyond the scope of his narrative and is brought in only as a parallel to the equally merited and equally unexpected overthrow of Bernabò Visconti by his nephew Giangaleazzo, is nevertheless appropriate to the general theme of his history in that it gives the impression that decline is both a compensation for excess and a punishment for sin. It is one of a class of events on the one hand mechanically determined by fate, on the other demonstrating the failure of evil. As such it grafts the quality of inevitability on to a morally comforting interpretation of human action. Fortune works inexorably, being free of the element of choice inherent in divine intervention in history yet, as understood by Dati, has the same effect through the same miraculous means as the will of God in Giovanni Villani's representation of the past.

It is important to keep in mind the ambiguity of Dati's conception of fortune if one is to appreciate the nature of the role he allots it in resolving the conflict between Florence and Giangaleazzo Visconti. It is no mere tendency of power he visualises as he refers to it in his narrative but an actively interfering force that is as much responsible for luring Giangaleazzo into his evil ways as with casting him down from the peak of success when he has confirmed himself in them. Already in explaining the growth of the tyrant's ambition, Dati distinguishes the influence of fortune as a temptress exploiting his weaknesses by deceptively conceding him her favours:

Already coaxing fortune, showing herself his friend, blew with favourable winds on the ships of his desires and his mind strained to the utmost height the hoisted spars; such dominions as either his forebears or any other tyrant of Lombardy had had did not suffice him, and it seemed to him that he had nothing unless he had all.[2]

Further on, in arguing away the significance of one of Giangaleazzo's early victories (over the Count of Armagnac whom the Florentines had brought

---

[1] Dati, *Istoria di Firenze*, 6, pp. 14–15.   [2] 18, p. 24.

into the country to oppose him), Dati resorted to the same idea – fortune was biding her time merely to entice him on.

But fortune had not yet decided to make an end of it; it wanted to keep him waiting a little longer, wanted to make him rise all the higher to give him a greater fall; and certainly it was a very astonishing thing, notwithstanding that it is said that foolish rashness soon leads to repentance, that the Count of Armagnac and all his troops were captured and killed in two hours.[1]

The improbable nature of the Count of Armagnac's defeat, which had besides issued from his refusal to take the prudent advice of Sir John Hawkwood, the English *condottiere* in the pay of the Florentines,[2] was for Dati (as it might have been for Giovanni Villani) an indication that more than natural forces were at play. The later failure of the Florentines to follow up their victory at Mantua over Giangaleazzo Visconti which, as Dati himself admitted, could have been explained by the reluctance of their allies to see Milanese power completely destroyed was equally laid at the door of fortune that 'had not yet determined its day which it reserved for a greater blow such as afterwards befell'.[3] In his comments on both these engagements Dati was above all concerned to emphasise that their outcome was fated rather than naturally caused. Practical considerations which might have contributed to the determination of these events – such as, in one case, the arrogance of the French and their ignorance of Italian methods of warfare, in the other, the influence on the allies of Florence of the need to preserve the balance of power – were mentioned, but only as precipitating factors. Because the time was not yet ripe for Giangaleazzo's defeat, what one would have normally expected to happen had not done so; the Count of Armagnac's army, despite its numbers, had been quickly overwhelmed and the anti-Milanese coalition had failed to press home its victory at Mantua. Superficially things had turned out in both instances as they had as a result of human weaknesses. Yet in the context of the whole war these particular conditions revealed themselves as manifestations of a wider tendency, the operation of fortune.[4]

---

[1] 38, p. 39.   [2] 39, p. 39.   [3] 59, p. 54.

[4] Hans Baron in the first edition of his *Crisis of the Early Italian Renaissance*, II, 508, expressed the view that here in Dati 38 (p. 39) 'the fortune simile is used as an artistic device for emphasis, but not in place of causal explanation, for immediately afterwards, the disastrous defeat in the battle is traced to the fact that the French knights met their doom because of the arrogant belief that no one in the world could resist them'. I differ from Baron's opinion as here expressed in my interpretation of this passage in Dati's *Istoria* for two reasons: first, from other references to 'fortune' in this work, I feel it is clear that Dati does intend it to be understood as an active cause of events and not just as a metaphorical expression; secondly, I take Dati's reference to the contribution of the folly of the French knights to their defeat as intended not to replace fortune as a cause but to be included with-

This set the pattern and dictated the tempo of events. Giangaleazzo's mistakes in strategy might be attributable to imprudence, but this imprudence itself arose from the working of a mechanism which subordinated action in individual situations to broad historical trends. With reference to the rashness of the Milanese tyrant in pressing on with his designs against Mantua, Dati remarked '...had he gone step by step, he would have proceeded more surely; but fortune always wants to keep for herself some loophole through which she can intervene beyond remedy by human wit'.[1] Giangaleazzo's impatience became an instrument of fortune, helping to draw him up more quickly and more vulnerably to those dangerous heights from which he would inevitably fall.

It is the identification of ambition with the fatal propensity of power to rise and decline that distinguishes Dati's 'fortune' from the providence of earlier chroniclers. Although the effects of both forces were virtually the same, the manner in which they were realised was necessarily different. Divine intervention could suspend the normal functioning of nature; fortune had to work through it. Hence, if fortune was to play the same historical role as providence, the tendencies inherent in its action had to be built into the workings of nature. Human passion had to become the agent by which the results formerly secured by the will of God were now achieved.

To a certain extent, of course, even according to Giovanni Villani's view of things, vices had involuntarily contributed to the triumph of virtue. Despite themselves, evil men had worked towards their own downfall. But this had been within a framework of divinely ordained history in which the self-destructive character of wickedness had been less the underlying cause of the triumph of right over wrong than an attribute instilled into such action by God to provide mankind with a fitting demonstration of its true nature. Men were hurt when they did evil so that they might learn to do

in it as a manifestation of its working. In support of the latter point, I would refer to 59 (p. 54) where Dati follows his political explanation of the failure of the allies to pursue the Visconti armies to Milan after the battle of Mantua with the statement 'But we rather say that fortune had not yet determined its day, which it reserved for a greater blow which later came' ('Ma diciamo più tosto che la fortuna non aveva determinato ancora il dì suo, che lo riserbava a maggiore percossa come poi fu'). It is clear from this that, for Dati, fortune is considered the underlying cause determining the outcome of a series of events which individually, however, might be brought about by particular sets of circumstances which only had the long-term effect they produced because the influence of these circumstances was consistent with the tendency of fortune. In fairness to Baron it should be stated that the passage quoted above does not appear in the second edition of his *Crisis* where he concedes that in Dati's *Istoria* 'the image of Fortune's turning wheel is made to take the place of a genuine explanation' (p. 171). In view of this, the remarks above should be taken as a defence of the interpretation of Dati suggested in my text rather than as a statement of disagreement with what I take to be Baron's revised opinion on this point.

[1] Dati, *Istoria di Firenze*, 56, p. 51.

good; but it was through the divine will acting directly rather than through the natural consequences of men's own behaviour that the right side won out in history. Dati's 'fortune' by contrast, personified though it was, manifested itself in the actual effects of human action. Tyrants rose and fell, in Dati's view as in that of Matteo Villani, because the lust for power drove them on and eventually caused them to overreach themselves. They were thus punished for their moral transgressions, but through purely natural means, not by immediate divine intervention.

It is this ambiguity in Dati's conception of fortune – making of it at once an arbiter of history and a property of action – that forces him to implant in human impulses themselves the tendencies present for Giovanni Villani in the overall historical process. The story of the rise and fall of earthly power becomes for Dati a study of human appetites; his villain, Giangaleazzo Visconti, is irresistibly drawn through his fated course by the influence and consequences of his own desires. Significantly, these are compared to such basic addictive urges as sex and greed. Explaining Giangaleazzo's resumption of his intrigues against Florence after his reverse at Mantua had compelled him to make peace, Dati likened him to a woman whose physical desire causes her speedily to forget the pains of childbirth.

Just as agony and fear induces in a woman who gives birth such a hatred of carnal intercourse [that] as a result of the pain she is disposed never to engage in it again; and afterwards, that anguish over, it seems to her a thousand years before she can return to the usual embraces, so it happened to the Conte di Virtù that, when with peace made he considered himself out of danger...the inner poison worked and he reverted to his customary desires.[1]

And later Dati compared Giangaleazzo to a sailor who, having narrowly missed being wrecked, is nevertheless drawn back to the sea by the lure of wealth.

When the seafarer has escaped from a fierce storm at sea, he resolves out of greed for gain to resume his accustomed voyages, not believing that he will ever again encounter a storm or the terror of experienced dangers, for man in his natural disposition always hopes for that which he wants and not the opposite – so did the mind of the Duke...follow its nature with more ardent heart and heightened spirit.[2]

It is the irresistible, ungovernable character of Giangaleazzo's impulses that Dati clearly emphasises in these picturesque metaphors. The tyrant is a gambler whose very determination to win condemns him to lose. He cannot help himself because his passion drives him on. Why, Dati's

[1] 46, p. 44.   [2] 61, pp. 56–7.

imaginary questioner asks him at one point in the dialogue, did the Duke of Milan not realise, despite his excellent councillors, that what he aimed to do would overstrain the resources of his state? The chronicler replies that his anger and emotion so blinded him that he lost all foresight: 'his great and impetuous hatred conceived towards the Florentines' prevented him from tempering 'his passion for what he immoderately desired which gave him false hope of soon obtaining that which he could not have had in all eternity, that is, possession of Florence...'[1]

According to Dati, the ultimate exhaustion of the Milanese war-effort was predictable even at this early stage in the conflict. Some of the Florentines, so he held, had 'made reckonings with pen in hand' which proved that 'either the Duke would be overthrown by the force of his enemies or, if he defended himself with the troops that he retained in his pay, the inordinate expense would make him come to grief...'[2] Thus the Milanese tyrant's insistence upon pursuing his goal reflected, in Dati's view, the subordination of rational calculation to the dominance of an uncontrollable impulse that could not but bring to disaster those who fell under its sway. The overcoming of his last obstacle, 'the hedge' (as Dati put it) 'that would not let him advance any further,'[3] namely Florence, became such an obsession to him as the one impediment to the attainment of his goal, the kingship of Italy, that he refused to admit the impossibility of surmounting it and so paved the way for his own downfall.

The impulse which bore Giangaleazzo on towards catastrophe was the force of his own ambition suddenly frustrated at the point when his objective seemed almost within reach and when the removal of the one remaining impediment to its satisfaction ceased to be a question of rational policy and became one of imperative emotional need. The acquisition of Bologna in 1402 which appeared to bring Giangaleazzo within sight of his goal was, to Dati, the culminating step leading to his ruin: 'now the Duke,' the chronicler wrote, 'found himself in the most fortunate state in his estimation and with the greatest and most noble dominion that ever there was; here is the pinnacle from which henceforth one must descend as far as until now one has risen, but the decline is with much greater impetus and fury.'[4]

The peak of the Duke's success marked, as Dati explicitly stated elsewhere, no more than the turn of the tide, the fullness of fortune that signalled its impending decline.

Just as on the western shores of the ocean, when the tide rises, the water in certain places covers with its waves a great area of land and, when it has risen as far as it should, it recedes in a little time with faster flow and leaves the sands

---

[1] 92, p. 72.   [2] 90, p. 71.   [3] 93, p. 72.   [4] 99, p. 76.

uncovered, so does noble fortune to some whom for a space of time it raises aloft and, when it chooses, turns and pulls down with an overwhelming rush.[1]

The action of fortune, in this description of it, has the regularity of a force of nature. It realises itself through human impulse in the immediate instrumental sense; but it also dictates that decline shall follow rise with the inexorable certainty of a law. Fortune as an autonomous tendency in history is here confused with the urge to power which erodes the achievement of the end it seeks. The mixed derivation of the concept as understood by Dati enables the element of the supernatural to be eliminated from it by making the tendency it assumes operate as a natural law. It thus reverts to its original sense of a counterpart in the human world of the rising–falling rhythm of the physical one – an assimilation of the cycle of night and day, the seasons, the tides, the orbits of the planets, to life and history. In so doing, it casts off, at least outwardly, the religious overtones that had, in the Christian Middle Ages, led it to be identified with the will of God, although it still preserves the morally corrective character of the process it secularises.

While vestiges of the providential view of history continue to cling to it, it is effectively free from the dependence on a transcendental reality which buttressed this. It no longer needs direct divine intervention because it attributes to the self-induced consequences of natural inclinations the tendency for good to overcome evil which had formerly been considered divinely ordained. Fortune, in Dati's understanding of it, becomes the framework of a structure of interpretation that appears valid purely in terms of this world, yet which satisfies the demands that history shall be just, in accordance with the expectations of a religious age.

But it does this at a cost, namely that of forcing upon events a meaning that, properly speaking, arises not from them but from a predetermined assumption that good shall necessarily prevail over evil. In this sense, Dati's interpretation of history, whilst on the surface more objective than that of the chroniclers of the fourteenth century in its elimination of any overt suggestion of the supernatural, in fact achieves its appearance of naturalism by constraining objective facts into an arbitrary pattern of significance. If we compare Dati's account of the Florentine–Milanese war with the anonymous chronicler's, it becomes evident that it is precisely those features which give it its semblance of a scientifically worked out explanation that have been superimposed, largely out of motives of prejudice, upon the plain historical reality.

The emphasis on causation that distinguishes Dati's *Istoria* from earlier

---

[1] 106, p. 80.

chronicles and makes it at times sound surprisingly modern in approach is also what leads it to misrepresent the haphazard confusion of accident, as a coherent, logically connected process in which the roles assigned the participants are fixed by the contribution they are required to make to the fated outcome of the struggle. Thus, rather unexpectedly, Bernabò Visconti, the notorious Milanese tyrant whom Giangaleazzo Visconti overthrew, is presented in a relatively sympathetic light and, as the enemy of the great villain of Dati's history, is shown as a man just in his severity and redeemed, besides, by a repentent end.[1]

If he was outwitted by his nephew who treacherously seized and murdered him, it was, Dati argued, so that God might free him from the bondage of his temporal possessions and allow him to atone for his sins.[2] The anonymous chronicler, writing at the actual time of Bernabò's death, rather more plausibly drew the opposite conclusion, that by it 'God, the just avenger', punished him and his sons for his iniquity, brutality and faithlessness.[3] From his more neutral point of view, the latter author saw both uncle and nephew[4] as immoral, cruel and irreligious, and regarded Bernabò, by reason of his bestial barbarities, as being if anything the worse of the two. Such a judgment, however, Dati was unprepared to allow, partly no doubt because by the period he composed his narrative the earlier Milanese ruler had long since ceased to inspire terror and had become no more than a figure of semi-legendary memory, but also to ensure that nothing detracted from the blackness of the deed that was to set Giangaleazzo on his path to worldly greatness. The poisoning of Bernabò was for Dati the initial act by which Giangaleazzo committed himself to the devil by sacrificing all to the quest of earthly power. It was therefore important that it should be represented not simply as the removal of one tyrant by another but as the temporal ruin though spiritual redemption of a repentant sinner effected by an unrepentant one.

By reducing to a single movement the sweep of action that took Giangaleazzo to the peak of success and then denied him its fruits, Dati saw the historical truth in its broad lines; the motives of decision, the strategic principles underlying the Milanese conquest were discerned with the deceptive clarity of hindsight and inconvenient details that did not fit the pattern were overlooked or re-interpreted consistently with the overall trend of events. As a result the psychology of the people concerned came to be determined by their appointed historic role: Bernabò, the natural self-

---

[1] 9, p. 18. [2] 11, p. 20.

[3] *Cronica volgare di anonimo fiorentino* 1385, 19.

[4] The anonymous chronicler's appraisal of Giangaleazzo's character is given in 1402, 14.

seeking man, harsh in his capriciously savage punishments, yet capable of redemption once the temptations of power were removed; Giangaleazzo, the mechanically conditioned slave of ambition, driven by his single obsession towards his destined end; the rulers of Florence, dedicated to the cause of freedom, assured of eventual victory through their perception of their opponents' weaknesses but, in the early stages of the struggle, before his intentions had become clear to them, vulnerable to his guile and treachery. In order to make Florentine policy appear consistently purposeful, Dati tended to rationalise its motives, making it spring not from short-term expediency but from long-range considerations of civic interest. Where these had been overlooked, as in the failure to intervene and save Verona and Padua from the Duke of Milan in 1387-8, he found an explanation in the misconstruction of Giangaleazzo's aims by the Communal government. Its members were blinded because none suspected the malice concealed beneath the tyrant's feigned friendship; also it was felt, according to Dati, that it was up to the Venetians rather than the Florentines to contain Milanese expansion in this quarter:

because such enterprises and defences cannot be undertaken without cost, it was the advice of the wise that money should not be spent to buy into strife, seeing that this was what the Venetians were doing and it not being realised that the Count's thoughts extended any further. But at this time there arose certain developments in Tuscany which caused the tyrant's mind to be revealed.[1]

Up to this point, in Dati's view, the Florentines did nothing to curb Milanese expansion in Northern Italy because they underestimated its eventual scope; but henceforth, its nature identified, they confronted it with a purposeful and well-conceived containment policy. This neat picture of the situation however overlooks, as one would expect, some of the more intricate complications of the diplomacy of the period. The Florentines did not intervene to save Verona or Padua not because they were unwilling but because they were unable to do so. The essential point which the contemporary narrative of the anonymous chronicler[2] brings out but which Dati omits to mention is that Giangaleazzo Visconti secured control of Verona after having made an alliance with the Carrara of Padua to whom he promised Vicenza[3] and of Padua after having won the Venetians over to his side in return for undertaking to cede them Treviso once he had overcome the Carrara.[4] Florentine efforts which were in fact made to reconcile the

---

[1] Dati, *Istoria di Firenze*, 19, p. 27.
[2] *Cronica volgare di anonimo florentino* 1387, 3; 1388, 7.
[3] D. M. Bueno di Mesquita, *Giangaleazzo Visconti* (Cambridge, 1941), p. 74.
[4] *Ibid.* p. 79.

Venetians with Padua failed because Francesco da Carrara was not prepared to pay the price the Venetians required for their friendship, namely his withdrawal from Friuli which he had occupied.[1]

The Florentines were therefore certainly not indifferent even at this stage to the threat which the expansion of Milanese territory represented to them. Of this the anonymous chronicler was well aware, for he commented on rumours that Giangaleazzo Visconti, after his successful seizure of Verona, was about to assume the title of king in the following terms: 'It displeased the Florentines much that the Conte di Virtù was making himself so great, and it also displeased them that he wanted to take the name of king which he used...'[2] The same writer also reported that, on receiving the reports of its ambassadors, the Florentine *signoria* set up a *balìa*, or special committee, to look into the situation,[3] so gravely concerned was it with recent developments in Lombardy. Dati, on the other hand, through his ignorance of these facts, was able to make the policy of the Commune seem more consistent and its rulers more effectively in control of the position than the prevailing diplomatic climate would allow. Preoccupied as always with the end-result and doubtless forgetful after the lapse of years of the exact point at which the Florentines had become apprehensive of the growing strength of Milan, he chose an explanation plausible in view of the subsequent course of events rather than that suggested by the circumstances of the time. Whatever happened tended to put down, given his historical method, to design rather than to accident. For instance, the defeat of the numerically superior Milanese army at Mantua was held up as a triumph of strategy: 'it is the way with battles,' Dati wrote with reference with it, 'that reason wins'.[4] Many valiant men, he stated, had affirmed that 'in our times no more magnificent battle could be recalled than that was'. The general impression left by his account was of a handfought, skilfully contrived victory. The anonymous chronicler's contemporary or near-contemporary description of the same engagement scaled it down to less heroic proportions. According to him, the battle was won because the enemy panicked after a surprise attack. Caught off their guard, the Milanese besiegers fled, abandoning their equipment, and did not defend even the inner bastion of their camp with any resolution because most of them were trying to escape across the Po. Thus, 'the Duke of Milan's troops were completely defeated on both land and in the Po River, almost without a blow being struck...' Of Carlo Malatesta, commander of the forces in Florentine pay, the anonymous chronicler remarked rather scathingly that he 'was much honoured for this

[1] *Ibid.*   [2] *Cronica volgare di anonimo fiorentino* 1387, 34.   [3] *Ibid.*
[4] Dati, *Istoria di Firenze*, 58, p. 53.

victory, notwithstanding that little skill or wisdom or prowess was displayed in it by anyone'.[1]

The tendency on Dati's part retrospectively to gild history by attributing
fortuitous and partly fortuitous end-results to carefully calculated fore-
thought is equally apparent in his reflections on the final failure of Giangaleazzo's attempt to take Florence. Whether the Milanese tyrant would have
succeeded in his designs against the Tuscan Commune had he lived is of
course open to conjecture, but in the event it was his death by plague in
1402 which foiled his adroitly laid plans to capture the city. For Dati, this
explanation was in itself too simple, too much dependent on mere chance,
to be the critical factor in the resolution of a conflict between what were to
him symbolic protagonists of tyranny and republican freedom. Its result
must, he felt, reflect the fundamental nature of the two opposed powers,
being the outcome of the collision between the self-destructive power-urge
of the Milanese despot and the methodically ordered resistance of the
Commune of Florence, in a word between self-consuming impulse and
self-conserving rationality. In a passage, part of which is quoted earlier in
this chapter,[2] he contrasted the over-extension of Milanese resources
entailed by the ungovernable ambition of the Duke with the restraint of the
rulers of Florence who deliberately limited the numbers of their troops to
what they could afford, confident that, if they followed a defensive strategy
and kept their economy viable, the war-machine of their enemy would
sooner or later collapse under its own weight. Later, speaking of the ex-
tremely grave situation that faced Florence after Giangaleazzo Visconti had
gained control of Pisa, Siena, Perugia and Bologna and won the good will
of the lords of Lucca, the Casentino and Romagna, thus virtually en-
circling the Tuscan city, he remarked that, despite their drastic predicament, the Florentines,

...had never any fear of being conquered, that is subjected, since their minds
were so opposed and averse to him in their every thought and in every eventuality
there seemed to them to be many remedies – as to the valiant and sure heart a
way and remedy is never lacking – and always they comforted themselves with
a hope that made it seem that they had the thing securely in hand, that is that the
Commune cannot die and the Duke was a single mortal man so that his state
would end with himself.[3]

The issue of the conflict was decided for Dati not so much by the caprice
of circumstance as by the essential nature of the two political forces opposed

[1] *Cronica volgare di anonimo fiorentino* 1397, 14.
[2] Dati, *Istoria di Firenze*, 90, pp. 70–1. See page 121 above. See also Bueno de Mesquita,
Giangaleazzo Visconti, p. 211.   [3] Dati, *Istoria di Firenze*, 97, p. 74.

in it. The republic was collective, permanent, its policies the fruit of rational deliberation. The tyranny was the manifestation of the will of one man, geared to the extension of his power which at once sustained it and drew it towards the fatal climax of its life-cycle. Despite all appearances to the contrary, it followed that the former must win since it enjoyed the inherent superiority of reason, order, self-control over the compulsive but self-destructive emotional urges animating the latter. Necessarily and predictably the victory of Florence had sooner or later to come because in the nature of things what it stood for had ultimately to prevail.

Set against the historical record, the impression of the certainty of the triumph of Florence which Dati strove to convey breaks down on the very point of the assurance of the Florentines in their ability to avoid defeat which he most strongly emphasised. It may well be that the Milanese threat was as empty as its sudden collapse made it subsequently appear; but it is clear from other sources that it did not seem so at the time. Giangaleazzo's policy of the slow strangulation of the trade on which the wealth and therefore also the power of Florence rested by bringing the city-states surrounding it under his control or influence was well-conceived and, had it been applied over a long period, might well have weakened the capacity of the Tuscan Commune to resist to the point where it would have been an easy prey for him. As Bueno de Mesquita makes clear in his biography of Giangaleazzo Visconti, once the Milanese had gained control of Bologna and Pisa and compelled Paolo Guinigi of Lucca to deny the Florentines the use of the port of Motrone as an outlet for their trade, only 'the long and arduous road across the Apennines to Romagna remained open', and this 'was too difficult to cope with the bulk of the Republic's commerce'.[1] Archival sources which Bueno de Mesquita quotes confirm the desperate plight of Florentine trade at this period which, if prolonged, would certainly have made the Commune more vulnerable to an attack from without.

At the same time, it was weakened from within by divisions of which Dati says nothing, but which the anonymous chronicler records. A plot in 1400 which was barely foiled would, if successful, according to this writer, 'certainly have brought Florence under the rule of the Duke of Milan'.[2]

The financial resources of the Commune were also less adequate to the conduct of a protracted war against Giangaleazzo than Dati's work suggests. If the number of troops in Florentine pay was kept relatively small it was not, as Dati would have it, because the city's administration was

---

[1] Bueno de Mesquita, *Giangaleazzo Visconti*, p. 287.
[2] *Cronica volgare di anonimo fiorentino 1400*, 11.

sufficiently confident of victory not to feel the need to enlist more men, but that it could not afford to do so. Both in 1392[1] and 1397[2] the number of mercenaries in the service of the Commune was cut down because the expenditure required to maintain larger forces had become insupportable. In 1401–2 plans to bring the Emperor, Rupert of Bavaria, back into Italy to oppose the Duke of Milan came to nothing because it was beyond the means of Florence to equip an army equal to that which Giangaleazzo had under his command. The Emperor had been induced to intervene in the war in Lombardy in the previous year with the promise of lavish Florentine subsidies. After he had been ignominiously defeated in an early encounter with the Milanese and had promptly retreated to Germany, the Florentines had withheld payment of the later instalments of the money they had agreed to supply. In the ensuing negotiations, the Emperor had at first accused the Florentines of bad faith but had later become reconciled with them on recognising their inability to raise the sums they had originally undertaken to furnish.[3]

The defencelessness of Florence was thus at this stage to a significant extent the result of the critical state of the Commune's finances. Dati may have been partly right when he ascribed the withdrawal of the Emperor from Italy to the bribes he had received from Giangaleazzo Visconti;[4] but his explanation failed to take sufficient account of the relation between available resources and the cost of effective intervention against the Duke of Milan. The Florentines sought the aid of the Emperor because they could not themselves afford to field an army in Lombardy that would match that in the pay of Giangaleazzo; yet the very limitations of their financial means which compelled them to take this step made it impossible for them to support, at least on a permanent footing, imperial forces capable of withstanding the Milanese ones. The superior strength of their enemy, in an economic no less than a military sense, placed them in an insoluble dilemma that left open to them only a policy of passive resistance. Far from being the outgrowth of confidence, this in fact was the last resort of despair. That this was the mood in the city at this time the anonymous chronicler testifies. On hearing the news that the Emperor had retired to Trent after the defeat of some of his men in a skirmish with Giangaleazzo's troops '...the Priors, the Ten of the Balìa and all the other citizens were speechless with the great grief that this happening aroused in them and, looking at one another without saying anything, all remained silent.'[5] Later,

---

[1] *Ibid.* 1392, 12.   [2] *Ibid.* 1397, 23.
[3] *Ibid.* 1401, 8–14; 1401, 17; 1402, 1.
[4] Dati, *Istoria di Firenze*, 76, pp. 63–4.
[5] *Cronica volgare di anonimo fiorentino* 1401, 11.

when Bologna fell, the situation of the city became even more desperate and its enemies were convinced that it could no longer hold out against Giangaleazzo.[1] It was at this point that his death suddenly reversed the fortunes of the war by relaxing the pressure on Florence and loosening the grip that had held together as a single state the miscellaneous territories under Milanese control. The transformation that this wrought in the Florentine position engendered that mood of civic pride and self-confidence in which Dati wrote and which he mistakenly projected back to the period of the city's greatest peril when it seemed about to succumb before the Milanese tyrant's apparently irresistible advance. Relief on escaping from the closely averted danger undoubtedly contributed to that sense of the fatefulness of the Florentine victory which animated his work. The recovery of the city in the swift switch of its fortunes was no mere trick of circumstances but a proof of the resilience, the latent strength of its people and institutions.

Dati's account of the climax of the struggle between Florence and Giangaleazzo Visconti must be judged in the light of the overall pattern of his interpretation. Considered independently of other evidence, it suggests a sense of political realities of an unusually high order. Read against the background of other contemporary testimony such as the anonymous chronicler's and of facts available from other sources, it reveals the limitations of a work written from recollection several years after the events it describes. Although I substantially share Hans Baron's estimate of Dati's significance as a historian,[2] I would tend to rate less highly than he does Dati's realism and the penetration of his political judgments and explanations. In my opinion, the unity and clarity of Dati's view of historical situations often arises from oversimplification and sometimes from distortion. On the other hand, those of his shrewder judgments which are accurate are not as exceptional among writers of his time and class as one might at first suppose. For instance, his perception of the inter-relatedness of political developments in Lombardy and Tuscany in 1387–8 which

---

[1] *Ibid.* 1402, 9.

[2] Baron, *Crisis of the Early Italian Renaissance*, pp. 171–2. After conceding that Dati's work compares unfavourably with Bruni's *History of the Florentine People* in that it is partisan, draws a picture of 'unalloyed black and white', alternates 'between reasoned penetration and still confirmed accumulation of irrelevant detail, between the exploration of causality and the naive attitude with which the hand of God is discovered in both success or failure, or the image of Fortune's turning wheel is made to take the place of a genuine exploration', he nevertheless maintains that 'a closer study reveals that these flaws are mostly on the surface of Dati's work; they do not prevent him from carrying through the analysis of the political, moral, and economic factors in the crucial events of the Florentine–Milanese duel with a penetration that leaves everything previously achieved far behind.' It is this latter statement that I personally would be inclined to qualify.

Baron refers to as an indication of the relative modernity of his approach[1] is shared by the essentially orthodox anonymous chronicler.[2]

At the same time, there is no doubt that Dati's *Istoria* does occupy the important position that Baron has claimed for it as a work transitional in character between the fourteenth century chronicles and the historical writings of the humanists. Closely reasoned and methodically ordered around a single theme, it has, despite the absence in it of the elegance of style typical of the writings of Renaissance Latinists, something of the structural unity of a humanist discourse. Together with many of the virtues of early Renaissance historiography, it has however also some of its faults, notably a tendency to smooth over the rough edges of the historical narrative in order to achieve an effect that is fitting rather than necessarily right. Events work themselves out in conformity with principles which, while they teach a wisdom that is practical and ostensibly grounded in experience, in reality derive from traditional notions of the obligatory consistency of life with moral precept.

While in these respects, Dati's *Istoria* anticipated some of the characteristics of Renaissance historical writing, it was still more closely linked than the works of the humanists to medieval ways of interpreting history. Not only in crudeness of style and naiveté of outlook but in the presence of vestigial traces of traditional patterns of interpretation, it betrays its affinity with the Florentine chronicles of the fourteenth century. The element of the supernatural, outwardly eliminated, is inwardly present not only in the reappearance of providence in the guise of fortune, but also in the continued inclination to see the triumph of good, even if secured through natural processes, confirmed by miraculous signs. The catastrophe which concluded the historic drama of Giangaleazzo's rise and fall is accompanied, like the catastrophe of the ruin of the Hohenstaufen in Giovanni Villani's *Chronicle*, by a prediction of the eventual outcome of the

---

[1] *Ibid.* p. 170. 'He tries to work out a scheme of analysis that makes the reader sense the constant impact of the dislocations in Northern Italy on the relations among Tuscan states. As a consequence, he is incessantly intent on discovering connections of more than merely provincial extent behind every local event; he tries to lay bare the relations which exist between the happenings in regions geographically far removed from one another. In this new interest we are confronted with the ultimate cause of Dati's bold attempt to break away from the disconnected annalistic enumeration of near and distant, weighty and trifling events that had been the fashion of the chroniclers of the Trecento.'

[2] See, for instance 1387, 34; 1388, 10; and in particular 1389, 24 where the anonymous chronicler states (cf. Dati 55, p. 50) that 'it was advised by all that a way should be found to make war in Lombardy, since they were very sure that the cities which he held by force would, if they saw the emblems of the Florentines, rebel against the Conte di Virtù'. (– 'e per tutto fu consigliato che si trovava modo che la guerra fosse in Lombardia però chelli si rendeano molto certi che le città ch'egli, tenea per forza se vedessero le'nsegne de' Fiorentini si ribellerebbono a' detto Conte di Vertù).

conflict made at a point when all indications suggested that events would take an opposite course. When Florence was apparently in desperate straits in 1402, it was reported, according to Dati, that 'a holy hermit of the *contado* of Arezzo had said that of a certainty the Duke would die in that year...'[1] In giving this piece of information, Dati qualified it by remarking that 'notwithstanding that little credence was accorded it by the leading citizens, the people who have an ear for such things took comfort from it...' Despite this disclaimer, revealing in its way of the prevalence by this time of a more sceptical attitude towards such prophesies, the inclusion of this detail in Dati's account of events is not without significance. It falls too neatly into the pattern traditionally appropriate to such situations to be accidental, or to have merely the casual relevance Dati appears to concede it. It can be taken as a surviving trace of an older, supernatural type of explanation which Dati has rationalised and secularised but which betrays its underlying presence by the persistence of some of its accidental features, now however causally isolated and redundant. Inserted at this critical point in the narrative, it does, however, still have psychological force since it endorses rational argument with the appeal of the emotional prompting that, as the darkest hour precedes the dawn, so the very extremity of the predicament of the city (if correctly interpreted) presaged its imminent deliverance.

Avoidance of explicit reference to the supernatural does not in a case like this obviate recourse to a suggestion of it for atmospheric effect. There is the same evocative use of it in Dati's account of Giangaleazzo's death: '...the night that he died there was in all his land such a terrible tempest of the air, that is rain, wind and lightning and earthquakes that it seemed that the world should be undone, and at that point the proud tyrant rendered up his wretched soul to him who had earned it.'[2] An earlier chronicler might have spelt out the moral in terms specifically linking the turmoil of nature with the divine (or diabolical) castigation of the expiring sinner; but Dati merely recorded – or more probably invented[3] – the coincidence of the storm and Giangaleazzo's end; yet the intended impression depends for its effect on the survival of the superstitious belief that a major crisis in the human world has its counterpart in a corresponding disturbance of the physical one. Here again the point Dati wanted to stress, that Giangaleazzo's failure flowed naturally from the character of his actions, was buttressed by an oblique reference back, through one of its interconnecting links, to a world-view which underwrote such a conclusion.

---

[1] G. Dati *Istoria di Firenze*, 97, p. 74.   [2] 100, p. 76.
[3] According to Pratesi (*ibid.* footnote 2), no other source mentions this tempest.

The intermeshing of omen and event is further brought out in Dati's comments on the Duke's fatal illness, the onset of which, he notes, occurred on the eve of St John's Day, the feast of the patron saint of Florence. 'And it was a notable and miraculous thing that the day of St John's Eve, when in Florence there began a great presentation of banners, in the most magnificent festival held in the world, exactly at that hour of vespers there began within the city of Milan the palpitations of the illness that killed him. . .'[1]

It is striking that, although many of Dati's observations on history have an unmistakably modern ring, he is, in his evident faith in the miraculous, conservative even by the standards of his own day. What distinguishes his account of events from that of, for instance, the anonymous Florentine is his insistence on seeing every incident as impregnated with moral significance to the point where it acquires, despite the apparent rationalism of his method, a kind of supernatural dimension. One has the impression, as in earlier, unquestionably medieval chronicles, that life is being held in place by the framework of an external order which at critical points in time, breaks through and reveals itself.

Comparing the treatment in the two works of one particular episode, the reign of Charles of Durazzo as King of Naples, one becomes aware of a difference, not between moralising and non-moralising (for the anonymous Florentine, rather a-typically, also discovers in it the hand of God) but between explanation in essentially religious terms and ethical judgment. The incidents both deal with may be summarised briefly. Queen Joanna was excommunicated by Urban VI because, from the beginning of the Great Schism in 1378, she supported the anti-Pope Clement VII; Charles of Durazzo, who had been her protégé, had invaded the Kingdom of Naples with Urban VI's backing, deprived her of the Crown and had her murdered. Subsequently, he too had fallen out with the pope and been excommunicated; on his return to Hungary (of which he had also been made King) he was attacked at his own coronation, wounded, deposed and later killed in captivity.

The anonymous chronicler saw these events in a light consistently unfavourable to Charles. As a child this man, according to his account, had been saved at Queen Joanna's pleading from being blinded on the orders of her father. She had then taken him into her household, brought him up and, when he had come of age, had made him her heir. She had treated him 'as though he had been her son.' As a reward for these favours, he seized her throne, had her imprisoned and executed. When he himself met

---

[1] 110, p. 82.

a violent death, it was because God, so the anonymous chronicler insisted, had chosen thus to punish his sins.

Truly God the Just Lord then meted out to the said Charles of Durazzo his just deserts for such a great injustice that he had done, for this King Charles...died among common, ignorant, savage and cruel people and, if one examines it closely, of the same death that he had first made the noble Queen Joanna die, who was in truth a royal lady.[1]

While the conclusion of this story is expressed in religious terms, its point is to condemn inhumanity. The intervention of God is, in a sense, superfluous since the punishment of Charles of Durazzo for his sins does not follow from any miraculous suspension of the laws governing the natural order but from the tendency for the violent to die by violent means, for those who take up the sword to perish by the sword. The anonymous chronicler, in his account of this incident as in that of other similar ones in his chronicle, is above all preoccupied with the prevalence of ingratitude and savagery in the human world. The only difference between his reaction in this case and in others is that, at the early point in his work when he described the fitting end of Charles of Durazzo, he had not yet lost faith in divine justice. Men might be perverse but they paid for their perversity. Later, the accumulated evidence of the impunity with which evil was done in the harsh age in which he lived reduced him to a more neutral moral attitude. Yet, even here, when he felt it appropriate to bring God into history as the rectifier of human wrongs, he did so without distorting explanation or motivation. There is no suggestion that Charles of Durazzo's death did not take place for adequate political or natural reasons: the implication is merely that those who seize power by violating all moral laws render themselves vulnerable to overthrow by those who do to them as they have done to others. Thus they bring upon themselves their divinely ordained fate.

Dati's view of this series of events is coloured not by this kind of judgment of the quality of Charles of Durazzo's actions but by their tendency to help or harm the Church. His victory over the numerically superior forces of the excommunicated Queen Joanna was, according to Dati, 'a miracle to show that the pope is Vicar of Christ and that that which is binding on earth is binding in heaven, and to show that Pope Urban was a true pope and that his excommunication should be feared and not despised...'[2] On the other hand, his own overthrow and death issued

---

[1] *Cronica volgare di anonimo fiorentino* 1385, 18.
[2] Dati *Istoria di Firenze*, 32, p. 35.

from his failure to reward the pope for his support, his seizure of Church lands and his own excommunication.

Afterwards, the king having increased in power and forgotten the benefits received from the pope, [and] having great desire for lordship, took many lands which were by right the Church's and many benefices against the will of the pope, for which reason the pope, offended, excommunicated him; and thus excommunicated, having been elected King of Hungary, he went for the Crown, took it and after a few days was attacked in the hall by certain barons and killed, and died excommunicated.[1]

In this interpretation, Dati reverts to what is, in effect, an archaic view of history, substantially that of Giovanni Villani in its naive identification of right with the cause of the Papacy and wrong with that of its enemies. The emphasis on the miraculous nature of events which take not the course one would expect from outward appearances but that dictated by the inner rhythm of history is part and parcel of this view of things. It assumes ultimately the dependence of phenomenal world on the supernatural and the decisive influence on the outcome of any development of forces acting upon this life from beyond it. It is not without significance that the passage quoted above, in which Dati relates Charles of Durazzo's death and his excommunication, is immediately succeeded by the following one:

And I do not want to remain silent on the augury which was proclaimed to him; granted that these are things that one should not make fundamentals of faith, nevertheless they are not altogether on that account to be disdained on every occasion, and when a man can do the same thing a sure way he should not proceed by a dubious way. On the 31st December, 1386 there was a major eclipse of the sun, that is an obscuration at the third hour, and on that day the king had determined to take the Crown, it being the day of the feast of St Sylvester. He was told some time beforehand that that day was the day of the eclipse. 'My Lord, do not do it on that day for it is the last day of the year, the last of the month, the last of the week (since it was Saturday) and the last of the lunar month, and an eclipse of the sun.' He, to show that his great mind cared nothing for these things, said: 'I wish it nevertheless and we shall see what will come of this action.'[2]

Dati added to his record of this prognostication the following sentence: 'I do not however judge it further but have chosen to relate it as a noteworthy recollection.' The comment is characteristic, serving as it does to disassociate the author from the superstitious point of the story whilst at the same time enabling him to make it. Despite it, the conclusions to be inferred from the passage are of a piece with Dati's general views of the causal process determining events. If the results of actions followed from

---

[1] 33, p. 35. [2] *Ibid.* pp. 35–6.

some form of ultimately miraculous divine intervention, then it was to be expected that they should be signalled by suitably extraordinary omens. A particularly unusual set of coincidences was likely to betoken some untoward occurrence if physical reality did reflect in its aberrations disturbances in the human and spiritual worlds.

Beneath the pragmatic skin of Dati's interpretation of history, there lies concealed, as an examination of its underlying structure reveals, the skeleton of a magico-religious conception of life. In many ways it is regressive for its age; yet paradoxically it is its very regressive characteristics that provide the reinforcement which enables the new insights it contains to be central to its structure rather than an incidental element within it. By combining the sense of fatality and of underlying world-order inherited from the past with a presumption of the autonomy of nature, Dati could attribute to the working of politics a regularity and rationality which no truly objective analysis would have enabled him to deduce from it.

The shape of history was the same for Dati as it had been for Giovanni Villani but the qualities that ultimately determined the course of events were different. To the earlier chronicler, there had simply been those who were on God's side, and those who were against him, those who supported the cause of the Church and those who, out of obstinate perversity, opposed it. This kind of distinction was by no means foreign to Dati; he too held to the old Guelph view that the interests of Florence and the Papacy were, or should be, identical.[1] When they were not, as during the War of the Eight Saints, he ascribed this to the presence on the papal throne of men misguided enough not to see eye to eye with their faithful Tuscan ally.[2] But his belief that Florence and the Church should properly be in harmony with each other did not play the central part in his interpretation that it did in Giovanni Villani's. For him, the true virtue of his city which had enabled it to prevail over its enemies was not its espousal of the cause of the Church but the character of its values. And the fatal flaw which had brought Giangaleazzo Visconti to his ruin had not been his incidental godlessness but the compulsive urges of his tyrannical nature. The mechanism of causation was, in his representation of history, translated on to a different plane from that on which it had operated for Giovanni Villani. The essential responses that governed it were men's not God's. The inherent tendency of a course of action, not the divine judgment upon it, became the immediate determinant of its outcome.

This secularisation and generalisation of the qualities on which the issue of historical developments depended had the side-effect of creating a need

[1] 158, p. 121.   [2] 160, p. 122.

for a new supporting framework of validating traditions. What Giovanni Villani could do directly by invoking the unquestionable authority of the Church, Dati had to do obliquely by linking what he considered to be the essential features of Florentine life to models that commanded universal respect and admiration. It is in this connection that one must understand his continual recourse to Roman example to substantiate the claims of Florence to enjoy the especial virtues that he discovered in her. Adapting traditional legends relating to the Roman foundation of the city and the division in its early population between those of Roman and Fiesolan stock,[1] he evolved an ingenious mythology of his own to reinterpret the customary view that Florence was 'the daughter and creature of Rome' in terms linking not only the histories but also the ethos and values of the two cities. According to this, in the early stages of Rome's independent existence, when society was still primitive and rough, its leading citizens had sent their sons to be brought up and schooled in Tuscany 'so that they might be reared and nourished in virtue and good customs since in Tuscany moral virtues, fine habits and noble refinements were practised more than in any other province of the world and most of all honouring the gods and learning how to make sacrifices...'[2] As a result of having inculcated in them such self-discipline and piety, the Romans had subsequently become the masters of the greater part of the world. Mindful of their debt to their Etruscan teachers from whom they had learnt to render honour and reverence to the gods and to behave with justice and virtue, these being in their own opinion the accomplishments that had enabled them to make and hold their extensive conquests,[3] they had resolved to repay what they owed by establishing a city in the middle of Tuscany in a place 'where the air was best, most suitable and pleasant and the water better than in any other possible site, a city marvellously beautiful, built in the likeness of Rome, and which should be called Romula, that is, the little Rome.'[4] It was, Dati continued, also set in this location, at the foot of the hill on which stood the Etruscan stronghold of Fiesole, in order to keep in check this latter city and to this end was settled by colonists 'chosen by the senators from all the noblest families and clans that there were at this time in Rome.' Eventually of course, when the place had come to be called Florence, this original Roman stock was diluted by the amalgamation of the population with that of Fiesole. The dire consequences of this, as retailed in popular legend, in early chronicles and by Dante and Giovanni Villani were, however, played down by Dati according to whom 'the families which descended from

---

[1] See Rubinstein, 'Beginnings of Political Thought in Florence', pp. 198–227.
[2] Dati *Istoria di Firenze*, 149, pp. 108–9. [3] 150, p. 11. [4] 159, p. 112.

Fiesole have all diminished, like bad seed, and the good Roman seed has remained.'[1] The notorious social discord within the city, traditionally attributed to the mixed provenance of its people, did not figure in his assessment of the legacy of its origins.

Whilst the materials out of which Dati constructed this myth were all to hand, either in popular legend or available in classical works,[2] the combination and treatment of them are original and are clearly influenced by the desire to emphasise similarities between Rome and Florence at the expense of differences. The inconsistency of his attitude towards the Etruscans, who are praised at one moment as the teachers of Rome and the embodiment of all virtue and religious devotion, and damned the next as the forefathers of the inferior element in the Florentine population, arises in part from imperfect assimilation of material from contradictory sources. But it is also due to a desire to combine what the Florentines derived from the Etruscans of antiquity to what they owed to their Roman ancestry. Dati was predominantly concerned to establish the essential affinity between the qualities which had made Rome great and those, in his opinion, possessed by his fellow-citizens. It was therefore important to him to trace to a Tuscan source the distinctive virtues of the Romans while at the same time emphasising the ethnic and cultural continuity between Rome and Florence. His point that Florence was a 'little Rome' built on the model of the parent city was elaborated by a comparison of the topography of the two places:[3] each had a St Peter's at its entrance within the walls, and a St Paul's on the same road outside them, and a St Lawrence and a St Stephen's both adjoining the city boundary and lying on the other axis of the street plan. The Florentine Mercato Vecchio was at the junction of the two principal thoroughfares of the town as the Capitol was in Rome. This correspondence in the form of the two places was, to Dati, evidence of the deliberate intention of the Florentines, who had rebuilt their city after it had been burnt by Totila, to preserve its character as a miniature Rome. The connection between the two was not to be merely the accident of the founding of the younger city by inhabitants of the older, but something more essential, more enduring. The reference made by Dati to the debt

[1] 159, p. 122.

[2] Dati himself gives the authority of Valerius Maximus for his statement that noble Romans sent their children to be educated in Etruria. Livy (IX, 36) would appear to have been the ultimate source of this information.

[3] Dati *Istoria di Firenze*, 151, p. 114. It is to be noted that the Florence which is here matched with Rome is the original nucleus of the city, not the enlarged fourteenth-century town. Dati owed his belief that the town-plans of Rome and Florence corresponded to the earliest Florentine historical writings, notably the *Chronica de origine civitatis* and *Libro Fiesolano*. See Hartwig, *Quellen und Forschungen zur ältesten Geschichte der Stadt Florenz*, I, 55–6.

owed by the Romans to Etruscan teaching is clearly introduced to under-line this. It was not just that Florence was the heir of Rome: both in fact participated in the same tradition, one which had its roots in Tuscany, which Rome had then taken up, brought to perfection but which was still alive in the soil where it had first arisen – in the institutions and customs of Florence. Rome meant to Dati not simply an empire and civilisation but the capability of achieving what its citizens had achieved through adherence to a code, learnt from the Etruscans and now transmitted to the Florentines. The capacity to reproduce what Rome had been, to copy and revive, resided in a method valid wherever civic virtue and strict religious observance were practised.

The pragmatic and virtually relativistic standard by which Dati judged the qualities that attracted divine favour and worldly success is brought out by his discussion of the role of religion in raising the Romans to greatness. How was it, asks the questioner in his dialogue, that they owed their victories to performing sacred rites when these were directed not to the true God, but to pagan deities? Dati answered that 'because they believed that they were making that sacrifice and doing honour to the true God, whom they did not know, the true God permitted that they should acquire merit for it on earth as they sought...'[1] In other words, it was the intention and intensity of their devotions rather than the substance of their religion that really mattered.

The implications of this are clear. The value of religious – or for that matter, one might add, ideological – beliefs depended not on their specific content but on their quality. By adopting such a view, Dati was able to regard as effectively equivalent quite different attitudes and ideas, provided that they reflected the same underlying disposition and expressed the same

---

[1] 149, p. 110. A question which remains open is the extent to which Dati might have been influenced by the humanists in expressing the view stated in this quotation and his relatively flattering references to the Etruscans. I have not been able to discover any writings of the Florentine humanists, prior in date to Dati's *Istoria*, with which he could have been familiar and which might have suggested his remarks either on Roman religion or on the Etruscans, although the first book of Bruni's *Historiae Florentini Populi Libri XII*, written in 1415, expresses a view of the significance to Florence of the Etruscan heritage not dis-similar from Dati's (*Rerum Italicarum Scriptores* n. ed. XIX pt 3, p. 9). Whether this means that Dati was influenced in what he wrote by what his humanist contemporaries were saying at the time, and later wrote down, or whether it indicates that the humanists them-selves gave more sophisticated expression to popular beliefs which Dati here naively reflects, is difficult to determine. In all likelihood, both traditional notions and popular distortions of humanist ideas contributed to what Dati here says: while the general shape of Dati's interpretation of history is clearly traditional, his emphasis on Roman republican-ism could well derive from the humanist school of thought, the origin of which Hans Baron has so ably traced in his *Crisis of the Early Italian Renaissance*. Further examination of this subject would, however, clearly be necessary, before any firm conclusions on this point could be reached.

general standards. There were lines of connection running through history between what to him were manifestations of persistent tendencies, articulated variously in changed circumstances, yet basically of the same nature.

His most striking application of this principle linked the Florentines' support of the Guelph cause with the anti-tyrannical and anti-aristocratic attitude allegedly derived by them from their Roman forefathers. In an interestingly argued passage which deserves to be quoted at length, he remarked that, although the Florentines had on the whole sided with the Guelph party, this had not always been the case. Indeed, the opposite had originally been true,

for the ancient Florentines who attained eminence supported the imperial and lordly party, and the multitude held them in odium out of fear of coming under a tyrant, as Rome had done under Caesar from having let him make himself too powerful; and for this reason they have always dragged down to the ground the great and powerful, so that these might not exceed the common measure; they have acted like the good gardener who prunes and cuts back the branches of the trees which extend too far so that they may last longer and bear better fruit and not give shade nor harm the soil and other seed; and at the foot of those that are lean they put moisture to nourish them; and that people has this nature for the reason that it is born and descended from those Romans who, under the rule of liberty, acquired the lordship of the world and brought Rome more peace, tranquillity and honour than it ever had, who if they returned now to the world would be the enemies of Caesar and of anyone who disrupted that popular state and government and reduced it to tyranny. And therefore these Florentines, born of those free Romans, following their nature, always suspect those who might overcome and take away the liberty of their popular Communal government, and for this reason are hostile and opposed in intention to whoever purposes, through tyranny and pride, to overcome their liberty, as do those who, because of their nobility, disdain to remain equal to others and seek office over others in perpetuity, through force or through deception as tyrants, or through imperial provision, as vicars. And they [the Florentines] have fortified themselves with the help of the Church which is free, and have always helped to defend the liberty of the Church against certain emperors and kings who wished to usurp it; thus the pastors of the Church and those devoted to them have always been of help to the Florentines in the defence and maintenance of such liberty and at the present time all those anciently of the imperial persuasion have been so reduced that there is no longer anyone of contrary mind on grounds of party, but all are united, and are born and live in Guelph convictions more than in any other city or place in Italy today.[1]

The equations on which the logic of Dati's argument in this passage rests are those, on the one hand, between the Guelph cause and liberty and on the other, between liberty and the Roman republican tradition. Each of

[1] 158, pp. 120–1.

these identifications is made on the basis of the common nature of the two supposedly equivalent terms. It was in the nature of the Church to defend its liberty and therefore it also supported the Italian Communes in the protection of theirs; they, in turn, aided it because it stood for freedom from imperial control. Equally, it was in the nature of the Florentines as the descendants of free Romans to resist the aristocratic pretensions of the leading families among them. Their inherited characteristics induced them to bring the great down to the common level for the general good of the state and, since their aims in doing this coincided with the essential interests of the Church, they became its inseparable allies. Differences between the Romans and the Florentines, or between Communal and papal aspirations, were irrelevant to the basic unity of purpose that bound them indissolubly together. Just as the observance of the Roman religion could have the same effects as adherence to the one true Church because it was animated by the same desire to serve God and obey his commandments, so the concern with the preservation of freedom gave an identical value to the attitudes of societies widely separated in time or to institutions serving quite divergent ends.

The line which Dati's argument takes here has significant implications in two respects. In the first place, it enables him, by seeing Florence at once as the ally of the Papacy and the heir of Rome, to use justifications valid for its defence in one role to support it in the other. Since it was ultimately freedom from the oppression of empire or tyranny that both the Commune and the Church were fighting for, why should not their enemies in either case suffer the same divine retribution? Self-seeking worldly power that offended God also violated the standards of justice and moderation of a free and virtuous society. Its ruin could plausibly be considered to be effected in both instances by the same means.

In the second place, Dati's identification of liberty as the essential link between ancient Rome and fifteenth-century Florence led him to enhance the standing of the Roman republic and degrade that of the empire. The spirit that had survived in the institutions and customs of the Tuscan Communes had been that of the republic which therefore became, to his mind, the true Rome. That of the Caesars to which it had become conventional in the Middle Ages to look back as the original expression of the universal commonwealth that men should ideally unite their corporal selves in, as they had their spiritual selves in the Church – this became for Dati, as for his successors during the Renaissance, merely a perversion of the vigorous civic society which by its dedication to freedom, justice and piety had earned the title of mistress of the Mediterranean world. Caesar himself, far from being the majestic figure of medieval legend, became the prototype of tyrant, the equivalent in ancient times of the despots of fifteenth-century Italy who sought, in the pursuit of their sterile power, to destroy the regenerative seed of liberty.

What is remarkable about the Roman ideal, as Dati here presents it, is that it not only closely corresponds to that of the early humanists but is also deeply rooted in the traditional notions exemplified in Giovanni Villani's interpretation of history. The qualities for which the republican Romans are extolled are explicitly the Guelph virtues – love of freedom, opposition to tyranny, devotion to religion. And their enemies are condemned for their self-seeking and ultimately self-destructive ambition. What has happened is that the old view, according to which those who sacrificed spiritual for material good became fatally embroiled in the retributive cycle, has been refurbished. It has lost its specific religious connotations but retained the essential character of its distinction between good and evil, together with the link between the inherent nature of sin and the means of its punishment. For Dati, as for Giovanni Villani, the good are those who submit to God, accept the deprivations of this life, disciplining and moderating their desires in the light of reason and moral law; the wicked, on the other hand, 'seek the good things of the world,'[1] making the satisfaction of their bodily urges the single purpose of their existence. They go not only against divine commandment, but against reason broadly interpreted to cover the sense of the measure of things, the awareness that all excess eventually exacts its own penalty. Directing their energies to physical ends, they condemn their achievements to the transitory fate of the physical world.

From its flux only what represents an absolute principle is secure: for Giovanni Villani, the Church; for Goro Dati, the communities which, in the permanence of their values, defeat the corroding fluctuations of change. 'The Commune cannot die and the Duke was a single mortal man...' – the statement is a pointer to the drift of Dati's thought. Although he was speaking only of Florence, the idea was capable of a wider extension. In nature, the single entity perished; the collective survived. A way of life and a principle of government that promoted the common good brought man into compliance with his ideal social end, as a gardener, by pruning, shaped trees into their proper, fruitful form. The endurance of what the Roman republic had stood for was more than the continuation of a tradition; it was proof of its universal character, of the conformity of its institutions with the rightful life of man.

[1] 149, p. 110.

What the Church had been for Giovanni Villani, the civic heritage, with all that it implied, became for Dati – at once a point of stability in history and a guide to human conduct. The process by which one had come to replace the other in this focal role can be traced in the changes in interpretation perceptible in the historical writing of the intervening period. Already in Matteo Villani's continuation of his brother's work, the essential shift is made: the ambiguity of the term 'Guelph' permits support of free institutions to displace loyalty to the Papacy as the key element in the concept it describes. The inability to link the fortunes of Florence with those of the Church makes it necessary to ground this designation of the city's political allegiance on a new base, that of the Roman tradition. The defence of liberty, the Commune's stake in the Guelph cause, is reinterpreted as a defence of the heritage handed down to Florence from the Roman and pre-Roman past. Hence is born the myth of the persistence of Communal freedom and the arrogation by the medieval emperors of powers properly belonging to the Tuscan people. What Dati was later to write on this subject represents no more than a development and refinement of the basic ideas Matteo Villani had put forward.[1] By tracing back to the free urban communities of ancient Italy the authority of the Roman state, this chronicler had by implication established the republic rather than the empire as the fountainhead of the tradition which Florence had inherited. Also, it was he who, in his psychological explanation of the self-destructive tendency of tyranny, anticipated Goro Dati's method of dealing with the history of the rise and fall of Giangaleazzo Visconti. By rendering in naturalistic terms the patterns of the old religious interpretation, Matteo Villani's work pointed the way to a new set of historical values and ideals. The later Florentine chroniclers of the fourteenth century confirmed the trend towards a more pragmatic approach to judgment and explanation. Their writings reflected a climate of thought disposed to regard the physical and spiritual worlds in isolation and so increasingly to subtract the supernatural from the sphere of material reality. While the need for history to have a religious or moral meaning was not denied, in practice the failure to detect any consistent structure or direction in the course of events militated against the connection of historical fact with tenets of ideological or theological belief.

Dati, in trying once again to show that history had significance and a lesson to teach, was insensibly affected by the changes in outlook that had taken place since Giovanni Villani had proposed his conventionally reli-

---

[1] See pp. 81–83 above for a discussion of the passage in Matteo Villani's chronicle (IV, 77) in which these views are elaborated.

gious interpretation of the past. Although Dati's picture of the inner workings of history closely resembled in form that of the earlier chronicler, he felt compelled to re-express it in terms of the operation not of divine, but of natural law. As his historical ideal he substituted for the Church, the intermediary between God and man, the Romans, the embodiment of the natural virtues. Order which had depended on the divinely instituted design for the world, with its checks and balances, rewards and punishments, now issued from a method, a principle of organisation, one peculiarly associated with a particular kind of society, that exemplified in ancient times by republican Rome and in Dati's day by the Florentine Commune. In one view of things, God kept the world in equilibrium, in the other nature did; and those who acted in accordance with its rules could secure for themselves the success and the stability that its fluctuations denied to those who failed to do so. Essentially the strategy which Dati praises the Florentines for following in their war with Giangaleazzo Visconti is one based on a discernment of the limits of political action and of the appropriateness of responses to the prevailing conditions. Whereas the Duke of Milan went on in one headlong rush, the Florentines knew when to be bold, when to be restrained. It is significant that in describing the Florentines' conduct of the war, Dati compared their tactics at different stages of it to that of the two Roman generals who were later to be taken by Machiavelli[1] as symptomatic of the alternative tendencies of human action, audacity and caution, that needed to combine with the appropriate circumstances to achieve lasting success – Scipio Africanus,[2] and Fabius Maximus.[3] Roman example confirmed what the contemporary experience of Florentine strategy taught because both illustrated the one method, the expression of societies which, inwardly responsive to the natural balance of things, manifested the same balance in their policies.

Between the medieval historical interpretation of Giovanni Villani and Dati's proto-Renaissance adaptation of it there lies a gulf, but also the link of a common morphology. One has succeeded the other not through reaction, but as a result of the altering of the value of terms within accepted equations and relationships. Fundamentally, only one thing has changed from which everything else has followed: the supernatural which was previously immanent in the world and the directing force of history is now only present in the guise of the natural. Material reality still behaves in much the same way but its autonomy is accepted. God rules it through its own inherent tendencies rather than by immediate intervention. His

---

[1] N. Machiavelli, *Discourses on the First Ten Books of Livy*, III, 9.
[2] Dati, *Istoria di Firenze*, 35, p. 37. [3] 55, p. 50.

removal from the centre of the historical stage means that the part he has played has to be distributed among others, to become the collective responsibility of nature and man. Order, goodness, justice, the earthly manifestations of God's will, become therefore attributable to the actions of such forces in the world as can most appropriately be represented as producing the same end-states through the same means as, in the old interpretation, were dictated and fulfilled by divine command.

CONCLUSION

DONALD WEINSTEIN, in a recent article,[1] has traced the persistence in fifteenth-century Florence of a strain of apocalyptic belief, linked with the myth of the city's destiny, that was to find expression in Savonarola's prophesies and the favourable response of his contemporaries to them. He sees this as influenced by earlier legends of the role of Florence as the daughter of Rome and champion of the Guelph cause, but considers it also to have reflected an adjustment by Florentines to the changing conditions of the late fourteenth century, an adjustment which, according to him, manifested itself in two forms:

One product of this re-thinking, as Hans Baron has shown, was civic humanism, with its ethics of individual freedom and civic responsibility to an idealised free republic. Another, and probably related development was the new assertion of Florence's mystical destiny to religious and political supremacy... Weakened by private greed and beset by godless and tyrannical enemies, the Florentines would cleanse themselves, unite in a spirit of communal love and assert their dominance in a new age of spiritual perfection and grace.[2]

The division of the old Dugento and Trecento traditions into these separate streams which Weinstein distinguishes provides the clue to the at first sight paradoxical co-existence in fifteenth-century Florence of two seemingly contradictory tendencies – the growth of a more naturalistic outlook on the one hand, and a periodic resurgence of an apocalyptic view of the world on the other. While one might have expected the development of humanism to have been accompanied by a progressive rejection of the supernatural in all spheres of life, in fact what it appears to have brought about was rather the splitting off of the rational elements of the culture of the past from the mystical ones. This opened the way not only for a more secular conception of man's nature and destiny, but also for a more anti-natural interpretation of the action of spiritual forces. In the tradition which took up those residues of the old world view which humanism had failed to absorb, these came to be seen more as contributing to the attainment of a millenarian ideal than as shaping the course of events to make it accord with the dictates of a providence manifesting itself in history: hence the predilection which Weinstein has observed in late fifteenth-century Florence for transforming the previous faith in the city's historical role

---

[1] D. Weinstein, 'The Myth of Florence' in N. Rubinstein (ed.), *Florentine Studies* (London, 1968), pp. 15–44. [2] *Ibid.* pp. 43–4.

into a conviction that it was destined to become a New Jerusalem by resisting and eventually transcending the evils of this world.[1]

Belief in the supernatural seems at this period to have revived with renewed intensity but in a form closely linked with apocalyptic prediction. That this was the case not merely in Florence but also elsewhere in Italy is borne out by the evidence of two histories, Angelo de Tummulillis' *Notabilia Temporum* and Stefano Infessura's *Diario*. In the latter, references to miracles,[2] astrological signs,[3] tempests[4] and omens[5] proliferate in the relatively short final section of the work that, significantly, follows the report of the preaching in Rome of a prophet of unknown origin, dressed poorly like a beggar who predicted that in the year 1491 in which he spoke many tribulations would befall Rome which would later, in 1492, extend to other parts of Italy until in 1493 the church was freed of temporal domination and the 'angelic pastor' came who alone cared for 'the life of souls and the spiritual life'.[6] In the bulk of Infessura's *Diary* preceding this passage, such indications are seldom mentioned[7] and it would therefore seem reasonable to infer that this author's sensitivity to phenomena of this nature from 1491 onwards was a result of his awareness of their possible meaning in the light of the prophecies he had heard in that year.

In Angelo de Tummulillis' *Notabilia Temporum* the connection between an apocalyptic reading of history and the recording of ominous events is even clearer. Not only does his narrative of events open with an account of one of the prophetic visions of St Brigit,[8] but later (in the sixty-second chapter of his work) he explicitly links the occurrence of 'signs in the sky and portents on the earth, in the air and in all the elements' with predictions made around 1450 by the Spiritual Franciscans, to the effect that God would 'shortly inflict on the people many ills', with worse to follow in the future and that these visitations of divine wrath would be accompanied by appropriate astrological and other prodigies.[9] From here on, Tummulillis' history changes, like Infessura's *Diary* at the corresponding point, from a straight description of political events that has run from its second to its fifty-ninth chapter into an account of historical occurrences, interspersed

---

[1] *Ibid.* pp. 15 ff.

[2] Stefano Infessura, *Diario della città di Roma*, ed. O. Tommassini (Rome, 1890), pp. 270–1, 272–3.

[3] *Ibid.* pp. 264, 266. [4] *Ibid.* pp. 267, 291.

[5] *Ibid.* p. 280. [6] *Ibid.* pp. 264–5.

[7] I have been able to find only one reference to a comet, on p. 75. There is also an account of an eclipse immediately preceding the passage in question, but this would almost certainly have been written after Infessura had become influenced by these prophesies.

[8] Angelo de Tummulillis de Sant' Elia, *Notabilia Temporum*, ed. C. Corvisier (Livorno, 1890), I, pp. 4–5.

[9] *Ibid.* LXII, pp. 57–8.

and at times interwoven with allusions to eclipses,[1] comets,[2] changes in the colour of the sun[3] and moon,[4] miracles,[5] earthquakes,[6] storms, floods and climatic peculiarities[7] There are also, in the section of the work that follows the report of these prophesies, occasional digressions containing detailed astrological predictions,[8] or referring the prognostications of further apocalyptic preachers[9] or arcane prophetic writings.[10]

The re-emergence of this preoccupation with supernatural signs in historical interpretation and political myth-making in the late fifteenth century has a significant bearing on the conclusions of the present study. The evidence of the Florentine chronicles of the fourteenth century suggests a progressive weakening in the course of that period of the sense of connection between the spiritual and natural levels of reality. The structure of the historical process which for Giovanni Villani had arisen from the action of supernatural forces upon the natural would had become for Goro Dati something that owed its form to the tendencies of human nature and of 'fortune', conceived as a secularised providence, a morally directed natural law. At the same time, the omens, astrological indications, miracles and other preternatural signs which had been an integral part of Giovanni Villani's historical universe, though still sometimes mentioned in deference to previous convention, lost their relevance as symptomatic pointers to the direction of historical change. Yet, as subsequent developments were to show, this did not mean that faith in the supernatural as such declined. The revived interest shown by the late fifteenth-century writers in portents and astrology reveals a continued willingness to make reference to such indicators of the spiritual reality underlying the material surface of life. But the close connection between this renewed preoccupation with supernatural signs and apocalyptic predictions does make one thing clear: that such phenomena were now not linked with the normal functioning of the world but were taken as omens of the impending approach of a millenium or final cosmic cataclysm. For Giovanni Villani

---

[1] *Ibid.* LX, p. 55 (the record of this precedes the report of the prediction by two chapters), LXIII, p. 71, CLXIII, p. 136, CXIV, p. 136, CLXXII, p. 143, CCXIII, pp. 189–90.

[2] *Ibid.* LXVIII, p. 63, LXII, p. 71, LXXIV, p. 72, CXXVIII, p. 108, CXXIV, pp. 146–7, CCIX, p. 181, CCV, p. 184, CCXI, p. 188.

[3] *Ibid.* LXXI, p. 70, CLXII, p. 135.

[4] *Ibid.* CVI, pp. 90–91, CXVII, p. 100.

[5] *Ibid.* CLI, pp. 124–6, CCVIII, p. 187, CCXXVII, p. 210–11.

[6] *Ibid.* LXX, p. 69, LXXXIII, p. 78, CXII, p. 91, CLI, p. 121, CCXXI, p. 205.

[7] *Ibid.* LXVII, p. 62, LXIX, pp. 63–4, CXXXVIII, p. 166, CLXVIII, pp. 139–40, CLXXVII, p. 149, XCX, pp. 173–4, CXCVIII, p. 178, CCII, p. 182, CCXIV, p. 191, CCXXIII, pp. 206–9, CCXXXVII, pp. 219–20.

[8] *Ibid.* LXIII, p. 58, LXIV, p. 59, LXXV, pp. 72–3, CLXXIX–CLXXX, pp. 151–61, CXCLX, pp. 179–80, CCXVI, p. 192.   [9] *Ibid.* CCXV, pp. 191–2.   [10] *Ibid.* CXXXII, p. 112.

they had served as confirmation that history in its natural form had a spiritual and moral significance. Stefano Infessura and Angelo de Tummulillis, on the other hand, ignored them until the possibility of some violent transformation of the historical process made them worth observing as signals that the last days were at hand.

The supernatural was important to both, but for different reasons. It is in the light of this, I believe, that the changes in outlook reflected in the chronicles I have considered should be interpreted. The evidence that these chronicles provides shows not that there was any rejection of belief in spiritual forces, but that the sense of connection between the natural and the supernatural was weakened. One result of this weakening was the evolution of the humanist tradition which offered substitutes in terms of the realities of this world alone for older conceptions of order relying upon the interdependence of this world and the next. Another was the growing association of the supernatural with the sinister, catastrophic and abnormal. As spiritual powers lost their relevances to the explanation of natural processes, their manifestations came to seem by their presence to threaten, rather than reinforce, the order of the natural world.

The development illustrated in the Florentine chronicles I have examined reveals one side of the transformation of the composite world-view of the High Middle Ages into two independent and incompatible substitutes for it, the one intensifying its naturalistic base, the other its otherworldly overtones. The conclusion to be drawn from the way in which that development came about appears to be this: the merging of the elements which underlay Giovanni Villani's interpretation of history depended upon a consistency between the religious meaning he ascribed to political events and their actual outcome. When this failed to hold, two avenues remained open: either the rejection of an intractable world, the adversities of which could be seen as prior indications of its coming dissolution, or the attribution of the aberrant course of things not to divine wisdom but to human folly. Giovanni Villani himself, in the apocalyptic forebodings of the closing chapters of his work, appeared inclined to take the former course. Had he survived the plague and lived to have to square its ravages with his basic assumption that God's judgments were reflected in history, he might perhaps have been attracted, as for instance Cola di Rienzi was in 1350,[1] three years after the Black Death, to the chiliastic prophecies of the Fraticelli. But his brother Matteo, true to the pragmatism that had informed Giovanni's efforts to find confirmation of his religious and ideological beliefs

---

[1] Cola di Rienzo, *Epistolario*, ed. A. Gabrielli (Rome, 1890), letters xxx–xxxii, pp. 92–141, xxxv, pp. 149–79, xxxvii, pp. 181–9, xliii, pp. 197–202.

in the resolution of events, chose instead to try to preserve the principle that whatever happened was just, and so, to dissociate God from the calamities which he was compelled to record, saw human weakness rather than the working out of a divine design as the essential determinant of what occurred in the world. Later Florentine chroniclers, subject to the same general cultural influences, took even further the divorce between secular history and a supernatural order of significance. As they did so, portents and astrological signs increasingly lost their relevance to historical explanation even though much of the shape of the old interpretations was unconsciously taken over by the new, through the acceptance of moral assumptions that re-formulated as values inherent in the working of the natural world the principles formerly derived from religious belief.

The change this represented issued, however, not from the growth of a more secular mentality but from the adoption of the more congenial of two possible ways out of the difficulty of applying traditional preconceptions to conditions that evolved in directions these did not anticipate. The point of departure for this development was not really the changes in historical circumstances that set it off, but the original conviction that the various levels of reality, as they were understood in the fourteenth century, were so directly related that the meaning of history in its transcendental sense could be spelt out in terms of the immediate issues of Italian politics. This committed the validity of a whole structure of interpretation to the soundness of one application of it in a way that ultimately could only lead to its undermining.

It remains to ask why the motive arose to anchor a general medieval Christian view of history specifically in a particular political context. Up to a point, the answer to this question is self-evident. All medieval chronicles took it for granted that God's judgment was manifested in history. But this does not entirely explain the formulation of this principle not only in terms of one set of circumstances but also with the distinctive overtones which Giovanni Villani gave it. Since it was not his acceptance of it but the way he applied it which was to make the traditional view of the world it implied vulnerable to change, it is necessary to inquire further what it was about his interpretation of the past and of his own time that made its specific points of reference so essential to it.

Fundamentally, the answer lies, I believe, in the underlying structure of Giovanni Villani's view of history. For what he was doing was showing not merely that events were expressions of the will of God, but that they naturally fell into certain patterns, governed by inherent tendencies of human action, through which divinely ordained ends were realised. It was the absorption into his interpretation of a rational method, together with a number of assumptions of a fatalistic character, linking misfortune with evil and excess that established the close and necessary connection between his evidence, his mode of argument and his conclusions which meant that, as one altered, so the substance of the view of things all these implied had to be modified.

Though ostensibly Christian, Giovanni Villani's conception of the world assimilated an extensive legacy of pre-Christian notions and attitudes. Foremost among these was the primitive magical belief in the sympathetic relationship between spiritual forces and physical reality. More relevant, however, to the form of Giovanni Villani's interpretation of history was the family of ideas, ultimately in all likelihood of astrological origin, which represented the lives of men and of nations as a series of cycles passing through the stages of growth, fulfilment and degeneration. Combined with the conviction that evil must be atoned for, the residues of this in Giovanni Villani's cultural inheritance produced an understanding of human behaviour and historical development as processes in which a surfeit of success or good fortune led on to vices bringing in their train the disasters that were at once the divinely ordained punishments and the natural consequences of the sins which had provoked them. This basic model of the situations that constituted the human world seen through time in history – the rise and fall of men and powers as a result of their susceptibility to the temptations that would ultimately destroy them – implied a correspondence between the actual outcome of events and the moral quality of the motives of those acting them out. It therefore went beyond the minimal requirement set by Christianity that God's will be fulfilled through the revelation of the vanity of all that this life contained, a revelation that would turn men's minds from their temporal preoccupations to the eternal ends of their existence. And of course it also bound the role of divine providence in history up with a particular reading of definite political situations, since the essential characteristic on which the functioning of this model depended was that right and wrong had to be precisely identifiable for the explanation it suggested to be discernible.

What exposed Giovanni Villani's interpretation of events to the kinds of contradictions that arose in his work and in that of his successors between what it sought to prove and the materials that had to be used to prove it was not that it was Christian in intention, nor that it was Guelph in its ideological colouring, but that it was a composite of two elements that could only be reconciled if what actually occurred was what morally ought to occur. The first of these was the sense of a world governed by an order – the stars, men's passions, nature, the spiritual forces lying beyond the confines of material reality, all contributing to an organic, rhythmically operating cosmic design of which they were interdependent constituents. The second was the religious belief in the necessary consistency between life and moral principle and the identification of what was good in terms of its relation to the cause of the Church, or specifically of the Papacy.

There were really three levels in Giovanni Villani's conception of history which can be traced back to the sense of world-order which he had inherited from his Christian and pre-Christian past, but which were placed in a fixed relationship in his interpretation of the events of his time by the need to give a particular moral direction to the lessons he sought to draw from those events. The first was that of direct manifestations of the supernatural, omens and astral signs; the second that of human action considered as falling into a morally self-rectifying rhythm; the third that of the immediate issues of Italian politics seen primarily in the light of the conflicts between Florence and its enemies, the Papacy and its Ghibelline antagonists. The magico-religious basis of the structure that held these levels together had been fluid and flexible, capable of adaptation and readaptation to changing circumstances and points of view. Once, however, it was frozen into a particular form by having introduced into it the idea that life not merely reflected the underlying harmony of the elements that made it up but also demonstrated what was right and what was wrong, then a shift in any part of this structure had to be accommodated by corresponding adjustments to the rest of it. Failing this, some degree of freedom of adaptation could be achieved by reconciling two of its levels and disregarding the third. Given that political incident provided the foundation in objective fact on which all interpretations of it had to rest, this left open two possibilities: either events could be related to a naturally operating mechanism which secured the triumph of good and the discomfiture of evil through the tendency of human passions to overreach themselves; or they could be seen as immediately affected by spiritual forces which acted directly upon them through a suspension of the laws normally governing the physical world.

What had been the conjoined parts of a total view of reality were in consequence separated. On one side of the division a rational order modified and replaced a religious one: on the other, the supernatural, redundant to the physical world, detached itself from it, assuming the character of abnormality that was to distinguish it throughout the early modern period. There was no break, at least immediately either with the sense that a harmonious order underlay existence or with faith in the spiritual as such. Nature, idealised to denote a set of values as well as the substance of physical reality, replaced providence as the regulative force maintaining the balance and equity of things. The supernatural, increasingly alienated from ordinary experience (which in view of the enhanced stature of nature, became intelligible without it), receded to the fringes of life, the former province of apocalyptic forebodings, of the sinister and monstrous that had not found a place within the integrated framework of the medieval world-picture but which had defined, with morbid intensity, the zone of chaos lying beyond it. In the process, it lost none of its power to inspire conviction – indeed this was in some ways heightened by its removal from the sphere of the usual to that of the exceptional – but it began to attract a different kind of attention. On the one hand, it became an object of esoteric interest as its manifestations were thought of less as tangibly evident occurrences involving physical reality than as mysteriously activated phenomena of the psychic world. On the other, in proportion as it ceased to be part of the familiar order of things, it became more and more to be associated with the forbidden and menacing, providing the channel of expression for the fears that the abandonment of a spiritually centred view of existence unconsciously aroused. Peripheral to the ordinary course of life, yet still unquestionably real, the supernatural offered the means by which doubts could be rejected, unease at repudiation of old beliefs allayed, through the attribution of whatever challenged assurance in the prevailing order to the malignant forces of the other world.

The separating out of the natural and supernatural elements in the medieval conception of reality in the long run undermined faith both in a rationally organised, harmonious nature and in the overbearing presence of spiritual powers. Each preserved independently for a time the appearance of self-evident truth with which the past had endowed it but, since ultimately both depended on the structure of which they had originally formed part, neither could subsist permanently without the backing of the other. The interval between the disintegration of the medieval synthesis and the working out of the ultimate implications of its collapse was, however, to prove significant in enabling the formal characteristics of the medieval world-view to be carried over into that which replaced it. The transference of a set of assumptions appropriate to a conception of reality grounded upon the supernatural to one positing a self-sufficient nature was, on the one hand, to give coherence and universality to the newly emerging picture of things but, on the other, to introduce inconsistency into its very basis. The expectation fundamental to it, that experience should conform to a predetermined order would force adaptations on it, and erode even further the certainties remaining to it from its medieval inheritance.

It is in the context of this background that the evidence of the fourteenth-century Florentine chronicles needs to be assessed. In one sense, they illuminate the processes by which attitudes changed; in another, they reveal the underlying nature of the new by showing how it evolved from the old. From a study of them it is possible to reconstruct the dynamic, prompting the successive transformations of outlook of which the shift from the medieval to the modern world-view was to be only the first: the system that they disclose is one in which a chain-reaction of definition, discrepancy, re-adjustment and re-definition is precipitated by an initial, inherently contradictory set of demands, the imbalance of which is preserved in its subsequent displacements by a continuing insistence on matching the substance of reality with a pre-conceived idea of order. The movement so produced is not only self-perpetuating but entails in addition a shedding of the beliefs with which discarded conceptions of the world have been identified, with a consequent progressive whittling away of the capital of magico-religious convictions and their metaphysical derivatives.

These chronicles, defining as they do points of application of conventionally accepted notions of the world to the detail of historical circumstance, bring out, more clearly perhaps than other evidence from this critical period of the fourteenth century, the way that adjustment of interpretations to conditions, under the influence of the insistence on their conformity to each other, wrought the new from the old. Though not themselves important expressions of intellectual attitudes, taken together they achieve, by the naive literalness of their approach, something of the effect of a slow-motion representation of the stages of a movement, the more striking manifestations of which confront us only in the isolated perfection of completed gestures.

Also, by reaching back to stray vestiges of beliefs buried in the cultural subsoil of their age, they draw together, albeit in a loose and tangled fashion, strands of thought the discrimination of which throws light on the underlying form and origin of the shapes the interpretation of history took in their time. By the very refusal of their authors to order and select they succeed in embracing an entire scene, rejecting none of its confusions but grounding the present they depict in a framework of meaning anchored deep in the persisting traditions of their past. They are still chronicles because they issue from a sense of the world that had had a continuous existence, from the beginnings of the civilisation of which they were a late expression, to their own day: they accept the inherent value of the event for its own sake as a necessarily significant element in the universal scheme of things; they are still inspired by the primitive wonder out of which the apprehension of the order they assume had initially arisen; they still see time shadowily sketched against the ultimate truths of eternity. But they stand as well on the threshold of history, in the modern understanding of the term, by their progressive disengagement of action from the web of total world significance and its resultant isolation in the self-contained field of its own operation. On the one hand, they make meaningful for their own time the legacy of the many layered tradition of which they were a culminating expression; on the other, they prepare the way for the separation of the human world into a self-sufficient universe of its own in which history, in common with other secular studies, could become a new, more selective inquiry into the natural causes of events.

APPENDIX 1

THE SOURCES OF
GIOVANNI VILLANI'S 'CHRONICLE'

Despite having been the object of scholarly attention for a considerable period, the problem of the sources of the earlier books of Giovanni Villani's *Chronicle* has never been fully resolved. Otto Hartwig[1] and Pietro Santini[2] examined the question in their studies of early Florentine historiography and the former published a number of the surviving sources in his *Quellen und Forschungen zur ältesten Geschichte der Stadt Florenz*. Together with Martin of Troppau's chronicle of the lives of popes and emperors[3] and a work known as the *Gesta Florentinorum* of which the original text has been lost but which Schmeidler has reconstructed from other sources,[4] these provided Villani with the bulk of his information on Florentine and general history up to about the end of the third quarter of the thirteenth century. From this point on, however, the relationship between Villani's *Chronicle* and its possible sources is much more doubtful. This is partly because there is some disagreement as to whether certain works which contain accounts of events that correspond to Villani's (notably the chronicles of the Sicilian Vespers edited by Sicardi)[5] have been used by him or whether they have subsequently been copied from his narrative. The coincidence of the period from 1280 onwards with Giovanni Villani's own lifetime (he was born no later than 1276) raises the further problem of determining how much of what he records of occurrences in these years not mentioned in other surviving sources is derived from his own observation and the testimony of his contemporaries and how much must be assumed to have been based on written works known to him but not to us.

In view of the differing degrees of certainty with which Villani's sources can be established for the periods before and after c. 1280, I shall consider separately the question of the relationship to earlier historical works of the sections of his chronicle covering the years up to 1280 and that of the provenance of the factual information he reproduces on events between 1280 and 1320.

(i) The first segment of Giovanni Villani's *Chronicle*, consisting of Book I and the first three chapters of Book II (with the exception of the initial chapter of the work which is in reality an introduction), is clearly derived from a version of the

---

[1] Hartwig, *Quellen und Forschungen zur ältesten Geschichte der Stadt Florenz*.
[2] Santini, *Quesiti e ricerche di storiografia fiorentina*.
[3] Martini Oppaviensis, 'Chronicon Pontificum et Imperatorum', in *Monumenta Germaniae Historica Scriptorum*, XXII, 377–475.
[4] As the first appendix of his edition of the 'Annals' of Ptolemy of Lucca in *Monumenta Germaniae Historica Scriptores*, Nova series, VIII, 243–77.
[5] In *Rerum Italicarum Scriptores*, n. ed. XXXIV, part I.

Chronica de origine civitatis which also survives in a slightly different form under the title of the *Libro Fiesolano*. Of the three manuscript texts of this which Hartwig published,[1] one is in Latin and the other two in the vernacular, and Villani probably used one of the vernacular renderings of the *Chronica* version of this work.

The remainder of Book II, Book III and the initial chapters of Book IV of Villani's *Chronicle* are based upon information drawn from Martin of Troppau and doubtless also other general chronicles of the same type. This section covers the period from the advent of the Goths to Italy to the eleventh century and is largely concerned with recording the lives and exploits of kings and emperors, the barbarian incursions into Italy, the rise of Mohammedanism and so on. Chapters 1–3 of Book III and chapters 6–7 and 10–14 of Book IV deal, however, with Florentine history, the former describing the events following the re-founding of the city by Charlemagne, the latter those associated with the taking of Fiesole by the Florentines. Villani's source for the earlier group of chapter is, once again, the *Chronica de origine civitatis*, but he has transposed the account of the re-building of Florence which this contains from the aftermath of its destruction by Totila to a point in time two and a half centuries later. Chapters 6–7 of Book IV derive from a well-established Florentine tradition concerning the capture and destruction of Fiesole by the Florentines and the subsequent absorption of the population of Fiesole into that of Florence. Chapters 8, 10, 11, 12, 13, 14 of the same book describe the city so created, the first in terms of its walls and topography, the rest in terms of the families then residing in it. For this information, Giovanni Villani must have been indebted to a source now lost or to oral tradition.[2]

---

[1] Hartwig, *Quellen und Forschungen zur ältesten geschichte der Stadt Florenz*, pp. 36–65.

[2] The question of the provenance of Villani's information on the early history of Florence is inextricably bound up with that of the authenticity of the Malispini chronicle, which deals with this subject, though much more briefly, and with the relationship between Villani's work and Dante's *Divine Comedy*. The view that the Malispini chronicle was a forgery, composed in the late fourteenth century and itself derivative of Villani, was first put forward by P. Scheffer-Boichorst in 'Die florentinische Geschichte der Malespini eine Fälschung', *Historische Zeitschrift* XXIV (1870), 274–313 and has recently been re-stated and, in my opinion, conclusively argued by C. T. Davis in 'The Malispini Question' in *A Giuseppe Ermini* (Spoleto, 1970). R. Morghen, in a number of articles of which the most important are 'Note malispiniane', *Bullettino dell'Istituto Italiano per il Medio Evo* 40 (1920) 105–26, 'Dante, il Villani e Ricordano Malispini', *Bullettino dell'Istituto Storico Italiano per il Medio Evo* 41 (1921), 174–94, 'Ancora sulla questione malispiniana', *Bullettino dell'Istituto Storico Italiano per il Medio Evo* 46 (1931), 41–92, has plausibly, though, to my mind, not convincingly supported the opposite thesis. Other writers who have engaged in this controversy are noted in C. T. Davis, 'The Malispini Question', note 9, p. 219. The same author's earlier *Dante and the Idea of Rome* (Oxford, 1957), pp. 244–62 gives a survey of the state of opinion on this question up to its date of publication.

In this appendix, it will, in view of the opinion stated above, be assumed that the Malispini chronicle is a work posterior to Villani's and therefore not one of its sources.

As to the question of the possible dependence of Villani on Dante, it can only be said that, while Villani, at least when he came to compose the final version of his work, was undoubtedly familiar with the great poem of his contemporary, the references to the explicit facts of early Florentine history contained in the *Divine Comedy* (for instance in

For the period from 1080 to 1278, in other words for the section of his *Chronicle* that runs from Book IV, c. 23 to Book VII, c. 55, Giovanni Villani's main source was the *Gesta Florentinorum* which no longer survives in its original form but which was so extensively used by other early fourteenth-century chroniclers that it has been possible for Schmeidler to reproduce what is presumably the bulk of it.[1] The priority of this to Villani's work can be established from its use by Ptolemy of Lucca whose *Annals* (composed between 1303 and 1308)[2] make frequent reference to it. One hundred and thirty-four of the chapters out of the two hundred and five in this stretch of Villani's *Chronicle* refer to subject-matter with which the *Gesta* deal and owe the bulk of the facts contained in them to this source. Some of this material may have been derived by Villani from a thirteenth-century Latin chronicle by Sanzanome which also has the title of the *Gesta Florentinorum*[3] but is far more restricted in its coverage and far more diffuse in style than the other work that bears the same name. Since, however, the basic information included in Sanzanome seems to have been absorbed into the other *Gesta*, it is more plausible to assume that Villani took it from the latter source which he must in any case have used, given the evidence of his other borrowings from it.

Of the other chronicles on which Giovanni Villani drew for his account of events between 1080 and 1278 it is possible to isolate only the history of the popes and emperors of Martin of Troppau, the so-called pseudo-Brunetto Latini chronicle, published by Hartwig[4] and by Villari[5] and Brunetto Latini's own *Livres dou Trésor*[6] – if one excepts Ricold of Monte Croce's *Liber Peregrinationis* which, as has already been indicated in the text of this book,[7] is the source of the twenty-ninth chapter of Villani's fifth book, recounting the fantastic origins of the Tartars. The three works mentioned do, however, between them touch on the subject-matter of about half of the chapters in this part of Villani's *Chronicle* that cannot be traced to the *Gesta*, although the information they contain is frequently not as full as that which Villani gives. Other sources unknown to us must therefore be presumed to have provided him with further factual material that enabled him to elaborate and expand his narrative.

Of these three authors, Martin of Troppau is the one on whom Villani de-pended most – for his references to general European history with which the

Inferno xv, 61–2) are neither sufficiently precise nor sufficiently full for Villani's account of the first stages of the growth of his city to be in any significant measure based on them. It is more plausible to assume a common source or tradition on which both Villani and Dante drew than to posit the derivation of the chronicler's narrative at this point in his work from the scattered allusions in the *Divine Comedy* to what must have been in the early fourteenth century fairly generally accepted beliefs about the Florentine past.

[1] See note 4 on p. 155, above.
[2] Schmeidler, 'Die Annalen', p. xxvii.
[3] Published by Hartwig, *Quellen und Forschungen zur ältesten Geschichte der Stadt Florenz*, I, 1–34.
[4] *Ibid.* II, 221–37.
[5] P. Villari, *The First Two Centuries of Florentine History* II, 1–80 at the conclusion of the volume.
[6] B. Latini, *Li Livres dou Trésor*, ed. F. J. Carmody (Berkeley, 1948).
[7] See p. 35 above.

Gesta dealt only in passing. From the anonymous chronicler once identified with Brunetto Latini, or possibly from a source on which that author drew,[1] Villani obtained his account of the origins in 1215 of the Guelph–Ghibelline feud in Florence (v, 38) and various other odd bits of information, including the taking of the Cross by numerous Florentines in 1188 on the eve of the Third Crusade (v, 13). His borrowing from this source was in all likelihood more extensive than this suggests, however, since there is a gap in the only surviving manuscript of this chronicle between the years 1248 and 1285. Some of the material relating to this period in Villani's *Chronicle*, the origin of which is unknown, may well have come from the lost portions of this work. From Brunetto Latini himself, Villani derived much of what is most characteristic of his treatment of the reigns of the Emperor Frederick II and his heirs and of the coming of Charles of Anjou into Italy. Latini's *Trésor* appears to be the only one of his sources that yielded Villani not merely information but also an interpretation of the history of his recent past on which he could build his own conception of the significance of the events of his time. Villani's portrait of Frederick II owes a great deal to Latini as do his strictures against the Hohenstaufen and his explanation of their misfortunes as divine retribution for their defiance of the Church. In point of fact, Villani's whole view of the age preceding his own which Neri considered to have been influenced by Dante could more accurately be seen as a reflection and extension of the passages in the *Trésor* that represent Frederick II and Manfred as the great Guelph historical villains who contribute to their own destruction through their sins and their divinely induced blindness to the effects of their own actions, Manfred by the murder of his father, and Frederick II by his ingratitude to the Church which had nurtured, crowned and protected him. Indeed, the very phrase Villani uses to explain decisions made by the Hohenstaufen that turned out to their own detriment – 'God deprives of sense he to whom He wishes ill' – echoes Brunetto Latini's 'Mais hons pense une chose et Deus repense tout autre; car quant il voit tourbillier un home, il li tolt tot avant la veue; c'est a dire son sens et sa bone porveance.'[2]

(ii) For the period from 1278 on, Giovanni Villani had at least two identifiable sources – a continuation of the *Gesta Florentinorum* in the version published by Hartwig[3] from a manuscript in the Biblioteca nazionale in Naples (XIII, F, 16) and

---

[1] See the discussion below of the possible objections to assuming that Villani drew directly on the pseudo-Brunetto Latini chronicle.

[2] Latini, *Li Livres dou Trésor*, p. 76.

[3] Hartwig, *Quellen und Forschungen zur ältesten Geschichte der Stadt Florenz*, II, 271–96. I follow Hartwig in assuming that the close verbal parallels between this work and Giovanni Villani's *Chronicle* indicate that it was one of Villani's sources. My grounds for accepting it as such are the evident interrelationship between it and other versions of the *Gesta* (which, having been used by Ptolemy of Lucca, must be anterior in date to Villani) and the correspondences between entries in it relating to the period after 1278 and other minor chronicles that appear to be independent of Villani's. The possibility that this chronicle, published by Hartwig, was written after Villani's and based on it cannot, however, be excluded with absolute certainty, although it would seem very unlikely that a work could have been produced from Villani's text alone, the earlier portions of which bore such a close resemblance to the *Gesta* family of chronicles. Professor Charles Davis, with whom I have been in correspondence since the original text of this Appendix was written and to

the pseudo-Brunetto Latini chronicle already mentioned (or one of its sources). In addition, he probably drew on an account of the Sicilian Vespers and its historical aftermath which may or may not have been the *Leggenda di Messer Gianni di Procida* published by Sicardi in vol. XXXIV, part 1 (pp. 63–78) of the new edition of the *Rerum Italicarum Scriptores*.

Otto Hartwig,[1] following Amari,[2] argued that, although Villani's account of the Sicilian Vespers was undoubtedly related to that given in the *Leggenda*, the latter was copied from Villani's *Chronicle* and was hence not its source. Sicardi, in the introduction[3] to his edition of the chronicles of the Sicilian Vespers in the volume of the *Rerum Italicarum Scriptores* indicated above, challenged this conclusion. The case made by neither Hartwig nor Sicardi seems to me in any sense conclusive: both use what is basically the same evidence, but interpret it in different ways. In favour of Sicardi's hypothesis there is, however, the circumstance that Villani's chapters on the Sicilian Vespers and their consequences are very much fuller and more detailed than any that precede or follow them up to the point where Villani himself is in a position to describe events. This suggests either that Villani used the *Leggenda*, or that he had another source on which the *Leggenda* was based. It appears to me highly implausible that he could have constructed his extensive account of the Vespers and the developments that surrounded them from the scattered references – letters, chronicles etc. – that Hartwig lists[4] as some of the possible sources of this section of his historical narrative: on the basis of the remainder of the text of the earlier books of his *Chronicle*, one would have expected much briefer entries on a few key events had he in fact pieced together his story of the rebellion and its results from the disparate kinds of material Hartwig mentions and not the connected, coherent account he in fact gives. Running through the seventh book of his *Chronicle* from its fifty-seventh chapter onwards, there are blocs of continuous narrative dealing with the Vespers and the subsequent war for the re-acquisition of Sicily that cover chapters 57–75, 85–7, 93–6, 102–5 and 117 and contrast with the short, fragmentary notices of isolated facts in the intervening sections of this part of the work. Thirty-six of the fifty-eight pages taken up in the Dragomanni edition of Villani's *Chronicle* by Chapters 57 to 117 of Book VII are about the prelude to the revolt of the Vespers, its

whom I am indebted for his comments on it, has suggested a further possibility – that the Neapolitan manuscript published by Hartwig, like the Orsucci manuscript nr. 40 in the Archivio di Stato in Lucca, might have incorporated additions drawn from Villani in its later sections while remaining substantially independent of Villani's *Chronicle* in those parts based on the *Gesta*. This, of course, could only have been the case if Hartwig were wrong in his dating of the Neapolitan manuscript in question and it had been composed not a decade or so after 1309 (when its text breaks off) but in the 1340s when the Orsucci manuscript was written. If one provisionally accepts Hartwig's dating, the version of the *Gesta* he published has to be acknowledged as one of Villani's sources. However, if further studies disprove it, then it will have to be assumed that it probably incorporates considerable sections of an earlier work on which Villani drew.

[1] O. Hartwig, 'Giovanni Villani und die *Leggenda di Messer Gianni di Procida*', *Historische Zeitschrift*, XXV (1871), 233–71.

[2] Amari, *La guerra del Vespro siciliano*, III, 268.

[3] *Rerum Italicarum Scriptores*, XXXIV, part 1, iv–lxxvii.

[4] Hartwig, 'Giovanni Villani und die *Leggenda di Messer Gianni di Procida*', pp. 265–6.

occurrence and the events flowing from it. In view of its length, the detail which it contains and the way that it is woven together, one can only assume that the history of the Vespers and the ensuing hostilities which Villani provides must have as its basis a single fairly comprehensive source, even if it may have been filled out at certain points with information from other less substantial ones. Whether this source was the *Leggenda*, which is undoubtedly closely connected with Villani's account,[1] or another work on which the *Leggenda* was based or which was derived from it, or whether Villani used a chronicle unknown to us, and Amari and Hartwig were right in considering the *Leggenda* and the other narratives of the Vespers resembling it to have been composed later from Villani's text, one can say on the basis of the evidence of Villani's *Chronicle* itself that there must have been an extensive narrative source on which its author drew. Most probably, though by no means certainly, this was the *Leggenda* or some later rendition of it, possibly in the Italian translation and continuation of Brunetto Latini's *Trésor* of which Amari and Sicardi[2] have published the relevant sections.

If one excludes the chapters describing the events surrounding and following the Sicilian Vespers which have been indicated above (31 in number, covering 36 pages), Villani's account of the period between 1278 and 1299 (Book VII, c. 56 to Book VIII, c. 35) is reduced to 104 chapters taking up 91 pages of the Drago-manni edition. With the exception of those devoted to the war between Florence and Arezzo (VII, 115, 120, 127, 131–2, 138, 140), to the continuing hostilities between the Aragonese and the Angevins that may be presumed to have been derived from the same source as the earlier account of the Sicilian Vespers (VII, 125, 130, 134–5; VIII, 13, 18, 29), to Flemish history (VII, 133; VIII, 4, 19, 20, 32), to events in Florence following the *popolani-magnati* clash of 1292–3 (VIII, 1, 8, 10, 12) and paradoxically to developments in the Near East (VII, 83, 101–1, 129, 145; VIII, 35), these tend to be short, fairly perfunctory notices of isolated events. Of the seventy-five chapters left after the elimination of the sequences listed above, forty-three record information contained in the continuation of the *Gesta* published by Hartwig or in the pseudo-Brunetto Latini chronicle. In addition there are entries in these two sources dealing with the episodes in Florentine history, the war between Florence and Arezzo, the Angevin–Aragonese conflict, the fall of Acre in 1291 and the battles between the French and the Flemish which touch on the subject-matter of the groups of chapters in Villani's *Chronicle* already mentioned but do not deal with it as fully as Villani does.

From this, it would appear that Villani had fuller information than known sources provide on the Campaldino campaign against Arezzo in 1291 and its sequel, on political developments in Florence in the 1290s, on the political prelude to the war between Philip IV of France and the Flemish (which he was to be in a position to report on at close quarters in 1302–4), and on the events occurring in the Near East in the last two decades of the thirteenth century. This he must

---

[1] For some of the parallels between the two works see Sicardi's introduction to *Rerum Italicarum Scriptores*, n. ed., XXXIV, part I, cxviii–cxix.

[2] Amari, *Altre narrazioni del Vespro siciliano*, pp. 238 ff. and *Rerum Italicarum Scriptores*, n. ed., XXXIV, pt. I, 91–116.

have derived from the oral or written testimony of his older contemporaries, or perhaps from other chronicles now no longer extant. Most of the routine factual material of which the remainder of this section of his *Chronicle* is made up was clearly drawn from the continuations of the *Gesta* to which he had access and from the pseudo-Brunetto Latini chronicle or possibly from one of its sources.

Of the continuations of the *Gesta Florentinorum*, that published by Hartwig and already alluded to is clearly the one that bears the closest relationship to Villani's work. Another which has some affinity with Villani's *Chronicle* is the *Cronichetta*, edited by Santini from the Magliabechiana manuscript xxv, 505.[1] Simone della Tosa's *Annals*,[2] although completed no earlier than 1346 and therefore later in their date of composition than the corresponding sections of Villani's *Chronicle*, may also incorporate material from a source which Villani used, though in view of the lateness of the time of its completion, the possibility of its own dependence on Villani cannot be entirely excluded.

Hartwig's *Gesta* and the Santini *Cronichetta*, the one ending (albeit in a truncated manuscript) in 1309, the other in 1321, must both be presumed in view of their close relationship with the *Gesta Florentinorum* either to antedate Villani's *Chronicle* or to derive from sources antedating it and covering the period up to the first decade of the fourteenth century. The main problem with the latter of these two works, as with the chronicle of pseudo-Brunetto Latini is, however, to establish whether Giovanni Villani drew directly upon it or used sources on which it was in turn based. The minor chronicles of this time tend to interweave elements of the same store of information in differing combinations to an extent which makes it virtually impossible to determine where a particular historical fact was first recorded. If one compares Hartwig's *Gesta* with the pseudo-Brunetto Latini chronicle, one finds, for instance, correspondences between the wording and substance of entries running up to the year 1292 which also have their counterpart in Villani's *Chronicle*.[3]

In addition, there are odd correspondences between the pseudo-Brunetto Latini chronicle and Santini's *Cronichetta*, some containing information not in

[1] Santini, *Quesiti e ricerche di storiografia fiorentina*, pp. 89–144.
[2] Published by Manni in *Cronichette antiche di vari scrittori del buon secolo della lingna toscana*, pp. 125–71.
[3] The location of the correspondences between the three works is tabulated below. The page references are to Hartwig's *Quellen und Forschungen*.

Villani	pseudo-Brunetto Latini	Hartwig's *Gesta*
VII, 106 108 110 111	p. 228	p. 286
VII, 112 115	p. 229	p. 286
VII, 128	p. 229	p. 287
VII, 145 146 153	p. 232	p. 290

Hartwig's *Gesta*, but with significant variations in dating and detail, though occasional similarities in wording.[1] It would be reasonable to conclude from these two sets of indications that the authors of both Hartwig's *Gesta* and of the pseudo-Brunetto Latini chronicle used a common source going up to 1292 and that Villani besides employing Hartwig's *Gesta*, drew on the pseudo-Brunetto Latini and possibly also Santini's *Cronichetta* or on some of the sources these works in turn depended on. Beyond this, it is difficult to make connections with any degree of certainty.

However, the Santini *Cronichetta*, though the information it contains is closely related to that included in Villani's *Chronicle*, is much more specific in its use of dates in this period, and it would therefore have been surprising if Villani had consulted it and not reproduced all the detail he found in it. This raises the possibility of his employing yet another chronicle based on it, or a more generalised variant of it. Also, there are very few verbal parallels between the Santini *Cronichetta* and Villani's *Chronicle* and, while most of the dates given in both works correspond, there are occasional discrepancies between them.[2] This suggests that though the material both authors used is often the same, neither had direct knowledge of the other's text. The similarities between the two chronicles are likely, in view of this, to be due either to a common source or to the employment by Villani of a more generalised derivative or variant of Santini's *Cronichetta*. The evidence of discrepancies between the account of events after 1309 in Santini's *Cronichetta* and that in Villani's *Chronicle* (outlined below) supports this conclusion. That Villani used the pseudo-Brunetto Latini chronicle directly can also be questioned. If in fact Simone della Tosa did base his account of the years 1285–1310 on a work other than Villani's *Chronicle*, this source would have contained all that Villani could have borrowed from pseudo-Brunetto Latini in a form much more closely resembling the corresponding sections of his own text. And even if Simone della Tosa did copy from Villani rather than another chronicler, the possibility still remains open that what Villani and pseudo-Brunetto Latini have in common is derived from a shared source, and not from the use by one author of the work of the other.

The exact derivation of Villani's account of the history of the last two decades of the thirteenth century is clearly difficult to determine with any accuracy. However, the substance of the sources on which he drew, of which the principal one was undoubtedly the version and continuation of the *Gesta* edited by Hartwig, can be reconstructed from the surviving chronicles of the period immediately preceding his own. These contain the bulk of the material he used outside

[1] Cf. Villani VII, 154, 155; pseudo-Brunetto Latini, p. 232, Santini, p. 121.

[2] Cf. Villani VII, 106 where date of Pope Martin IV's death is given as 24 March 1285 and Santini p. 119 where it is recorded as 5 March; Villani VIII, 28 where peace between Bologna and Marquis of Ferrara is placed in the year 1299 and Santini p. 122 which dates it 27 December 1298; Villani VIII, 44 which dates the capture of Gubbio by the Guelphs 23 June 1300 and Santini p. 123 which dates it a day earlier; Villani VIII, 45 which says that the Blacks were expelled from Pistoia in May, 1301 and Santini p. 123 which has them expelled on 5 June of that year. There are many more examples of such discrepancies over the years 1302–21, but also, as in the period 1285–1301, a considerable number of correspondences (see note on next page).

the special areas indicated above, on which he must have had fuller information than the cursory account of events these chronicles could provide.

For the section of his work dealing with the first two decades of the fourteenth century, Villani would have gone on drawing on Hartwig's *Gesta* and whatever source, derivative or version of Santini's *Cronichetta* was available to him. There are signs, however, that in his historical narrative from 1300 onwards, and particularly after 1309, Villani was becoming more independent both of Hartwig's *Gesta* and whatever work it was that formed the link between the text of his *Chronicle* and Santini's *Cronichetta*. His accounts of events in Florence in 1300-5 (VIII, 39-43, 49-50, 59-60, 68-72, 74), of developments in Flanders in 1302-4 (VIII, 55-8, 76-9) of relations between the popes and Philip the Fair of France (VII, 62-4, 66, 80-1, 91-2) and of the descent of the Emperor Henry VII into Italy (VIII, 101-2; IX, 1, 7, 9, 11, 14-15, 20-9, 31-53) which take up between them the greater part of the space he devotes to the years 1300-1313 (97 out of 145 pages in the Dragomanni edition) are too full and detailed to have been derived exclusively from the chronicles of the *Gesta* type which do little more than list isolated historical facts. It is also significant that the divergences between Villani's text and that of Santini's *Cronichetta* become more frequent from 1309 onwards[1] and that the description of the events surrounding Henry VII's journey to Italy in 1310-1313 given by the two chroniclers varies considerably.

This suggests that Giovanni Villani was probably to some extent drawing on his own recollections and written records in filling out his account of occurrences in the first decade or so of the fourteenth century. We may also conclude that whatever other sources he had for the period up to 1320, we can, from surviving chronicles, establish a secure relationship between his text and that of other extant manuscripts (or the sources of those manuscripts) only up to about 1309. This is the date at which Hartwig's *Gesta* breaks off and Santini's *Cronichetta* begins to reveal serious divergences from Villani's *Chronicle*. It is also the year before a thirteen-year gap in Simone della Tosa's *Annals*, the occurrence of which at this point may indicate the conclusion at it of the source on which that author drew.[2]

It is probable, in the light of the text of Giovanni Villani's *Chronicle*, that he continued to use some annalistic chronicle (perhaps the lost concluding pages of Hartwig's *Gesta*) for the years 1314 to 1319 since chapters 63 to 105 of his ninth book which cover this period are mostly short notices of isolated events such as might plausibly have been derived from this kind of source. However, in the absence of historical works from which Villani can definitely be shown to have borrowed for his account of occurrences over this space of time, such a possibility can only be considered conjectural.

From about 1322 onwards, Villani's narrative of events is almost certainly

---

[1] There are clashes in dates between Villani VIII, 107, 108, 110, 119; IX, 8 and Santini p. 130, Villani, IX, 40 and Santini, p. 132, Villani, IX, 49, 52, 75 and Santini, p. 135, Villani, IX, 61 and Santini, p. 136, Villani, IX, 71 and Santini, p. 137, Villani, IX, 85 and Santini, p. 141, Villani, IX, 101 and Santini, p. 142, Villani, IX, 99 and Santini, p. 143, Villani, IX, 132 and Santini, p. 144.

[2] Manni, *Cronichette antiche di vari scrittori del buon secolo della lingua toscana*, p. 160.

predominantly based on his own observation or the testimony of his contemporaries.[1] Some of the material he used for his account of the years 1320-1 would, like his description of the salient developments of 1301-5 and 1310-13 have also doubtless have been culled from his own records or recollections. From such of his sources as can be traced for the period 1301-9 (and conjecturally for the subsequent decade) it would appear that they provided him with a framework of facts, placing events in their historical order, into which he could insert what were in effect (despite their division into the conventional chronicle chapters) continuous streams of connected narrative dealing with the key political episodes of the time.

APPENDIX II

THE DATING OF
GIOVANNI VILLANI'S 'CHRONICLE'

The text of Giovanni Villani's *Chronicle*, at least in the form in which it has survived, can be shown from internal evidence to have been begun no earlier than the 1320s, and, if one accepts the argument of Ferdinando Neri,[2] the early 1330s. The version we now have may even date from as late as the 1340s.

The scholars who have examined this question have pointed to a number of references in the early books of Villani's *Chronicle* to events subsequent to 1318. Cipolla and Rossi[3] demonstrated that chapter 41 of Book VII must have been written after 1318 since it mentioned the death of Henry, the son of Manfred and the last of the Hohenstaufen, which occurred on 31 October of that year. Busson,[4] followed by Neri,[5] pointed out that Book IV, chapter 4 of Villani's *Chronicle* mentioned Charles IV of France who came to the throne in 1322. Neri furthermore indicated that in chapter 38 of Book V the presence of the statue of Mars on a column at one end of the Ponte Vecchio was referred to in the past tense.[6] Since this statue was swept away in the Florentine floods of 1333 described in the first chapter of Book XI, he drew from this the conclusion that the fifth book of Villani's *Chronicle* could not have been written before that date. Professor Aquilecchia, in a recent article, has questioned this inference,[7] attributing the 'era' or 'was' in the passage in question to a later copyist and has also taken the allusion

---

[1] See Appendix II.

[2] F. Neri, 'Dante e il primo Villani', *Giornale Dantesco*, XV (1912), 1-31.

[3] C. Cipolla and V. Rossi, 'Intorno a due capi della cronica malispiniana', *Giornale Storico della Letteratura Italiana* VIII (1886), 231-2.

[4] Busson, *Die florentinische Geschichte der Malespini und deren Benutzung durch Dante*, p. 54.

[5] Neri, 'Dante e il primo Villani', pp. 2-3.

[6] *Ibid.*, p. 3.

[7] G. Aquilecchia, 'Dante and the Florentine Chroniclers', *Bulletin of the John Rylands Library*, 48 (1965-6), 40-1.

in chapter 4, Book IV to Charles IV of France to indicate knowledge of the accession of that monarch to the throne but not of his death which was to occur in 1328 and which Neri had felt to be implied by Villani's reference Charles IV as the last of Philip the Fair's sons.

As against this objection to Neri's later dating of Villani's *Chronicle*, it is worth noting however that, in the fifth chapter of its eighth book there is a reference forward to chapter 89 of Book X which records the canonisation of Celestine V in 1328.[1] This would seem to indicate that Book VIII, as we now have it, was composed no earlier than 1328. Since it is unlikely that Book VIII was written long after Book V, if both formed part of a continuous narrative of past events set down years after they had occurred, this strengthens the case for bringing the date of composition of Books IV and V forward to 1328 or 1333 rather than back to 1322.

The problem of deciding when Villani's work was produced is not resolved by a comparison of it with Dante's *Divine Comedy*. While both Neri[2] and Aquilecchia[3] have indicated numerous parallels between Villani's *Chronicle* and the poem of his great contemporary, these only prove that Villani must have written it no earlier than 1321 when the *Paradiso* would first have been available to him. Of more significance is the reference in the eighty-sixth chapter of Villani's tenth book (which records the death in 1328 of the Lucchese tyrant, Castruccio Castracane) to the Florentines' purchase of Lucca from Mastino della Scala and their subsequent loss of this city, both of which occurred in 1341. It might be deduced from this that, if the earlier books of Villani's *Chronicle* had been written as late as 1333, as Neri's evidence suggests, there is no reason to suppose that they might not have been produced even later since Book X which contains an account of events up to that date contains information that would not have been known till 1341.

An examination of the internal evidence provided by the text of Villani's *Chronicle* suggests therefore that its final form could only have been fixed fairly late in its author's life, in the 1330s or 1340s. Before, however, one leaps from this to the conclusion that it was substantially written in those years, one has to consider the improbability of supposing that the detailed account of events which most of Books VIII and IX and all of Book X contain could have been produced from recollection decades after the occurrences described in them. The argument from internal evidence leads ultimately to a 'reductio ad absurdum' that forces one to postulate the re-working in the last years of the chronicler's life of material drawn partly from other sources but also consisting to a considerable extent of the author's own previously recorded narrative of incidents which he had either witnessed or had knowledge of through the oral testimony of others.

---

[1] According to Mollat, *Popes at Avignon*, p. 249, the canonisation of Celestine V occurred on 5 May 1313. The fact that Villani records it as having taken place in 1328 and makes an explicit reference forward ('come innanzi al detto tempo faremo menzione') in VIII, 5, to what can only be X, 89, suggests that, when he wrote the earlier chapter, he was aware of the contents of the later one.

[2] Neri, 'Dante e il primo Villani', pp. 6–22.

[3] Aquilecchia, 'Dante and the Florentine Chroniclers', p. 43.

Giovanni Villani's own claim, made in the thirty-sixth chapter of his eighth book, to the effect that he was inspired to undertake his work in 1300, has been generally dismissed by scholars on the grounds that the commencement of his *Chronicle* at that date is inconsistent with the internal evidence of its text. The use by Villani, in his account of how he came to write his history, of a phrase expressing an idea borrowed from Dante's *Paradiso* (xv, 109–11) (juxtaposing the rise of Florence and the decline of Rome) has furthermore been taken by Professor Aquilechia[1] as an indication that the whole of this passage should be read figuratively as an attempt by its author to associate the composition of his work with the ideal date of the *Divine Comedy*. If, however, one interprets what Villani here says to mean not that he started writing the *Chronicle* we now have in 1300 but that it was in this year that he began the collection and compilation of what was eventually to constitute it, neither of these suffices to eliminate the possibility that it was in or around 1300 that the idea of composing his *Chronicle* first came to him. His employment of an expression taken from Dante in his justification for undertaking his historical labours seems not enough in itself to invalidate the literal sense of his testimony.

There is indirect evidence to indicate that, while Villani probably did not begin making a continuous account of what he saw or heard before about 1322, he does appear to have recorded some events on which we know him to have had first-hand information as early as 1301–4. An examination of the amount of space he devoted to the various years between 1280 and 1330[2] and the amount of specific information (notably exact dates) contained in the chapters assigned to each suggests that it was around 1322 that his narrative filled out into a detailed description of everything he knew to be happening; however, there are certain episodes in the sections of his work dealing with earlier years of which his account is so full that, in the absence of other sources on which he might have drawn, it is difficult to consider them to have been written two decades after the incidents described in them had occurred. In particular, Villani's chapters on political events in Florence in 1301 (VIII, 39–43, 49, 59–60, 68–72) and on the revolt of the Flemish against Philip the Fair of France (VIII 55–8, 76–9) are rich in detail to an extent which would have made it impossible for them to have been written from any other known chronicle of the period or from recollection years afterwards. Since we know Villani to have been in Florence and Flanders at the time when the occurrences related in these chapters took place, it seems reasonable to suppose that he kept some written record of them at or near the time they took place and that he later incorporated in his chronicle what he had then noted down. The survival in the text of this part of Book VIII of his work of the word 'presente' in association with dates (for instance in VIII, 58 where reference is made to 'del mese di Settembre presente' and in VIII, 82 where the phrases 'a dì 20 del presente mese di Maggio' and 'nel presente mese di Giugno' both occur) also suggests the possible assimilation into a subsequently composed narrative of passages written at or near the time when the events recorded in them actually happened.

It might be added that, apart from the manuscript published by Hartwig (Cod.

---

[1] *Ibid.* pp. 48–51.   [2] See below.

Nap. XIII, F16) as a version of the *Gesta Florentinorum*,[1] there appear to be no surviving sources that Villani can definitely be established to have used for his account of the period after 1300;[2] and the entries in this chronicle dealing with the first years of the fourteenth century are brief and cover in four pages the substance of chapters 37 to 99 of Book VIII of Villani's *Chronicle* which take up 92 pages in the Dragomanni edition of that work. Even allowing for Villani's verbosity, it would seem too much to postulate that he could, writing two decades later, have expanded the sketchy recital of events available from this source into the full account he himself provided without some written material of his own to draw on.

The question of when Villani began to write his *Chronicle* has, in view of what has been said above, really to be divided into three sub-questions:

(i)   When was he first inspired to start the preparatory work for the production of the history he was later to compose?

(ii) When did he start keeping a regular account of events?

(iii) When did he cast the work we now have in its final form?

The answer to (iii) must, in the light of the internal evidence of Villani's text, be some date between 1333 and 1341 – towards the beginning of this period if one assumes a relatively slow rate of composition of Books V–X, towards the end of it if one supposes that the author, at this stage recopying and revising earlier material, transcribed and expanded these parts of his *Chronicle* fairly quickly. The answer to (i) is probably some date shortly after 1300, if not 1300 itself when Villani himself claimed he was inspired to begin his *Chronicle*. The answer to (ii) is more difficult to determine with any assurance; but a study of the amount of space devoted to each year between 1280 and 1339 (Florentine style) and the number of specific dates (day and month or saint's day) mentioned within each does show up a significant pattern that strongly suggests that it was about 1322 that Villani began making a more or less continuous record of events.

Taking the Dragomanni edition of 1844–5 as the basis of such a study, we arrive at the results given on the following page. From these, it will be immediately evident that the amount of space and the number of specific dates between 1322 and 1329 is significantly larger than that in any preceding period covered by Villani's *Chronicle*. In fact, there is an average of over 32 pages and of 44 specific dates per year over this stretch of time, as against 8 pages and 3.5 specific dates for 1281–90, 5 pages and 1.3 specific dates for 1291–1300, 10 pages and 4 specific dates for 1301–10, 11 pages and 7.4 specific dates for 1311–20. While the sections of Villani's work dealing with the years up to 1320 contain patches of relatively detailed narrative, it is only from 1322 onwards that there is an even flow of uninterrupted description of events. Such fullness of coverage is explicable only if one assumes Villani to have kept a

[1] Hartwig, *Quellen und Forschungen zur ältesten Geschichte der Stadt Florenz*, II, 271–96.

[2] See Appendix I. It is likely that Villani also drew on at least one other work covering the period up to about 1309 which was also used as a source by the author of the 'Cronichetta' published in Santini, *Quesiti e ricerche di storiografia fiorentina*, pp. 89–144, but his borrowings from this presumed chronicle would not have been sufficiently extensive to make any significant difference to the depth of his coverage of the years 1300–9.

	Chapters	Pages	Specific dates		Chapters	Pages	Specific dates
1280	—	—	—	1305	14	5	3
1281	5	4	—	1306	4	3	2
1282	28	26	8	1307	5	8	—
1283	2	2	—	1308	12	9	1
1284	10	10	4	1309	13	6	10
1285	10	9	4	1310	15	9	11
1286	2	1	—	1311	26	12	21
1287	7	5	3	1312	11	11	11
1288	9	8	4	1313	9	5	3
1289	10	12	8	1314	9	6	6
1290	6	4	4	1315	7	5	3
1291	6	5	2	1316	6	5	2
1292	5	5	2	1317	9	7	7
1293	3	3	—	1318	8	6	5
1294	7	8	2	1319	6	3	6
1295	4	4	1	1320	21	14	11
1296	4	3	1	1321	12	8	6
1297	2	2	1	1322	56	30	22
1298	5	3	1	1323	48	27	37
1299	9	8	2	1324	47	25	29
1300	9	10	1	1325	63	37	81
1301	5	6	1	1326	31	23	31
1302	14	26	3	1327	51	42	43
1303	6	7	3	1328	55	54	66
1304	11	24	7	1329	25	21	27

more or less contemporaneous record of occurrences from this point in time onwards.

An examination of the parts of the table above relating to the years before 1322 reveals certain variations in the amount of space devoted to each that reflect the insertion into what is basically a series of short factual entries of occasional blocs of more detailed narrative. For instance, of the 64 chapters covering the years 1281 to 1287, 31 deal with the Sicilian Vespers and their consequences and are presumably drawn from the *Leggenda* of Giovanni di Procida[1] or, if this is not original, from some other source. All but four of the specific dates in this period are in these chapters. The exceptions are the dates of the death of Pope Martin IV (VII, 106), the election (*ibid.*) and death of his successor Honorius IV (VII, 113) and that of a fire in Florence on the night of the Carnival of 1287. The first three of these were probably taken from a continuation of Martin of Troppau's lives of the popes;[2] the fourth from oral tradition or some unknown written source. Of

---

[1] See Appendix I.

[2] That actually published in *Monumenta Germanica Historia*, XXII, 481–2, gives dates for these events that are, however, one day later than Villani's.

the 25 chapters on the next three years (1288–90), nine are concerned with the military campaign against Arezzo and related developments and these include twelve of the sixteen precise dates in this time-span. Where Villani drew the information for this from is not clear; but it is possible he might have been relying on oral testimony or on some written account now lost, of the Campaldino campaign. The brevity of the treatment accorded to the years 1291–1300 suggests that for this period Villani could rely only on vernacular chronicles such as the version of the *Gesta* published by Hartwig and the so-called pseudo-Brunetto Latini chronicle.[1] Of the thirteen specific dates in this period, seven can in fact be traced to these two sources.

Between 1301 and 1321 the main substantial blocs of historical narrative are those already indicated relating to the conflict between the Bianchi and Neri in Florence and developments in Flanders at the beginning of the fourteenth century, and the events surrounding the descent of the Emperor Henry VII into Italy in 1310–12. These account for the peaks in the totals of pages per year for 1302, 1304, 1310, 1311 and 1312. For the remainder of these years before 1320 Giovanni Villani's record of occurrences is relatively brief and would have been derived either from sources such as the *Gesta* published by Hartwig or from notes of outstanding incidents made by himself. The fuller coverage given to the years 1320–1 is probably due to his having begun around 1320 to make a more extensive record of events.

It would appear therefore, from the evidence presented, that between 1301 and 1319, Giovanni Villani contented himself with collecting material, writing occasional extended accounts of developments of outstanding importance and perhaps making notes of individual incidents (the increase in the number of specific dates per page from 1309 on makes the last possibility a likely one). Round about 1320, it would seem he began to take his task of recording day-to-day occurrences more seriously, but it was evidently not till 1322 or thereabouts that he really launched into the full description of events he was to keep up till his death. At some point ten to twenty years later, he appears to have gathered together all the material he had collected and written himself since about 1300 and produced with it his *Chronicle* as we know it today.

[1] Both are published by Hartwig, *Quellen und Forschungen zur ältesten Geschichte der Stadt Florenz*, the former, as has already been recorded, in II, 271–91, the latter in II, 221–37.

BIBLIOGRAPHY

ORIGINAL SOURCES

Chronicles studied

Dati, Goro, *L'istoria di Firenze dal 1380 al 1405*, ed. L. Pratesi. Norcia, 1902.

Stefani, Marchionne di Coppo. *Cronaca fiorentina*, ed. N. Rodolico. In *Rerum Italicarum Scriptores*, N. ed., vol. xxx, part 1, Città di Castello, 1927.

Villani, Giovanni. *Cronica*, ed. F. G. Dragomanni. 4 vols., Florence, 1844–5.

Villani, Matteo. *Cronica*, ed. F. G. Dragomanni. 2 vols., Florence, 1846.

Anon. *Cronica volgare di anonimo fiorentino dall'anno 1385 al 1409 già attribuita a Piero di Giovanni Minerbetti*, ed. E. Bellondi. In *Rerum Italicarum Scriptores*. N. ed., vol. xxvii, part 2. Città di Castello, 1915.

Other original sources consulted

Compagni, Dino. *Cronica*, ed. I. del Lungo. In *Rerum Italicarum Scriptores*. N. ed., vol. ix, part 2. Città di Castello, 1907–16.

Dati, Gregorio. *Libro segreto*, ed. C. Gargiolli. Bologna, 1869.

Hartwig, O. *Quellen und Forschungen zur ältesten Geschichte der Stadt Florenz*. 2 vols. Marburg, 1875 – Halle, 1880.

Infessura, S. *Diario della città di Roma*, ed. O. Tommassini. Rome, 1890.

Jordanes. *Gothic History*, trans. and ed. C. C. Mierow. Princeton, 1915.

Josephus, Flavius. *The Wars of the Jews*, trans. W. Whiston. 3 vols. London, 1889–90.

Latini, Brunetto. *Li Livres dou Trésor*, ed. F. J. Carmody. Berkeley, 1948.

Laurent, J. C. M. *Peregrinatores Medii Aevi Quattuor: Burchardus de Monte Sion, Ricoldus de Monte Crucis, Odoricus de Foro Julii, Wilbrandus de Olderborg*. Leipzig, 1864.

Malispini, Ricordano. *Storia fiorentina*, ed. V. Follini. Florence, 1816.

Manni, Domenico Maria. *Cronichette antiche di vari scrittori del buon secolo della lingua toscana*. Firenze, 1733.

Martini Oppaviensis. 'Chronicon Pontificum et Imperatorum'. In *Monumenta Germaniae Historica Scriptorum*. Hanover, 1872, vol. xxii.

Morelli, Giovanni di Pagolo. *Ricordi*, ed. V. Branca. Florence, 1956.

Otto of Freising. *The Two Cities*, trans. C. C. Mierow; ed. A. P. Evans and C. Knapp. New York, 1928.

Piur, Paul. *Petrarcas 'Buch ohne Name' und die päpstliche Kurie*. Halle, 1925.

Rienzo, Cola di. *Epistolario*, ed. A. Gabrielli. Rome, 1890.

Sercambi, Giovanni. *Le croniche*, ed. S. Bongi. 3 vols., Rome, 1892.

Tholomeus von Lucca. 'Die Annalen', ed. B. Schmeidler. In *Monumenta Germaniae Historica Scriptores*, Nova series, vol. viii. Berlin 1955.

Tummulillis de Sant' Elia, A. de. *Notabilia Temporum*, ed. C. Corvisieri. Livorno, 1890.

Villani, Filippo. *Le vite d'uomini illustri fiorentini*, ed. F. G. Dragomanni. Florence, 1847.

Cronache dei secoli XIII and XIV in Document idi Storia Italiana pubblicati della R. Deputazione sugli Studi di Storia Patria per le provincie di Toscana, dell' Umbria e delle Marche, vol. VI. Florence, 1876.

'Due cronache del Vespro in volgare siciliano del secolo XIII', ed E. Sicardi. In *Rerum Italicarum Scriptores*, vol. XXXIV, part 1. Bologna, 1917.

SECONDARY SOURCES

Amari, M. *La guerra del Vespro siciliano*. Milan, 1886.

Anderson, A. R. *Alexander's Gate, Gog, Magog and the Enclosed Nations*. Cambridge, Mass., 1932.

Aquilecchia, G. 'Dante and the Florentine Chroniclers'. *Bulletin of the John Rylands Library* 48 (1965–6), 48–51.

Arias, G. 'Nuovi documenti su Giovanni Villani'. *Giornale Storico della Letteratura Italiana*, XXIV, An. 17. 1899, 383–9.

Baldasseroni, F. 'La guerra tra Firenze e Giovanni Visconti'. *Studi Storici*, XI (1902), 365–407; XII, 1903, 4–94.

'Una controversia tra stato e chiesa in Firenze nel 1355'. *Archivio Storico Italiano*, Ser. V, L (1912), 39–54.

'Relazioni tra Firenze, la Chiesa e Carlo IV'. *Archivio Storico Italiano*, Ser. V, XXXVII (1906), 3–60 and 322–47.

Baron, H. *The Crisis of the Early Italian Renaissance*. 2 vols. Princeton, 1955. Revised edition, 1 vol. Princeton, 1966.

Humanistic and Political Literature in Florence and Venice at the beginning of the Quattrocento. Cambridge, Mass., 1955.

From Petrarch to Leonardo Bruni: Studies in Humanistic and Political Literature. Chicago, 1968.

Bartoli, A. *Storia della letteratura italiana III: la prosa italiana nel periodo delle origine*. Florence, 1880.

Bec, C. *Les Marchands écrivains: affaires et humanisme à Florence 1375–1434*. Paris, The Hague, 1967.

Becker, M. 'Un avvenimento riguardante il cronista Marchionne di Coppo Stefani conservato nei documenti giudiziari dell'Archivio di Stato di Firenze'. *Archivio Storico Italiano*, Anno 117 (1959), 137–46.

Brucker, G. A. *Florentine Politics and Society*. Princeton, 1962.

'The Ghibelline Trial of Matteo Villani (1362)'. *Mediaevalia et Humanistica* 13 (1960), 48–55.

Burckhardt, J. *The Civilisation of the Renaissance in Italy*. London, 1944.

Busson, A. *Die florentinische Geschichte der Malespini und deren Benutzung durch Dante*. Innsbruck, 1869.

Capponi, G. *Storia della repubblica di Firenze*. 3 vols. Florence, 1876.

Cipolla, C. and Rossi, V. 'Intorno a due capi della cronica malispiniana'. *Giornale Storico della letteratura Italiana*, VIII (1886), 231–41.

Davis, C. T. *Dante and the Idea of Rome*. Oxford, 1957.

'Il buon tempo antico'. In N. Rubinstein, *Florentine Studies*. London, 1968, 45–69.

'The Malispini Question'. In *A Giuseppe Ermini*, Spoleto (1970), 215–54.

Döllinger, I. von *Beitrage zur Sektengeschichte des Mittelalters*. Munich, 1890.

Doren, A. 'Fortuna im Mittelalter und in der Renaissance'. *Bibliotek Warburg Vorträge*, II (1923), 71–144.

Emerton, E. *Humanism and Tyranny*. Cambridge, Mass., 1925.

Fanfani, P. 'Instrumento dell'accordo e compagnia fatto tra Giovanni Villani e Filippo e Francesco e Matteo', *Il Borghini*, III (1865), 520–5.

Faraglia, N. F. 'Alcune notizie intorno a Giovanni e Filippo Villani il Vecchio'. *Archivio Storico per le province napoletane*, XI (1886), 554–61.

Fiumi, E. 'La demografia fiorentina nelle pagine di Giovanni Villani.' *Archivio Storico Italiano*, Anno 108 (1950), 78–158.

'Economia e vita privata dei fiorentini nelle rivelazioni statistiche di Giovanni Villani.' *Archivio Storico Italiano*, Anno 111 (1953), 207–41.

Frugoni, A. 'G. Villani "Cronica", XI, 94.' *Bullettino del Istituto Storico Italiano per il Medio Evo*, 77 (1965), 229–55.

Garin, E. 'La cultura fiorentina nella seconda metà del 300 e i "barbari britanni"' *Rassegna della Letteratura Italiana*, LXIV (1960), 181–95.

Gerola, G. 'Fra Moriale in Toscana'. *Archivio Storico Italiano*, Ser. V, XXXVII (1906), 261–300.

Gervinus, G. G. *Geschichte der florentinischen Historiographie bis zum sechszehnten Jahrhundert*. Frankfurt, 1833.

Hartwig, O. 'Giovanni Villani und die *Leggenda di Messer Gianni di Procida*'. *Historische Zeitschrift*, XXV (1871), 233–71.

Hyde, J. K. 'Italian Social Chronicles of the Middle Ages'. *Bulletin of the John Rylands Library*, 49 (1966–7), 107–32.

Lami, V. 'Di un compendio inedito della cronica di Giovanni Villani nelle sue relazioni con la storia malispiniana'. *Archivio Storico Italiano*, Ser. V, V (1890), 369–416.

Luiso, F. P. 'Le edizioni della cronica di Giovanni Villani'. *Bullettino dell'-Istituto Storico Italiano per il Media Evo*, 49 (1935), 279–315.

'Indagini biografiche su G. Villani'. *Bullettino dell'Istituto Storico Italiano per il Medio Evo*, 51 (1936), 1–64.

Lungo, I. del. *Dino Compagni e la sua cronica*. 3 vols. Florence, 1879–80.

Mazzoni, G. 'La questione malispiniana'. *Nuova Antologia*, 1 June, 1922.

Mehl, E. *Die Weltanschauung des Giovanni Villani*. Leipzig-Berlin, 1927.

'G. Villani und die Divina Commedia'. *Deutsche Dante Jahrbuch*, X (1928), 173–84.

Meiss, M. *Painting in Florence and Siena after the Black Death*. Princeton, 1951.

Mesquita, D. M. Bueno de. *Giangaleazzo Visconti*. Cambridge 1941.

Milanesi, G. 'Documenti riguardanti Giovanni Villani e il Palazzo degli Alessi in Siena'. *Archivio Storico Italiano*, n. ser. IV, part 1 (1856), 3–12.

Mollat, G. *The Popes at Avignon*. London, 1963.

Monte, A. del. 'La storiografia fiorentina dei secoli XII e XIII'. *Bullettino dell'Istituto Storico Italiano per il Medio Evo*, 62 (1950), 175–282.

Morghen, R. 'Note malispiniane'. *Bullettino dell'Istituto Storico Italiano per il Medio Evo*, 40 (1920), 105–26.

'Dante, il Villani e Ricordano Malispini'. *Bullettino dell'Istituto Storico Italiano per il Medio Evo* 41 (1921) 171–94.

Neri, F. 'Dante e il primo Villani'. *Giornale Dantesco*, XV (1912), 1–31.

Palmarocchi, R. *Cronisti del Trecento*. Milan–Rome, 1935.

Panella, A. 'Politica ecclesiastica del Comune fiorentino dopo la cacciata del Duca d'Atene'. *Archivio Storico Italiano*, Anno 71, II (1913), 271–370.

Panofsky, E. *Renaissance and Renascences in Western Art*. Stockholm, 1960.

Paoli, C. 'Studi sulle fonti della storia fiorentina'. *Archivio Storica Italiano*, Ser. III, XX, 1874, 164–85; Ser. III, XXI (1875), 453–74.

Pardi, G. 'Disegno della storia demografica di Firenze'. *Archivio Storico Italiano*, Ser. VI, 1 (1916), 3–84.

Renouard, Y. *Les Relations des Papes d'Avignon et les compagnies commerciales et bancaires de 1316 à 1378*. Paris, 1941.

Rodolico, N. 'Note statistiche su la populazione fiorentina nel XIV secolo'. *Archivio Storico Italiano*, Ser. V, XXX (1902), 241–74.

Rubinstein, N. 'The Beginnings of Political Thought in Florence: a study in medieval historiography'. *Journal of the Warburg and Courtauld Institutes*, V (1942), 198–227.

'Florence and the Despots: Some aspects of Florentine Diplomacy in the Fourteenth Century'. *Transactions of the Royal Historical Society*, Ser. V, II (1952), 21–45.

'Some Ideas on Municipal Progress and Decline in the Italy of the Communes'. In D. J. Gordon (ed), *Fritz Saxl: A Volume of Memorial Essays*, London, 1957.

Sackur, E. *Sibyllinische Texte und Forschungen*. Halle, 1898.

Sanesi, I. 'Di un incarico dato della repubblica fiorentina a Giovanni Villani'. *Archivio Storico Italiano*, Ser. V, XII (1893), 366–9.

Santini, P. *Quesiti e ricerche di storiografia fiorentina*. Florence, 1903.

Sapori, A. 'L'attendibilità di alcune testimonianze cronistiche dell' economia medioevale'. *Archivio Storico Italiano*, Ser. VII, XII (1927), 19–30.

Scaglione, A. D. *Nature and Love in the Late Middle Ages*. Berkeley, 1963.

Scheffer-Boichorst, P. 'Die florentinische Geschichte der Malespini eine Fälschung'. *Historische Zeitschrift*, XXIV (1870), 274–313.

Schevill, F. *History of Florence*. New York, 1936.

Thorndike, L. *A History of Magic and Experimental Science*. 8 vols., London, 1923–58.

Torre, A. della. 'L'amicizia di Dante e Giovanni Villani'. *Giornale Dantesco*, XII (1904), 33–44.

Varese, C. 'Una "Laudatio florentinae urbis": la Istoria di Firenze di Goro Dati'. *Rassegna della Letteratura Italiana*, LXIII (1959), 373–89.

'Aspetti e limiti quattrocenteschi della "florentina libertas".' *Rassegna della Letteratura Italiana*, LXIV (1960), 196–7.

Villari, P. *The First Two Centuries of Florentine History*. 2 vols. London, 1894–5.

Weinstein, D. 'The Myth of Florence'. In N. Rubinstein, *Florentine Studies*, London, 1968, 15–44.

INDEX

DATE DUE

MAR 1 2 1967

DEMCO 38-297